clean

clean

Lessons from Ecolab's Century of Positive Impact

PAUL C. GODFREY WITH **EMILIO R. TENUTA**

WILEY

Library of Congress Cataloging-in-Publication Data

Names: Godfrey, Paul C., author. | Tenuta, Emilio R., author.
Title: Clean : lessons from Ecolab's century of positive impact / Paul
  Godfrey and Emilio Tenuta.
Description: First edition. | Hoboken, New Jersey : Wiley, [2023] |
  Includes index.
Identifiers: LCCN 2022054078 (print) | LCCN 2022054079 (ebook) | ISBN
  9781394153367 (cloth) | ISBN 9781394153381 (adobe pdf) | ISBN
  9781394153374 (epub)
Subjects: LCSH: Social responsibility of business.
Classification: LCC HD60 .G643 2023 (print) | LCC HD60 (ebook) | DDC
  658.4/08 — dc23/eng/20221109
LC record available at https://lccn.loc.gov/2022054078
LC ebook record available at https://lccn.loc.gov/2022054079

COVER DESIGN: PAUL MCCARTHY
COVER ART: © GETTY IMAGES | SAEMILEE

SKY10041704_012323

Ecolab is a publicly traded company (ticker symbol ECL) headquartered in St. Paul, MN. Throughout the book we reference Ecolab, Nalco, and several specific products, solution sets, and services provided by Ecolab. For ease of reading, we have not inserted trademark or copyright designations where legal counsel might advise inserting them.

The following names, products, and services, are all registered trademarks of Ecolab, and are used with the company's permission:

List of product mentions here:

- ECOLAB®
- NALCO®
- 3DTRASAR™
- SMARTPOWER™
- AQUANOMIC™
- FILLERTEK™
- WATER FLOW INTELLIGENCE (no trademark marking)
- ECOLAB SCIENCE CERTIFIED™
- ECOLAB WATER FOR CLIMATE™
- ECOLAB3D™

To Robin, your love and support make me better every day.
—Paul

To my wife Dawn and children Evan, Rachael and Emilio Marco — My life, my love and my legacy
—Emilio

CONTENTS

PREFACE

There are a thousand hacking at the branches of evil to one who is striking at the root.

—Henry David Thoreau

The lack of a sustainable economy stands as a great, perhaps catastrophic, evil of our time. Climate change roils communities, natural landscapes, and markets. Discrimination and social inequality fester like an open sore and stain our ideals of democratic societies and free markets, and questionable ethics and practices by prominent firms and leaders erode trust in business as an institution. Many well-intentioned business, civil society, and government leaders create products, processes, and programs to address the latest crisis of sustainability, desperately hoping that these one-off approaches will move the dial on creating a more sustainable world.

Most of these efforts represent "hacking at the branches," however, because the roots of sustainability lie out of view, they represent the outcome of long chains of cause-and-effect relationships, and require a different mindset to strike at them. Unless leaders identify the root causes of the lack of sustainability, they'll remain focused on the branches and churn out more temporary solutions. They'll fail to make a lasting, positive impact. How can we help leaders identify those root causes and move toward real solutions? By finding successful businesses that strike at the roots and adopting the core principles that guide them.

This book presents a case study of Ecolab, a company that's been building a truly sustainable world for a century. My first exposure to Ecolab came in 2017. I was consulting for a multinational industrial water company to assess the strength of its competitors. They really wanted to know about Nalco Water, a subsidiary of the Ecolab corporation. They knew Nalco was good, and the more I learned, the more I shared their respect for the company. Nalco created great products, went to market with a strong value proposition centered on sustainable water management, and enjoyed industry leadership. I wanted to get a personal take on Nalco's competitive goals and vision for the future, so one Friday morning in June 2017 I dialed the corporate operator at Ecolab and asked to speak with someone who might know about "sustainability at Nalco." I prepared myself for the inevitable trip to the dead letter box we know as voice mail.

Emilio Tenuta, then vice president of Sustainability at Ecolab, answered his own phone. That never happens in corporate America. Never. We had a *great* conversation. Three things impressed me.

First was Emilio's fundamental kindness; he took a call from a total stranger and spent the better part of a half-hour talking to me about Ecolab. I think that comes from his solid Midwestern upbringing.

Second was his passion for Ecolab and its commitment to sustainability as the core of its business model and strategy. Ecolab competed in an old-school industrial sector with a very new-school, cutting-edge approach.

Third, Emilio impressed me with his, and Ecolab's, vision for the future. Water is central to almost every industry, and industrial water use happens at a scale that's hard for most people to fathom. Water is scarce, and water fouled through industrial processing becomes water unavailable for drinking or other life-supporting uses. What Emilio, Nalco, and Ecolab saw clearly was that the stewardship of water would be *the* defining business, societal, and global issue within a decade or two. Emilio described the expansive Nalco/Ecolab mission to avert a water crisis by helping major industrial users reduce, reuse, and recycle immense volumes of water.

Emilio, who will offer his take on every topic I raise in the book, commented on our meeting:

> When Professor Godfrey reached out to me back in 2017, it was a totally serendipitous encounter. He was looking for answers to some questions about Nalco and their products and someone put the call through to me. I picked up the phone and the rest, you could say – in keeping with the theme of this book – is history.
>
> In that very first call, Paul and I connected about Ecolab's core purpose: sustainability, a topic that is both near and dear to me and the focus of my work for the past 11 years. At Ecolab, we're proud of our long and successful history, which is rooted in the principles of sustainability. We have always followed the belief that we must conduct business ethically and sustainably, being true to what we do best.

For us, that means delivering exceptional business and sustainability outcomes at the highest return for our customers. Our business model is even more relevant today than it was a century ago. Why? Because our greatest opportunity is to drive sustainable development through innovative solutions that help companies around the world achieve outstanding results while minimizing environmental and social impact. That has never been more important than it is today when we are faced with unprecedented global challenges.

That phone call in 2017 sparked a productive partnership. We've worked together to produce two cases for business school students, one about the Nalco acquisition – literally a textbook case of M&A done right – and the second about the development of Ecolab's 2030 sustainability goals. We worked well together and decided that the 100th anniversary of Ecolab's founding in 1923 (Nalco appeared five years later in 1928) provided a great platform to collaborate on a book about Ecolab and its commitment to sustainability.

This book aims much higher than being a mere recounting of Ecolab's first hundred years, an homage to a successful company and its leaders. The book builds from a simple premise: Companies, from the largest and oldest enterprises to the smallest and youngest startups, can learn valuable lessons from Ecolab to propel themselves on their journey toward sustainability. Ecolab's "secret sauce" isn't secret, it's based on time-honored and well-grounded leadership principles. Most of those principles are eminently transferrable. I hope that as you read, you'll say, "My company, or my team, can do that," and that you'll invest the energy, money, and time to become a more sustainable company in your own sphere. A century of experience is interesting, but if the lessons of that experience help you improve yourself and your organization, then that's a book worth reading.

For me, that hundred years of experience distills down to two key lessons: Being a good business is part and parcel of sustainability, and for sustainability to work over the long term, a company must "yarn-dye" a few important perspectives, principles, and priorities. Ecolab is a good business in the ethical sense of "good business" as praiseworthy. The company isn't perfect, and we'll point to more than one poor decision or outcome, but it's for good reason that Ecolab regularly appears on the "best company" lists of several organizations. Its management philosophies and systems make it a great place to work and a valued business partner for customers, suppliers, and community stakeholders.

More importantly, Ecolab is a "good business" in a very traditional, economic sense of excellence along a number of key business metrics: market share, product and process innovation, and profitability. Nobel laureate Milton Friedman argued a half-century ago that executives had to choose between "social responsibility" and shareholder value. Ecolab reveals the error in Friedman's either/or logic. Here's a hint of what you'll learn in Chapter 1: $100 invested in Ecolab when it went public in January 1957 would have been worth $249,770 in January 2020. That's 5 *times* the return on a similar $100 invested in sector leader Procter & Gamble, and 34 *times* the return on the S&P 500.

"Yarn-dyed" is a metaphor for deeply embedded. I'll frame the metaphor with a question: Which shirt holds its color better and longer, one where the color was printed onto a previously white cloth or one whose cloth is made of dyed threads? You guessed it. Yarn-dyed fabrics hold their color better and longer than print-dyed ones. You'll read in these pages how many of Ecolab's best practices became "yarn-dyed." In fact, Ecolab used sustainable business best practices *decades* before sustainability came in vogue. When these practices become "yarn-dyed" into your company's actions, products, people, and culture, sustainability will flourish for you, just as it has for Ecolab. Yarn-dyed principles help leaders at any company identify the roots of sustainability and make lasting, long-term contributions to a better world.

Each chapter draws on the history of Ecolab or Nalco to illustrate how both good business and sustainability became yarn-dyed in the company, but the book is far more than a trip down corporate memory lane. We'll rely on well-established theories and frameworks of leadership, organization, and strategy to tease out the why behind the what of Ecolab's success. I've tried to make these ideas accessible because they are absolutely essential for you to realize that Ecolab's success is not accidental. You can't replicate Ecolab's history, but you can install and instill the underlying principles in your own organization.

ACKNOWLEDGMENTS

The two of us, Emilio and I, share the byline for the book, but we've been supported along the way and we'd like to spend some ink formally recognizing and thanking those who've made this book possible. For Emilio, that list begins with his companion of 36 years, Dawn, and his three children who inspire him every day – Evan, Rachael, and Emilio Marco. Paul thanks his colleagues at Brigham Young University, especially Kim Clark, Lisa Jones Christensen, and Ben Lewis, for their long-term collegiality and their short-term feedback on chapters in the book.

The team at Ecolab, including Heather Dubois, Jeanne Modelski, Nigel Glennie, Jennifer McClean, Lori Nelson, Scott Adams, Jeff Hunt, Angela Busch, Larry Berger, Gail Peterson, Paul Langlois, Laurie Marsh, Jose Prado, Michael Sawlsville, Sam Hsu, Varsha Shah, and Emilio's sustainability team – Oriana Raabe, Anja De Reus, Amie Hedblom, Dallas Tebben, Christian Hoops, Laura Kowalski, Anna Wertheim, Kyle Kapustka, Daniel Kopan, Meredith Englund, Iris Raylesberg, Geoff Townsend, Amy Hahn, Anna Sarvello, Eliza Chlebeck, Tom Vandyck, Megan Kaatmann, Sarah Bresnahan, Melissa Callejo, Lynne Olson, Raj Rajan, and Matthea Najberg – all went above and beyond in providing data, insights and inspiration.

Finally, the Godfrey family, particularly Paul's wife, Robin, has endured another book project and given their full support, including edits and feedback that have made the book better.

FOREWORD

By Maelle Gavet, CEO Techstars and author *Trampled by Unicorns*

Beyond our flourishing program partnerships and co-investments in a number of successful startups in the future of food and agriculture space, Techstars and Ecolab have a great deal in common. Although we are markedly different businesses operating in different spheres, and Techstars has been in existence for a tiny fraction of Ecolab's now century-long history of pioneering innovation, we share two foundational principles.

First, we both believe that whether a company is at ideation stage or post-IPO, two hackers at a kitchen table, or a team dispersed around the world, the concepts of sustainability and profitability are not mutually exclusive. Rather, the first increasingly informs and underpins the second. Ecolab has been an outlier in this regard, successfully developing a business strategy where sustainability, and what it terms eROI, are core to the very purpose of the company – and long before corporate bosses were talking in such terms or there was a bandwagon in sight. Furthermore, we both believe that the application of this approach, at a time when the climate crisis affects all organizations, must be sector-agnostic for it to have global and generational impact. Techstars has invested in more than 700 sustainability/climate-tech companies, but the principle of embedding sustainability and long-term thinking in a team applies not just to them but to startups in every area from AgTech to Web3, and FinTech to fashion.

Second, we share a deep conviction that sustainability – and the business performance, productivity, and growth it unlocks – can only be achieved through technology and digital enablement. Not only does Ecolab invent and develop new technologies, but innovation itself has become an ever-bigger part of its overall strategy. Whether it's in manufacturing, automotive tech, the paper industry, or in 30,000 McDonald's restaurants around the world, Ecolab develops direct technology that marries up with its onsite expertise across 40 industries to improve water quality, climate, health and food safety outcomes, and resilience at a time when all of these are under unprecedented duress.

One of the reasons I was so pleased to be asked to write the introduction to this book is that the ideas it contains are highly relatable and applicable to the hundreds, and soon to be thousands, of early-stage tech entrepreneurs Techstars invests in every year. Among the most important of these is how startups, from the get-go, should think about the holistic impact that their product or service can deliver for clients and communities. A robotics company, say, can not only offer its customers enhanced performance capabilities and productivity gains but also help drive down costs and reduce their carbon emissions and water footprint. A holistic approach for a transportation and logistics startup, meanwhile, would consider impacts on the environment and community stakeholders, as well as suppliers and employees, alongside successfully scaling its customer base.

Another defining area is leadership – and not just in the top-down sense. Standout leadership today is about staying true to your core values and empowering an entire organization – in Ecolab's case, 48,000+ employees – so that every single team member understands that a company doesn't exist in a vacuum but in a wider world in which all its impacts need to be taken into account.

Ecolab's inspiring leadership teaches us to build sustainably from the start. Think holistically. Take the long view. Consider our place in the world. Sadly, we live in an era where greenwashing is more widespread than many of us would like to admit, and window dressing and slick PR all too often replace the hard yards required to reduce negative impacts and build resilience. Ecolab is the antithesis to this approach. And it isn't "just" startups that can learn from them. So, whether you are formulating a strategy for a Fortune 500 company or are in your kitchen tweaking your first product, this book will help you connect your work with the most pressing issue of our time: creating a sustainable organization and society.

–ENDS–

clean

Chapter 1

THE CALL FOR A SUSTAINABLE WORLD

Tó éí iiná (Water is Life)

— Navajo saying

A mid the chaos, fear, and confusion of the early days of the COVID-19 pandemic lockdowns, something unforeseen appeared: clean air. People around the globe found themselves in various states of lockdown as offices, restaurants, schools, theaters, and almost everything else shut down. With nowhere for drivers to go, the number of cars on the road plummeted. The result? Global levels of PM 2.5, the particulate matter that generates haze in both skies and lungs, declined by 30–40% and concentrations of the nasty pollutant sulfur dioxide fell 25–60% worldwide.[1] In the crazy days of spring 2020, people from Tokyo to Tacoma, and from Boston to Buenos Aires breathed easier during the first months of a policy-induced global economic coma.

That global breath of fresh air reinforced two prevailing ideas about building a sustainable economy, in terms of both ecological renewal and human health. The first cemented the notion that dramatically reducing, if not eliminating, the fossil-fuel-powered internal combustion engine is an essential element. The second emerged from our collective consciousness as we experienced the outside world through Apple's Facetime, Facebook, Skype, Teams, or Zoom: digital technology would pave a golden road to a more sustainable world.

The pandemic experience validated the first idea; the second, less so. Consumer-facing apps from Amazon through Zillow can reduce travel, fuel usage, and foul air, as well as accidents, breathing disorders, and the stress and general mayhem that all come with commuting. That pristine view of the digital-economy-as-sustainable-economy gets murkier the farther we go back in the internet value chain. Movement from software to hardware reveals an expensive and extensive web of "server farms" that enable us to seamlessly connect to and transact over the web. As of 2020, there were 3 million of these farms, known as data centers, around the world, but 600 or so constitute the largest type, hyperscale data centers. These behemoths occupy up to 400,000 square feet (about 10 acres) and house up to 5,000 servers. An average data center may use up to 50MW of electricity a year, enough to power 32,500 homes in a developed country. All that electricity generates heat, and if the temperature in a center gets too high, the problems begin. At best, a center goes offline – at a cost of $8,000 per minute in lost revenue; at worst, 5,000 servers melt, at a cost of $75,000 to $100,000 each. Keeping those servers cool and functional

3

requires massive air conditioning capacity, and an average center will use *200 million gallons* of very clean water every year to keep servers cool. That's a year's worth of drinking water for up to 667,000 people, or a city the size of Portland, Oregon.[2] With the amount of data being produced and stored expected to grow *50 times* between 2019 and 2030, the expanding backbone of the internet presents its own sustainability challenge.

Where do the world's biggest server "farmers," from mega player Microsoft to specialist Digital Realty, turn to for help with managing their water needs? These "new economy" companies partner with a very "old economy" company for the most sophisticated and sustainable water management tools on the planet: Ecolab, founded in 1923, and its younger sister and subsidiary Nalco Water, founded in 1928. A sustainable digital economy depends very much on the deep knowledge, skills, and talents of companies with decades of experience in a sustainable industrial economy. The experience of Digital Realty, a San Francisco, California–based owner and operator of over 280 data centers in 50 metro areas around the globe, highlights the value of this knowledge and skill.

The core of the air conditioning system is a cooling tower, a very large unit that allows hot water – the heat generated by the servers – to cool by transferring that heat to the air. Digital Realty pays for the water it puts into that system and the water it discharges as sewage. The physics of a cooling tower, however, means that 80% of the input water evaporates during cooling, leaving Digital Realty to pay sewage charges for water it never returns to the system. Several US states, including California, offer an evaporation credit if a company can document its evaporation loss. Walter Leclerc, director of Environment Health and Safety for the company, brought in Nalco specialists to help document and claim those credits for one of its small centers in Los Angeles. The business result? Digital Realty now claims over $150,000 in annual evaporation credits just for that site.

That work, begun in 2015, established what is now a long-term partnership. Leclerc and Ecolab team members used tools such as the Smart Water Navigator™ to create a global water use plan, and they deployed Nalco's 3D TRASAR™ technology to implement the program along with Ecolab3D™ technology to document results. The partners worked together to create and implement a global water strategy and solution for data center management. As of 2022, Digital Realty used 30 million fewer gallons of water each year, consumed 17MW less electricity, and emitted 12,000 metric tons fewer greenhouse gases. That's good for the environment and the health of those living nearby. It's also good for the bottom line. Digital Realty has saved $8 million to date, for an ROI of 60%.[3] Walter Leclerc says of his experience with Ecolab, "I could not have done it without them. Their technology is fantastic, but it's the people that make the difference."

I open with data centers because this business highlights two issues that I'll come back to throughout the book. First, the challenge of sustainability is multifaceted and complex and will require a mix of both simple and complex, industrial and digital innovations and solutions. Second, very "old line" companies like Ecolab and Nalco will play a significant role in creating a truly sustainable world. My research on water management led me to Ecolab, a 100-year-old company that developed, expanded, and nurtured a sustainable business model as it grew from a single employee to a team of over 48,000, each of whom possesses and deploys world-class expertise in environmental and human health. That expertise drives product, process, and service innovations that keep Ecolab in the vanguard of companies pioneering a sustainable future.

Sustainability may be a recent concept, but the principles that deliver it are ageless. In what follows, you'll see that Ecolab's success relies on a disciplined, integrated, long-term, and sophisticated approach to business. These aren't just one-off or timely tactics; the roots of Ecolab's success come from its application of enduring principles of business success. Whether you are online or old-line, you can adopt these principles to help your organization and people create the expertise we all need to build a truly sustainable world.

THE CHALLENGE OF SUSTAINABILITY

Neither Emilio nor I know if the sustainability movement has an undisputed birthday, but we both trace a pivot point in sustainability to the first Earth Day in the United States, April 22, 1970. A burning oil slick on Cleveland, Ohio's Cuyahoga River in the summer of 1969 dramatically illustrated the extent to which the natural environment had been used as an industrial dumping ground, and that first Earth Day catalyzed the need for change.

Fast forward to 1987; the United Nations joined the growing movement by appointing the Brundtland Commission to propel progress through a clear definition. That group defined a sustainable economy as one "that meets the needs of the present without compromising the ability of future generations to meet their own needs."[4] That definition of sustainability holds today, but like most things in this space, it continues to be debated – refined by adherents and rejected by critics. At its core, a sustainable economy represents a complex compromise between two very old and deeply embedded ideas: progress and conservation.

The idea of progress, according to South African historian Jacobus Du Pisani, traces its roots back to the earliest days of the Hebrew (and eventually Christian) conception of history that portrayed time as linear and inevitably moving forward toward a clear end state. To the religious, that end state was either salvation or damnation. Progress, writ large, indicated blessing – and thus spiritual salvation. As the world secularized during the modern era, progress became embodied in the notion that economic, scientific, and social innovation would benefit people through an ever-improving material standard of living. The growth of the global population, increasing personal income, and increased longevity since the dawn of the Industrial Revolution in the late eighteenth century provide, for its advocates, powerful evidence of beneficial progress.

The need to offset the impact of progress through conservation traces back to ancient times as well. Indeed, Plato, Pliny, and other classical writers tutored their followers about the dangers of deforestation and environmental degradation caused by ever-encroaching human activity. The Industrial Revolution marked a pivot point where the scale and scope of economic activity began to seriously outstrip the planet's and its societies' ability to renew needed resources. Historians mark the industrial age beginning in 1800 and peaking around 1970, with perhaps the burning Cuyahoga symbolizing a high-water mark in the havoc the industrial economy could wreak. During that time, global population more than trebled from just under 980 million to 3.6 billion; however, manufacturing output grew *1730 times* over the same period.[5] That first Earth Day in 1970 – perhaps the beginning of the end of the industrial age – catalyzed a growing global concern for the potential dire outcomes for both people and the planet if societies failed to stabilize progress and conserve/ preserve our natural and social resources.

The Brundtland Commission's definition sought to balance the demands of many, including those representing billions living in so-called "developing" countries, for an upgraded standard of living with those who argued that the total cost of a standard life would end up destroying the planet and human societies. The commission's work acknowledged the importance of continued economic growth but recognized that decision-makers needed to include the long-term impacts of that growth on human and natural environments. Making trade-offs would become critical. A truly sustainable world would require policymakers, business leaders, and citizens to draw a fine line that separated meaningful from unchecked progress and cut precisely at the joint between appropriate versus stifling conservation. Many of the debates we see today showcase our collective struggle in drawing those lines and our imprecision in cutting at that joint. The conversations and arguments about how to make those trade-offs have become more sophisticated and more pressing as the years go by.

At a macro level, sustainability gave voice to two previously voiceless stakeholders: the natural environment and future generations. At an individual level, sustainability invited each of us, in our personal and professional roles, to adopt a much longer time horizon and broader view as we thought about what to buy, where to invest, and how to define our own progress. For business leaders, the Brundtland report birthed the concept of a triple bottom line, one focused on economic (profit), one on social (people), and one on environmental (planet) sustainability, or the 3Ps.

As the twenty-first century proceeds into its third decade, the language of sustainability has changed again. The 3Ps are still the same, but the focus has shifted from societal outcomes to corporate actions. The new terminology calls for environmental, social, and governance (ESG) performance. Activists, investors, and regulators each work to measure current ESG performance and encourage change and progress along each dimension at the business level. ESG measures provide a snapshot in time of how each company contributes to the 3Ps, and when ESG reporting becomes commonplace, the combined snapshots essentially become a movie that captures dynamic progress toward sustainable 3Ps.

Sustainability as a Business Problem

Managing a triple bottom line presents executives and leaders with a complex business challenge, and today no company or executive team can claim mastery. Sustainable business practices are and will remain a work in progress. Although complex, leaders approach the challenge from one of two well-known starting perspectives, one that views sustainability as a financial, physical, or technological problem to be engineered and the other that sees it as a set of natural relationships to be nurtured. Building a bridge requires a technical mindset, for example, while saving a failing marriage involves a relational one. The technical approach focuses on developing and deploying bundles of money and steel designed to solve the problem while relational approaches seek to influence the human psyche or social culture. Each mindset presents a different set of problems, proposes different processes, and opens a different opportunity set. Each constitutes a *weltanschauung*, a worldview or simply a perspective.

I'll talk much more about mindsets and perspectives in Chapters 2 and 3, but I'll lay out a few important elements here.

First, a purely technical or relational mindset captures the essence of very few problems. Building a bridge invites a technical approach, but new bridges change the relationships in a biological ecosystem, economic transactions in and between communities, and social relationships in affected families and groups. Engineers who fail to engage in relational analysis usually face stiff opposition, even when their technical specifications are impeccable.

Similarly, rescuing a sinking marriage always requires attention to relationship skills and status but often includes technical elements such as new jobs, new housing, and new knowledge. Surveys indicate that while relational issues lead to most marital breakups, money plays a leading role in almost one-fourth of divorces, and wise therapists explore economic as well as emotional and erotic challenges in relationships. Put simply, a single- (simple-?) minded approach to problems usually leads to simplistic and partial solutions.

Second, in terms of process, the technical view adopts a *coercive* approach to problem-solving. A knowing, independent actor can deploy technical resources to provide adequate (and sometimes exceptional) targeted solutions to isolated business problems driven by downside risk management or compliance with existing rules. In contrast, the relational view invites *collaborative* problem-solving. Interdependent actors marshal both objective (knowledge) and subjective (cultural) human and social capital to develop holistic approaches that recognize the larger system in which the problem lives. The relational approach emphasizes lasting solutions at the system, rather than merely the problem, level.

Third, technical and relational mindsets complement each other; each has advantages that overcome the disadvantages of the other. The technical attends to discrete problems and conceives efficient, cost-effective solutions to problems. However, my experience teaches that a tight, technical focus tends toward a whack-a-mole approach to thorny issues. The relational view uncovers elements that require time and energy to understand the inherent complexity of any issue and more time to build consensus around both underlying problems and solutions. Speed is not a feature of the relational approach. The upside? That focus on systemic and continuous contexts of issues means that solutions identify and center on core, causal human and social drivers of sustainability challenges. The time spent building consensus helps people make and follow through with the tough decisions that lead to meaningful progress.

Real and lasting progress around sustainability, financial performance, product development, productivity, or any other business challenge leverages the power of *both* views and seeks solutions that address technical and relational elements. Technical solutions provide the tangible and time-bound assets and actions required to solve problems such as sustainability while the relational element works to change the priorities and processes that constitute the deep causal structure of problems. Technical solutions look different than relational ones, but both contribute vital elements to lasting solutions.

Finally, which viewpoint opens the conversation matters because each mindset uncovers different opportunities and solution sets. The holistic approach of the relational view naturally invites us to consider the role technical elements can play in a solution. Marriage partners working on their relationship will eventually uncover needed financial or occupational adjustments. The converse, however, is not true. The technical view, with its analytic backbone, isolates and compartmentalizes problems; it often obscures a broader view of the larger human issues and undervalues the systemic context that surrounds any issue. The complex engineering specs that create a stable and lasting bridge are independent of the impacts of a changed commute on individuals and families, and the technical view will not naturally lead to a relational one. Which frame you employ first determines if and how well you'll see the other.

I spent so much time discussing these two overarching worldviews because they form the foundation of Ecolab's success. From its earliest days, the company has operated from a relational *weltanschauung*, and the ability to see its business and the world as first and foremost a set of relationships. That's how and why they've been practicing sustainability for a century. Your ability to adopt a similar perspective will, I believe, ultimately determine your success in driving sustainability into the bones of your organization. To foreshadow what you'll learn in Chapter 2, Merritt J. (MJ) Osborn founded the business that eventually became Ecolab on two fundamental beliefs: the dignity and common humanity of all people and the fact that the world is an integrated, interconnected, and interrelated system.

A relationship-first perspective grounded Osborn's private world of hearth and home, the system of commitments that created an employee-centered business firm, the transactions between that firm and its many stakeholders, and the final impact on local, regional, national, and international communities. One of those critical communities has been and continues to be the natural environment. For Ecolab, it's relationships first, technical solutions second. The goal of an earnest, honest, and mutually beneficial relationship with each stakeholder determines which technical solutions and what chemistry the company brings to the table in each case.

Sustainability as a Leadership Problem

You may believe you can find the perfect blend of technical and relational solutions to the problems you face; however, my experience teaches that no one (at least no one I know) perfectly balances a technical and relational orientation along a razor's edge. Instead, genetics, upbringing, education, and life experiences predispose us to either a technical or relational default setting of how we view the world. As we confront and manage problems and lead others toward solutions, either the technical or the relational perspective serves as our baseline for action, and as our paradigm of choice leads us to success – and each one leads to its own type of success – our commitment to that baseline waxes stronger. Over time, our perspective, or *weltanschauung*, becomes more stable and frames our approach to leadership and management.

This book is about leadership and management because they represent, in both my and Emilio's view, two keys that unlock the door to creating sustainable businesses and societies. I'll avoid quips and false comparisons, such as "management is doing things right; leadership is doing right things."[6] I'll also avoid simplistic ideas such as "management is simply controlling others or driving results," or "leadership is about motivating people and getting out of the way." Emilio and I have accumulated years of experience as leaders, and much of that work involved management; they fit hand in glove.

Leadership is the work that mobilizes people in a process of action, learning and change to improve the long-term viability and vitality of the organization in three ways: purpose, people, and productivity. *Purpose* is realized more effectively, *people* experience increased personal growth, meaning and purpose in their work and lives, and *productivity* is strengthened.[7] Management is a set of tools leaders employ to accomplish their work: they *allocate resources* based on purpose and priorities, they design *processes and products* that enable people to grow and thrive, and they *measure/report* the viability and vitality of their organizations in terms of productivity and performance.

Figure 1.1 illustrates the proper relationships between these elements in a thriving organization. I've employed alliteration to make the elements of Figure 1.1 easy to remember, and I'll return to each level of the pyramid throughout the book as I explain the principles Ecolab follows to create a sustainable enterprise. Your ability to execute on the different Ps of sustainable advantage will, to a large extent, determine your ability to create a sustainable organization and economy. The most important thing to remember is the base of the pyramid: How we lead and manage depends on our fundamental perspective.

Perspective provides the bedrock or core that informs everything that we do, whether individually or in relationships, from family to firm. That perspective generates a defined purpose and set of priorities, what we really want to accomplish. Purpose and priorities enable us to build a set of processes and products that in turn realize our ultimate aims. The right processes and products allow people to productively engage with markets

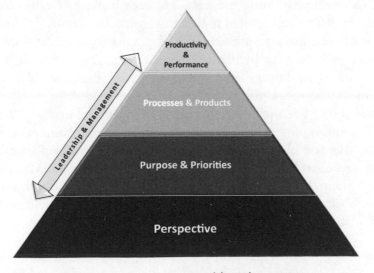

Figure 1.1 Creating a Sustainable Advantage

and stakeholders. Productivity drives performance. Leadership and management provide the fuel that brings the pyramid into being and keeps it aligned over time. Note that the arrow representing leadership and management runs both ways. Leadership enables performance, but performance informs and molds perspective. Positive performance deepens our commitment to our worldview while negative performance invites us to reexamine that view. Everything you read from here on in (and I encourage you to read every word!) builds on Figure 1.1.

ECOLAB AS AN EXAMPLE OF SUSTAINABILITY

MJ Osborn worked as a pharmaceutical salesman for most of the first decade of the twentieth century. Osborn noticed that the hotels he stayed in took rooms out of service for up to two weeks every time they cleaned their carpets. Osborn developed a carpet cleaner – *Absorbit* – that cleaned carpets in less time and required less labor and water, meaning that rooms would be back in service much sooner. Although customers paid more for *Absorbit*, their total cost of cleaning – factoring in labor, water usage, and downtime – declined enough that profits increased.[8] The product proved a boon for hotels, but not for Osborn – a container of *Absorbit* was so economical that Osborn saw few follow-on sales.

Osborn named his nascent company Economics Laboratory (EL) – "Economic" because it saved customers time, labor, and material costs, and "Laboratory" because the products were backed by laboratory research. In 1924, he acquired a chemical formula from a University of Minnesota chemist and introduced *Soilax*, an easy-to-use and measure dishwashing detergent. In 1928, Osborn rolled out a line of *Soilax* dispensers and other dishwashing equipment. EL became a provider of dishwashing solutions, not just products.[9]

Over the next century, the company developed and deployed a rather simple business model: Identify a pressing customer problem in cleaning/sanitation and develop a scientific solution that would save customers labor, maintenance, and downtime and preserve equipment. Customers would pay a premium for the company's products because the savings and regular on-site service provided by EL would more than make up for the price premium of the products. Sales grew from $35,000 in 1924 ($554,917 in 2021 dollars) to $12.733 billion in 2021: a nominal cumulative annual growth rate of 14% and a real (if we hold dollars constant) 11% CAGR. That's one of many impressive measures of Ecolab's economic success.

Economic Sustainability (the "Profit" Element of the 3Ps)

Osborn founded what would become Economics Laboratory – condensed to Ecolab in 1986 – when he was 44 years old; definitely not his first rodeo. He had enough experience in business to know what constituted a "good" business from a customer, employee, and investor perspective. You've already read about the company's sales growth, but there's more to the business story. MJ, as he preferred to be called, imbued his company with a perspective focused on profitable, prudent growth. We'll just hit the highlights, beginning with growth. EL entered *Fortune* magazine's ranking of the 500 largest industrial corporations in 1976 at number 500, and its revenue qualified it to be on that list through 2021, where it ranked 237th. Of the 500 firms on that list in 1976, only 69 (14%) remained on the list 45 years later. Of those 69, 36 fell in relative rank and 24 climbed up the list. Ecolab topped that list of climbers, moving up 263 spots against an average ascent of 87. Put simply, Ecolab grew in absolute sales, *and* it experienced the highest growth rate among a peer group of the country's largest companies.

In 1927, MJ laid out his primary measure of the firm's profit performance, a return on equity of 20%. His son and later CEO Edward B. Osborn refined that goal into a 20% return on beginning equity and added two more metrics: a return on sales of 7% and a prudent balance sheet that would be rated "investment grade." Table 1.1 presents data on Ecolab's historical performance. Return on beginning equity (ROBE) approximates 20% over the six and a half decades Ecolab has been publicly traded.[10] Return on Sales (ROS) misses the 7% mark over the long-term; however, since the second decade of the millennium, ROS averaged over 8%.

Table 1.1 Ecolab Financial Performance Through the Years

	Period	ROS	ROBE	Debt/ Equity	ROA	CapEx/ Sales	CapEx/ EBIT
Ecolab Average	Total	5.17%	19.16%	1.16	8.79%	5.60%	46.95%
Ecolab Average	> 2009	8.39%	18.38%	1.67	6.29%	5.03%	34.00%
Industry Top 1/4	> 2009	6.94%			5.38%		
Industry Median	> 2009	–12.32%			–13.75%		
Industry Median	No Date		16.00%			4.20%	36.93%
Investment Grade				2 or less			

Comparison industry is specialty chemicals.

An "investment grade" balance sheet proved too difficult to determine, and so I use Debt/Equity to measure balance sheet strength. Ecolab has maintained a strong balance sheet over its lifetime, well under the rule-of-thumb ratio of 2 that typifies an investment grade financial structure. I've added three other measures to compare Ecolab with its peers in the specialty chemicals industry: return on assets (ROA), capital expenditures as a percentage of sales (CapEx/ Sales), and capital expenditures as a percentage of cash flow, excepting depreciation (defined as Earnings Before Interest, Taxes, CapEx/EBIT)). Ecolab outperforms its peer group on every measure.

To make sense of Table 1.2, imagine two families living in St. Paul, EL's hometown in 1956. They learn that on January 1, 1957, shares of EL will be publicly available at $15 each. Each family sets up a fund for their posterity that invests $100 on January 1 of every decade and holds that investment until January 1, 2020. One family chooses to buy EL stock, the other buys shares in the low-risk S&P 500. Table 1.2 presents the results, by decade, of those investment choices.[11] In the most recent decade, our Ecolab investor more than doubled total shareholder return (price appreciation plus dividends less initial cost) compared with the S&P, $451 to $232. By the year 2020, the original Ecolab investment is 34.6 times the value of the S&P investment, almost $250K to $7,213. MJ would be pleased to see that his emphasis on shareholder return has played well through the decades.

Environmental Sustainability (the "Planet" in the 3Ps)

Ecolab's economic success has benefited thousands of shareholders; its work on environmental sustainability impacts billions. The company measures what it refers to as "clean revenue," revenue coming from products and services that have a demonstrated, and often certified, environmental or social benefit. Ecolab classified almost two-thirds of its 2020 revenue as "clean." Products that help manage water and the energy to move it, heat it, or cool it represent the major source of clean revenue. Packaging and delivery innovations also counted as "clean" revenue as they reduced the amount of solid waste generated.

During the pandemic year of 2020, Ecolab's products and services helped customers conserve over 206 *billion* gallons of water, enough to meet the drinking water needs of 686 *million* people – basically the combined population of the United States, Russia, Germany, the United

Table 1.2 Ecolab Stock Returns over Time — $100 Investment

		1957–2020	1957–1960	1960–1970	1970–1980	1980–1990	1990–2000	2000–2010	2010–2020
Benchmark	Opening Value	$100	$100	$100	$100	$100	$100	$100	$100
S&P 500	Ending Value	$7,213	$125	$5,800	$3,794	$2,825	$980	$231	$232
	CAGR	7.03%	7.54%	7.00%	7.54%	8.71%	7.91%	4.28%	8.76%
Ecolab	Number of Shares–open	6.67	6.67	4.84	3.03	4.29	3.42	2.65	2.21
Over Time	Number of Shares–2020	1,200.73	7.72	753.07	96.97	68.67	27.35	5.31	2.21
	Closing Price	$190.23	$20.66	$190.23	$190.23	$190.23	$190.23	$190.23	$190.23
	Appreciation	$228,314.05	$59.44	$143,157.00	$18,346.55	$12,963.00	$5,102.87	$909.45	$320.40
	Total Dividends	$21,456.81	$0.07	$13,457.27	$1,732.72	$1,225.82	$486.53	$92.33	$30.99
	Total Shareholder Return	$249,870.86	$159.51	$156,714.27	$20,179.26	$14,288.83	$5,689.40	$1,101.77	$451.39
	CAGR	13.22%	16.84%	13.05%	11.20%	13.21%	14.42%	12.75%	16.27%

Kingdom, and Italy. Customers burned 43 *trillion* fewer BTUs of energy, enough to power 672,000 US homes for a year – a city the size of Phoenix, Arizona. They avoided coughing up 3.5 million metric tons of CO_2 emissions, the equivalent of taking 389,000 cars off the road, or every private car in the state of South Dakota in 2021, and they discarded 77 million fewer pounds of waste in landfills, the equivalent of the waste produced by 43,000 US citizens, or the population of Mankato, Minnesota.[12] Those are annual numbers, so with each passing year, Ecolab's contribution to saving and renewing our planet grows. Osborn would be pleased with the direction he set with the water-saving *Absorbit* in 1923.

Social Sustainability (the "People" in the 3Ps)

EL garnered its first award for creating social benefits in 1970. EB Osborn wrote that year:

> I believe the stockholders will be interested in the role the Company plays in its attempt to do its part as a good citizen and to take an active corporate role in helping to reduce social problems. It was made the recipient of the Distinguished Service Award by President Nixon's Committee on Employment of the Handicapped [individuals suffering from mental and physical disabilities].

That program actually began in 1966 when company leaders designed a vocational training program for people with (primarily) cognitive disabilities in the Twin Cities. The program expanded nationwide in 1968, and in 1969 the company dedicated full-time corporate staff to the effort. "In accepting the above award," Osborn noted, "through joint industry-government cooperation we can expand this as well as other programs even further and can encourage other industries to exercise their corporate social commitments in this area."[13]

By 2020, that integral "corporate social commitment" landed Ecolab on several "best of" lists for corporate citizenship, including *Ethisphere's* list of Worlds Most Ethical Companies (14 years running), *Corporate Social Responsibility* magazine's Best Corporate Citizen list (7 years), *Fortune's* Most Admired Companies (6 years), *Selling Power* magazine's list of Best Companies to Sell For (5 years), and *Forbes* Best Employers for Women (3 years). If I wanted to give more than a sketch here, I could point to nine additional national or global social and environmental sustainability awards and recognition the company received in 2020.

Merritt J. Osborn's original objective in the social sphere was to create a company where employees wanted to work for their entire careers and where they wanted to become owners. He began a bonus program and one of the first employee stock purchase programs back in the 1930s, in the midst of the Great Depression, long before EL was a public company. That commitment to people lives on.

THE JOURNEY TO SUSTAINABILITY

The ensuing chapters build on the core architecture of Figure 1.1. How leaders design and execute their strategy, from perspective to processes, will determine their sustainability successes in terms of people, planet, and profits. Chapter 2 provides a detailed description of Ecolab's foundational perspective. No surprise here, but MJ Osborn imbued his company with what I term the RIGHT perspective during his 30 years at the helm. We'll travel back to the very beginning of the Osborn family in the United States and trace the origins of MJ's weltanschauung. Chapter 3 extends this discussion and describes how that perspective became, and remains, Ecolab's purpose and priorities.

Chapter 4 focuses on the role of executive leadership in creating a sustainable Ecolab, and I'll focus on the top, the six CEOs who completed a full term of service at the company. The company's success relied on more than just a single insightful or hard-working executive, and I'll tease out the fundamental and timeless leadership principles that these leaders used to grow the company over its first century. As Walter Leclerc noted in his work with Ecolab, "It's the people that make the difference." Those people who make the difference provide leadership at every level of the organization, people like Heather DuBois in the data center business. Chapter 5 illustrates the policies and the principles that allow Ecolab's people to grow as leaders, and how they help customers, suppliers, and communities to improve their own operations. Ecolab's 48,000+ leaders all help build a sustainable enterprise, and people inside and outside the company's ecosystem reap the benefits. All told, Chapters 2–5 focus on the leadership principles that will propel Ecolab into its second century.

That focus turns to management tools in Chapters 6–9. I'll take up products writ large in Chapter 6. The company has developed and sold hundreds, if not thousands, of products over its first century. While individually interesting, those products represent snapshots in time; the real story is the motion picture that details how Ecolab was, and continues to be, an Economics Laboratory of innovation and solutions to benefit each of the 3Ps. I'll complete that discussion with a discussion of the principles that drive the company's legendary customer service.

Osborn's company has used acquisition as a way to grow since the 1930s. The first acquisition was a license to sell Calgon, a competitive cleaning solution that, for a few years at least, offered customers a superior product. Ecolab would later develop a superior product and exit that arrangement. Since going public in 1957, acquisitions have become a staple of growth for the company; they've also provided a way for the company to acquire key technology and knowledge that all contribute to its ability to move the dial in each of the 3Ps. Chapter 7 considers how and when you can buy your way into greater sustainability.

It would be a truly awesome story if I could write that Ecolab had an unbroken string of successful acquisitions. They haven't. When they've made poor choices, whether a financial failure or just a strategic misfit, they've divested. Chapter 8 will tell some great stories about the failures, but I'll focus – as you can guess by now – on the principles that guide the company through the decision to shrink. Sometimes, paradoxically, we grow best through subtraction.

As the twenty-first century rolls on, the processes and skills needed to act effectively and intentionally in the "nonmarket" areas where firms operate become more important. You may be thinking of lobbying, but it's much more than just a simple relationship with the government. Relationships include working with individuals or organizations in both the public and nonprofit sectors of the economy. Chapter 9 will highlight Ecolab's work in multi-stakeholder collaborations, or collaboration on steroids. These require many of the same "non-market" processes and skills but deploy those skills across multiple groups of stakeholders in the private, public, and nonprofit sectors to create lasting, large-scale change.

As I noted in the preface, how Ecolab's leaders pulled those levers over time created a yarn-dyed commitment to a sustainable business, from perspective to performance. I hope to tease out lessons from Ecolab's experience that can help your organization move toward that same deep, yarn-dyed commitment to sustainability.

CONCLUSION

I end where I began, by thinking about Ecolab's work in the data center industry. Nalco products, services, and complete water management solutions help server farm owners win through reduced downtime, lower water and energy costs, and longer asset lives. Ecolab wins as it is organically growing a new and profitable business unit. The environment wins at two levels, when products and services reduce the impact of individual server farms and when they contribute to a sustainable digital economy. People win as well, particularly those working in server farms who have a cleaner and safer workspace.

I hope I've convinced you to remain curious about sustainability and about how Ecolab has been a practitioner long before the concept as we know it today became popular. I promise you a thoughtful and productive read; I'll offer summary and managerial insights along the way. I will offer my insights into the core text of what you read, and Emilio will close each chapter with his personal and unique comments based on a career at Nalco and Ecolab that spans five decades. After you read his thoughts below, turn the page and we'll take up the genesis of a sustainable *weltanschauung*.

EMILIO'S THOUGHTS

Doing Well by Our Customers to Make the World a Better Place

In the first chapter of this book, Professor Godfrey sketched out some of Ecolab's early history. In doing so, he highlighted several key themes and questions about sustainability, such as: What are the key characteristics of a sustainable business? What are the challenges from a business and management perspective? And how has Ecolab served as an example of sustainability in action?

In 100 years of doing business, one thing remains central to our purpose and our business model. Ecolab has both the ability and the responsibility to drive positive change in the world, within our company and with our customers and the communities in which we live and work. Our associates act with purpose and, together, we continue to do our part to help change the world.

Ecolab has always operated where sustainability and economic benefits align, helping our customers do more with less and living up to our responsibilities in our own operations. As he traces the history of Ecolab, Professor Godfrey recounts how our sustainability journey began. Environmental concerns weren't at the forefront for Ecolab or most businesses back in the 1920s. Or certainly not in the way they are now. Yet Ecolab did provide customers with many benefits that would now be defined as sustainability. Take for example a product such as *Absorbit* for cleaning contaminants out of hotel carpets or Nalco's sodium aluminate products, which were used to manage water on steam locomotives. Both led to sustainability benefits before sustainability was a business buzzword or top priority. As you'll discover throughout the book, both Ecolab and Nalco have had a consistent approach over the past century in building success sustainably by:

- *Working closely with our customers to uncover challenges as well as opportunities.* With nearly half of our 48,000+ employees partnering with customers at more than 3 million locations, Ecolab has a frontline view of the operational challenges that they face around water, energy, climate, waste, and costs. These close working relationships enable us to build trust and that, in turn, leads to partnerships that enhance our ability to solve complex industry problems.

  A case in point: our partnership with Digital Realty required a thorough understanding of how much water was being used, and where, in its more than 290 global data centers. That required a close collaboration with corporate and facility leaders across the enterprise to create and implement a global water strategy to improve and protect its operations, watersheds, and the communities in which it operates. Ecolab leveraged best-in-class tools such as the Smart Water Navigator™ and other unique solutions to minimize overall water risk, ensure reliable performance, and protect Digital Realty's operations.

  As this example demonstrates, we have a unique business strategy. We develop solutions for specific concerns that can then be applied to other customers as well as our own operations. This maximizes the reach of our solutions as well as our impact on the world.

- *Adopting a science- and evidence-based approach to solving customer problems.* From the very beginning, Ecolab's success has stemmed from two core benefits of our solutions. First, our expertise and approach to serving the customer are grounded in science. And second, we help our customers save time, labor, and material costs. The 2008 Nalco tagline "people you trust delivering results," remains true today. Personal service is still central to our business model and a strong relationship between customers and their Ecolab territory managers is key to our ability to deliver technical solutions, reliability and cost savings for customers. From water chemistry to health and hygiene, Ecolab has always been known for its expertise in helping customers solve complex problems through science. For instance, our high-technology field representatives use the basics of water chemistry to pinpoint solutions that enable customers such as Digital Realty and other large-scale data centers in water-stressed areas to optimize and conserve water. And our Ecolab Science Certified™ program, established in 2020, helps advance public health and food safety in hotels, restaurants, and other locations.

- *Making the business case for sustainability.* Value creation is the primary aim of any business. Because value drives growth. At Ecolab, we *know* that operational and sustainability goals can coexist without trade-offs. The solutions we provide deliver an exponential return on investment (eROI), which is how we quantify customer value at Ecolab. For Digital Realty, that meant gaining enterprise-wide visibility, measurement, and monitoring of water use. This enabled the company to track, trend, and compare water use across all data centers and quantify savings from water projects. Value creation also supports a positive, meaningful impact for our customers, partners, and communities. It illustrates our ability to deliver the best possible outcomes at the highest total return. In doing so, we help protect and advance people, the planet, and business health.

As the chief sustainability officer of the company today, I apply the same principles I did back when I was starting out as a newly graduated Nalco application engineer in 1984. Sustainability is embedded in our culture at Ecolab – it's core to everything we do. We act with purpose, we work together, and we do our part to help change the world. Although we didn't refer to it as sustainability back in 1984, the principle is the same: doing well by our customers to make the world a better place.

Chapter 2

PERSPECTIVE:
THE FOUNDATION
OF SUSTAINABILITY

He profits most who serves best

—MJ Osborn

The Osborn family had been in America for well over two centuries when Merritt J was born in 1879. Thomas Osborn left Ashford, in southeastern England, sometime in late 1637 for Britain's North American colonies. Osborn's arrival in New Haven aboard the Hector in 1638 would put him arriving with a large group of Puritan refugees escaping both religious persecution and conscription into the civil unrest that would spark the English Civil War within a few short years. Four generations later, MJ's father William would find himself in La Porte, Indiana, in a region we refer to today as Michiana.[1]

In 1856, William married Charlotte Armstrong, and the couple would parent eight children, seven of whom would live to adulthood. Sometime before 1870, the Osborn family moved to Buchanan, Michigan, where William bought and ran a business. Merritt was the eighth and final child, and he joined the family on Valentine's Day of 1879. Some 80 years later, he would reflect on the early influence of his family: "As to being a 'go-getter,' I came from a very large family, all hard workers, including my father, who was a furniture manufacturer."[2]

Sometime in 1886, William Osborn returned from a sales trip just in time to watch his plant burn to the ground. MJ remembered staring out the front window, watching the conflagration, and listening to the clang of the fire bells in a failed attempt to extinguish the blaze. The insurance had expired, and William was left with nothing but the family home. Merritt went to work at age ten tending horses and milking cows.[3] He remained in Buchanan until he completed his second year of high school. At that point, his brother landed him a job selling pharmaceuticals in Chicago at $5/week, with a workweek running Monday to Saturday from 8 a.m. to 8 p.m. Merritt met and married "a very fine girl," Susan Bartley, while working in Elkhart, Indiana, in 1901. They raised two sons together and celebrated their fiftieth anniversary before Susan passed away in 1956. Susan was a loyal companion, and MJ credited his desire to provide her with "everything she could possibly want" as one reason he founded Economics Laboratory.[4]

Merritt's brother started his own pharmaceutical business in New York City about 1904, and Merritt worked with him until the business failed due to a lack of working capital. Merritt moved to San Francisco with Eli Lilly right after the 1906 earthquake and fire. He and Susan

25

relocated to St. Paul in 1908 and lived out their lives in the Twin Cities area. He took a job with the pharmaceutical company Parke-Davis and then went to work for the Hamm Brewing Company of St. Paul, where he oversaw the national distribution of a new medicinal malt extract, Digesto. Hamm offered more money than Parke-Davis and more stability. Merritt noted, "While I had learned to like selling, I did not like traveling."[5] He soon ran all advertising for Hamm, including its beers.

Merritt left selling potions and began selling motion in 1911. He first sold White Motor Company trucks in St. Paul and then added the Overland and Willys-Knight dealership. When the Great War began, MJ found himself unable to obtain new vehicles, so he moved to used cars. This led to a brief stint at Nilson Tractor Company, a Minnesota firm launched by two Swedish brothers whose stubbornness clouded their judgment. Rather than sell a poorly managed company, the brothers preferred bankruptcy. Osborn liquidated the company and made all creditors whole (100% payback) and gave shareholders a partial return (60% of their invested capital).

After World War I, Osborn obtained a large Ford dealership and began selling cars. He later recalled:

> [T]he Ford Company were the toughest people to deal with in my experience. I sold my quota [500 cars a year + 100 tractors] and they raised it until . . . they seriously overloaded me beyond the limit of my bank credit and I told them to find me a buyer. This was in 1922 and we were in the midst of a depression and in my sell out, after paying my debts, I lost all but $5,000 of my earnings.
>
> "I never did like the automobile business and my mind then turned to my old love, the chemical business, but I did not have enough money to go into the pharmaceutical business with its multitudes of pills, tablets, solid and fluid extracts, elixirs, and the like. I gave the matter a lot of thought and, remembering in my traveling days how often the hotels had rooms out of service while their carpets were being cleaned (which in those days took ten days to two weeks), I decided to hire a chemist and formulate a product for cleaning carpets on the floor. It was then that I organized Economics Laboratory, Incorporated."

Osborn turned 44 the year he founded EL, well into middle age for a 1920s American male.

I open this chapter with an extended sketch of Merritt Osborn's early life for two reasons. First, I love history, and in so many ways, MJ lived a quintessentially American life, complete with setbacks, serendipity, and the success many could only dream of. Second, the lessons he learned in the first half of his life formed the fundamental perspective, or *weltanschauung*, that permeates Ecolab a century later.

WELTANSCHAUUNG: A PRIMER

Weltanschauung is a German combination of two words: *Welt*, a noun, means world, and *Anschauung*, the noun form of the German verb *schauen*, to look. A weltanschauung is literally a world look, which has been re-fined to a worldview or perception of the world. Encyclopedia.com tells us that a weltanschauung "is a comprehensive conception or theory of the world and the place of humanity in it. It is an intellectual construct that provides both a unified method of analysis for and a set of solutions for the problems of existence."[6] A weltanschauung provides an integrated perspective of life and the world that grounds how we act. As you'll recall from Figure 1.1 in Chapter 1, that perspective leads to a clear purpose and set of priorities – what really matters most – which beget the processes that guide action that drives performance. This chapter focuses on this perspective, and the next one illustrates how MJ's company turned its perspective into purpose and priorities.

The comprehensive nature of a worldview is divided into three components. First, our theory of the world describes *states of the world*, including which people are trustworthy and which are not, whether the world is fundamentally benign or hostile, and whether human capabilities remain relatively fixed or malleable through life. That description also defines our relationships with others, both human and nonhuman. Are we all equal? Am I superior? Inferior? You can think through the implications for business and key relationships with customers, employees, and suppliers that arise from those core assumptions about the state of humanity. Equality supports a collaborative leader, superiority a despot, and inferiority a coward.

Second, a robust weltanschauung articulates a set of *causal relationships* that link actions and outcomes. A theory of the world explains what causes what and why.[7] Causal relationships in business may be simple and readily accepted: "What gets measured gets done." Other causal structures feature complexity and contingency – for example, Fred Herzberger's two-factor theory of employee performance: some factors satisfy needs while others truly motivate; employing the wrong set of factors inhibits, rather than enhances, performance.[8]

Those relationships, what causes what, blossom into full-blown explanations of the world as they graft in notions about the fundamental state of things in the world. One tenant of industrial age management held that "constant supervision brings results" because people prefer loafing to working. This became known as Theory X. Today's knowledge economy leads to a different view of "autonomy brings results" because people prefer creativity to stagnation, or Theory Z.[9] You can see how these worldviews underlie leadership styles, organizational structures, and market strategies.

The final element of a comprehensive theory of reality rests in the *values*, or prescriptive component of a worldview: How *should* I act? What's desirable and what's to be avoided? The way we balance such fundamental choices as self-interest versus altruism, preservation versus exploitation, progress versus tradition, or how we regard elegant technical solutions versus deep relationships are informed by, and inform, our perspective on the world. When we combine the three components, the state of the world, the causal structure of the world, and which ends are worth pursuing, we have a theory of action, or to invoke a more popular term, we have a *business model*. That business model results in a set of *priorities* that every business leader hopes to accomplish. This is what matters most.

An individual's perspective arises from various sources. Genetics play a role in forming our core disposition, including basic personality traits and characteristics such as raw intelligence or emotional resilience, and those innate dispositions constitute our baseline, or "default," weltanschauung. Recent studies indicate that 40–60% of our core personality is inherited, so nature helps explain some portion of our worldview.[10] Nurture provides the other portion, with a mix of individual, family, and community/society experiences refining our fundamental perspective of the world. We have limited evidence of the role that nature played in MJ's worldview, but we have plenty of evidence about the family, community, and societal nurture that a mature leader brought to his new business in 1923.

THE PERSPECTIVE AT ECONOMICS LABORATORY AND ECOLAB

My research into the history of Ecolab – including reading 96 annual reports (no reports exist for 1923, 1941, 1942, and 2022) – reveals an enduring worldview built on five pillars: Respect, Integration, Growth, Humility, and Technology-driven progress (RIGHT). Each pillar describes a state of nature replete with models of causality, and each becomes value-laden over time. Merritt Osborn endowed his company with the RIGHT mindset.

Respect

If Ecolab has a primary perspective, it's respect. The Nilson Tractor incident I wrote about earlier provides an example of MJ's commitment to respect; he worked to liquidate the business in a way that made everyone as whole as possible. Respect recognizes other people's views as intrinsically valuable and equal to oneself, with independent, real, and worthwhile needs, even though those needs may differ from our own. Everyone has dignity, and that dignity drives relationships. The Golden Rule represents a foundational theory of causal action; indeed, a funeral tribute noted that "to anyone who knew MJ Osborn, it was apparent that he followed The Golden Rule – 'Do unto others as you would have them do unto you' – in all his dealings and relationships."[11]

EL, and later Ecolab, would continue to build on that first principle of respect for the customer. In 1966, EB Osborn – who committed himself to carrying on and extending his father's legacy – explained, "It is the company's objective and constant aim to render to our customers what we like to call *total responsibility* for end satisfaction with the product and its benefit."[12] Total responsibility would evolve into its current phrasing at the company: *Circle the Customer*. The idea is to completely embrace the customer with warm support. The priority is not to *sell* an arms-length customer as much as possible, but to *create* a relationship that generates ongoing value for both company and customer.

Respect permeates Ecolab and enriches interactions between people, inside and outside the organization. One of Osborn's original goals was

> to gradually build "a business family" that through the interest of the Company in establishing good working conditions, good pay, plus the opportunity to acquire additional income in excess of wage or salary thru dividends resulting from ownership of Company stock, plus incentives for accomplishment as would result in an atmosphere of "one for all and all for one."

Al Shuman, CEO from 1995–2004, told me that his most important priority was creating and maintaining a company that people wanted to work at and stay at.

Another manifestation of respect for people shines through in Ecolab's commitment to technical expertise. An Ecolab field associate should
know more about the customer's business – the industry and value chain,
not just the company itself – than the customer. Both company and customer benefit from this deep knowledge. In the course of my research,
I ran across the *Klenzade Dairy Farm Sanitation Handbook*, published in
1968 by EL's recently acquired Klenzade corporation of Beloit, Wisconsin. The book taught best practices for running a dairy, and fewer than
5 of its 300 pages contain any material about Klenzade products. I have
on my desk today the fourth edition of the *Nalco Water Handbook*, an
almost 1,400-page tome on water management, not on Nalco solutions.
The priority is to inform, not to sell.

Just as respect provides the bedrock for Ecolab, it also comprises the
footings and foundation on which sustainability builds. The sustainability
movement works toward abandoning a mindset of others as objects to be
exploited for our gain and invites us to see them as subjects of their own
lives. Sustainability requires that we see others as possessing a fundamental dignity. That dignity requires attending to their interests. Sustainable
growth also sees the natural and physical environment, planet Earth, as
a dignified subject unto herself, complete with her own set of very legitimate needs. Respect also points us toward the subjects who will inherit
that earth in the ensuing generations and requires that we take seriously
their needs for and right to a future filled with opportunities for growth
and development.

Integration

I believe that MJ's success derived from his ability to see the interconnected, interdependent, and fully integrated nature of the human and
non-human world. The genius of *Absorbit* lay in recognizing that hotel
owners had two tightly linked problems. They needed to clean carpets
and rugs – more important in the post-pandemic world of the early 1920s
than ever before – and they needed to make money by keeping rooms in
service. Where most had seen what management gurus Jim Collins and
Jerry Porras referred to as the Tyranny of the Or (clean carpets *or* rooms
in service), Osborn perceived the Genius of the And, that by cleaning
carpets in place, downtime – not to mention water usage – would drop
dramatically. Clean *and* in service.[13]

The introduction of EL's second product in 1924, the commercial dishwashing detergent *Soilax*, allowed Osborn to create a dishwashing solution, not just a soap. *Soilax* sold at a higher price than competing detergents, so Osborn developed a mechanical dispenser that helped customers meter *Soilax* to get optimal cleaning without overuse. EL sold less *Soilax* to each customer each year but gained customers for life as they realized the EL solution improved their bottom line. No pun intended, but EL and Ecolab would "rinse and repeat" that formula for the next century.

One powerful manifestation of that formula was the clean-in-place (CIP) solution for the dairy industry in the 1960s. A large commercial dairy runs milk through miles of tubing and piping as it moves from cow to container. In mid-twentieth-century America, cleaning those miles of pipe required disassembly and shut down of the dairy. (Do you see the corollary to *Absorbit*?) EL combined their chemicals with Klenzade's high-pressure hardware to allow farmers to clean and sanitize all that piping without disassembly or shutdown. By the mid-1960s, CIP technology had dramatically extended the shelf life of fresh milk and would later do the same for beer and other beverages. A perspective and priority of integration continues to energize Ecolab to build solutions to real customer needs.

Ecolab also sees communities as integral to its work. Fred Lanners, CEO from 1978 to 1982, began a program to train Laotian and Hmong refugees settling in the Twin Cities following the end of the Vietnam War. Ecolab paid refugees while it trained them to repair dishwashing equipment, and the company paid them to learn English. Technical skill and English proficiency carried far more value than either alone. Refugees, the Twin Cities, and local businesses all prospered. Today the Twin Cities hosts a very large and vibrant community of Laotians.

Doug Baker, CEO from 2004 to 2021, integrated Ecolab and St. Paul's civic interests. Ecolab leased its existing downtown office tower but needed to move headquarters to accommodate an ever-growing number of employees. Baker and his team helped find a new tenant for their old space, which helped keep the St. Paul downtown full. As a leaseholder, Ecolab had no legal obligation to find its own replacement; however, Baker noted, "I'm a loyalist; this is Ecolab's neighborhood. I am also a realist; we need each other. St. Paul is weaker without us, and we are weaker with an unhealthy St. Paul."[14]

To say that sustainability requires the perspective of an interconnected, interdependent, and integrated world seems both obvious and simplistic. It is nonetheless true despite its simplicity. Human life, from the family to the school to the community, becomes sustainable and resilient when people feel, and have, strong connections with each other. Making a dent in our greatest social challenges requires system-wide solutions that leverage the unique skills of different groups. As the English poet John Donne noted over a half-millennium ago, no [hu]man is an island. I'd add that neither is an island isolated from its surrounding biosphere. Restoring the planet to a more sustainable state requires that business leaders see their actions, and those of their companies, as supporting an interdependent and integrated effort to restore a healthy climate. The priority must be on holistic solutions.

Growth

Growth presumes a beneficent world; an unforgiving one hardly encourages the kind of risk-taking that leads to meaningful human progress. The early history of the Osborn family exemplifies a growth mindset. The patriarch, Thomas Osborn, fled the harsh political and social climate of seventeenth-century England for the new opportunities the Colonies might bring, and his descendants followed thousands of American pioneers in a great westward expansion they believed was their manifest destiny. During MJ's time as an auto dealer, he experienced the greatest decade of growth the auto industry ever knew. In 1910, 1 in 137 Minnesotans owned a car; a decade later 1 in 7 did, a *nineteen-fold increase* in the number of vehicles on the road.[15] Merritt saw the opportunity and the benefits that growth could bring, and so growth became a not-so-hidden priority that underlies the others at his company.

We noted in Chapter 1 that sales growth, profit growth, and increasing returns to shareholders were in 1923, and are in 2022, clear priorities at the company. MJ had a clear causal map of how sales and profit would grow; he laid out his philosophy in a 1953 letter to his associates: "He profits most who serves best."[16] I hope you see the *integrated* link between *growth* and *respect*. The pursuit of growth over the decades would lead EL into the consumer business in 1948, international markets in 1955, the dairy business in the early 1960s, industrial lubricants and cleaning products in 1965, and textile care and laundry services in 1973. The name change to Ecolab in 1986 followed its expansion into pest elimination in 1985. Expansion continued into the quick service restaurant cleaning business with the 1994 acquisition of Kay Chemicals, and Ecolab entered the water management business with its 2011 purchase of Nalco. Today the company is growing businesses in the life sciences, data centers, digital training, and predictive data analytics.

Growth also took place in the social and environmental spheres. Fred Lanners noted that in 1947 EL developed a spot remover for commercial dishware that eliminated the need for staff to use dirty hands and dishtowels to wipe spots off just-sanitized glasses, plates, and silverware. He boldly claimed that *"We made sanitation economically attractive, which did more to advance public health than all of the laws and enforcement put together."*[17] With the first Earth Day in 1970, Ecolab introduced its line of *Ecotemp* dishwashers and detergents, machines designed to provide the same level of cleaning and sanitation at lower temperatures. *Ecotemp* products continue to help institutional customers (hospitals, hotels, restaurants, and schools) save both water and energy in their ware washing operations. The company now makes and markets a high-temperature dishwasher, which seems the opposite of *Ecotemp*; however, the new machine works faster and requires less water and energy than competing products.

Lasting sustainability must combine preservation with progress; it will foresee and foster growth. Some critics see development and progress as the problem. However, prospects for a low-growth or no-growth future dim enthusiasm for the type of changes needed, increase the level of acrimony around changes, and needlessly extend the time horizon for action. I know from my experience in developing countries that economic growth improves public health, the rights of many marginalized groups, and as people's incomes rise, they become more concerned about preserving the natural environment.[18] Growth is not the enemy – unbridled or inappropriate growth is. Ecolab provides a template for truly triple-bottom-line (TBL) growth; it's not sustainability or growth, it's sustainability through growth.

Humility

Humility is a value deeply rooted in many theological traditions, including Christianity and its Puritan interpretation that motivated Thomas Osborn to leave England. Most people, however, misunderstand humility and see it as self-deprecation or a diminished view of the self. Psychologist June

Price Tangey refutes that false view. She argues that true humility lies in an *accurate* sense of self that recognizes and celebrates both *strengths and weaknesses*. The Puritan theology to which Thomas Osborn most likely adhered described this as "breaking the false self-confidence."[19] The death of his eldest sibling showed MJ at an early age that life was fragile and not guaranteed, and the fire he witnessed as a young child further deepened a perspective that people don't completely control their own economic destiny. The failure of his brother's business because of a lack of working capital only reinforced that lesson.

MJ knew his own strengths and the sad experience of the Nilson Tractor Company – the owners' pride and stubbornness scuttled a sale of the business – led him to an honest assessment of the prospects for EL. As he sold $50,000 of stock in the mid-1920s, he made sure investors knew that EL was a "blue sky" venture and they could – and likely would – lose it all. Sixty-plus years later, his successor Sandy Greve (CEO 1983–1995) bought ChemLawn, noting, "You only prove you are right or you're wrong later. But we're reasonably confident. We would not have taken action if we thought the risks were so high that we were foolhardy."[20] They seemed humble going in, but it would take four painful years for Greve to sell ChemLawn in 1991. The team had been foolhardy. Humility is about strengths and weaknesses. Humility shines through today in the continual development of Ecolab associates' technical expertise and the company's commitment to ongoing research.

Ecolab has always taken a humble stance in its relationships with governments and regulators. From its inception, MJ and others realized that working with health departments – seeing them as equal and valuable partners – would benefit the company, the government, the customer, and the general public. EB Osborn expanded that commitment to the environmental sphere in the late 1960s and early 1970s when he wrote that the government had a legitimate and vital role to play in solving the collective problem of saving energy and cleaning water. That commitment to work hand-in-glove with the government continues today. In 2020, Ecolab's *Sink and Surface* cleaner was the first product certified by the EPA to kill the COVID-19 virus in 15 seconds. The company recognized that its expertise (an element of humility) could make an impact. Ecolab also donated millions in cleaning supplies and grants to organizations, blunting the economic consequences of the pandemic.[21]

A sustainable future hangs on our collective ability to adopt a humble perspective. Admitting our role in creating the social and environmental challenges facing our world represents the necessary first step. Until we all admit we are part of the problem, real solutions will elude us. We must admit our failures, but a humble look at ourselves should also energize us with hope in our capabilities to solve intractable problems, whether in human or natural environments. Humility links with attitudes and assumptions about how we grow ourselves to a sustainable future. Strategies that work to mitigate our weaknesses and failures become invitations to stagnation unless we couple those strategies with faith in our latent abilities to create a world that future generations will be happy to inherit.

Technology

The final element in the RIGHT principles that were core to MJ Osborn's worldview is a very positive view of the role of technology. Merritt's father William became a manufacturing plant owner in the 1870–1880s, following the momentum of the ongoing and maturing industrial revolution. MJ began selling scientific pharmaceuticals at the turn of the twentieth century and jumped into the emerging technology of automobiles. He eventually named his company Economics Laboratory, the first word signifying savings and the latter that his products came from science-based technological research.

EB Osborn took pride in dedicating the MJ Osborn Research Center in 1965. The center brought together the company's 125 research scientists for the first time. That number exceeds 1,600 today, fanned out over the globe yet guided by the same core perspective. In 1969, EL developed a unique version of its logo, featuring an atom and nucleus, to highlight its commitment to research and new technologies. Based on 75 years of data, the company funds its research and development activities at just shy of 1.8% of sales.

Ecolab gets a lot for that investment. Patent output provides a common metric to compare research efficiency between organizations. I looked at Ecolab's patent performance over the decade of the 2010s compared to a large, well-known competitor, Procter & Gamble. Ecolab spends about one-tenth of what P&G budgets and generates about one-third as many patents. Behind the leader? No. Ecolab generates one patent per million dollars of R&D expense, but it takes P&G $3.44 million (that is 3.5 times as much) to generate a patent.[22] Ecolab's leaders and research teams have a highly efficient process. I'll describe in Chapter 6 how that process focuses not just on patents but on useful patents and products.

The company has long used technology and innovation to benefit communities and societies as well as customers. MJ wrote to his shareholders that

> early in 1942 the U.S. Army medical Corps commenced to show interest in one of our research developments, a patented organic chlorine germicide capable of maintaining stability for unusually extended periods in the presence of organic matter . . . in 1943, they had adopted our product [Mikroklene] as a "standard item" and had placed it on the U.S. Army Quartermaster's Table for use in sterilizing men's mess kits in barracks and field to prevent the spread of saliva borne diseases.[23]

In the mid-1960s, the Magnus (industrial) division had developed and deployed technology for cleaning up oceanic oil spills, an unfortunate but lucrative business during that time. Technological solutions continue to solve critical sustainability problems today. In 2018, Ecolab created the first EPA-approved laundry disinfectant to kill *Clostridium difficile*, a leading cause of healthcare associated infections.[24]

The debate over technology's role in creating a sustainable world rages on. Technology's harshest critics rightfully note that most of our ecological – and many of our social – ills sink their roots deep into the soil of technological innovation. We create technologies to solve existing problems, but these generate their own harmful byproducts. Despite that bleak view, I hold, as do many others, that new, appropriately bounded technologies mark the path ahead. Society can't go back to the days of horses, buggies, and outhouses to solve our crises, whether we are dealing with climate change or hospital-acquired infections. The challenge for every company and every leader lies in designing and bringing to market technologies that meet TBL criteria.

I close my discussion of perspective by returning to Chapter 1's two meta-worldviews – superordinate weltanschauungen – technical or relational. Respect, Integration, Humility, and Growth all ground themselves in relationships between others, or between the past, present, and future. Even the underlying role of Technology has a relational component: as practiced at Ecolab, technological progress manifests respect toward true customer needs. Integrated and humble technologies satisfy a TBL agenda, fostering growth for people, the planet, and profits. Figure 2.1 plugs the first content into the skeleton of sustainable advantage. I'll make two brief comments here.

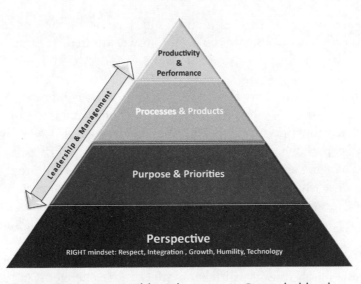

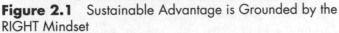

Figure 2.1   Sustainable Advantage is Grounded by the RIGHT Mindset

First, the RIGHT perspective is in fact the foundation from which Ecolab's sustainability advantage builds. As you'll see in the next chapter, perspective frames purpose and informs priorities.

Second, Figure 2.1 points the way to a "yarn-dyed" advantage. You begin with a clear weltanschauung or comprehensive perspective of the world. At Ecolab, that perspective traces its roots back centuries. MJ inherited some fundamental, baked-in assumptions about the state of the world from his family and early progenitors. His lived experiences in the late nineteenth and early twentieth centuries yielded a set of theories about what caused what, and why. I believe that, if pressed, MJ would be able to articulate some of these perspectives, such as respect for people, the desire for growth, and the role of technology and science in providing solutions. My sense, however, is that humility and an integrated view of the world were taken for granted by him – he never seems to act on any other assumptions – that he would have difficulty explaining these two perspectives. Whether easy to articulate or deeply tacit, perspective sets the stage for everything that follows.

LESSONS FOR LEADERS

A natural question for you should be, "But I don't have a century-old perspective and yarn-dyed values. What can I *really* learn from Ecolab?"

There are things you can learn and do to draw on the best of what the Ecolab case teaches. Below you'll find answers to that question and actionable steps to begin, or strengthen, the yarn-dyeing going on in your organization.

I'll begin my summary lessons section with some good news: You can do this. *Yarn-dyed* is a helpful metaphor, but organizations can change and evolve their perspectives, priorities, and processes. Now the bad news: Deep change like this takes work, real work, and lots of it over time. Changing a weltanschauung and the strategy and culture that rests on top of it will make many in your organization uncomfortable, as it requires personal, as much as organizational, change. That said, I suggest five things to keep in mind as you move toward a RIGHT mindset:

1. *Be realistic* about how much change you can effect and expect and how much time it will take to effect those changes. Startups and small organizations have an easier time; indeed, MJ built his worldview from employee #1 up, while everyone else entered an organization operating with the RIGHT perspective. The larger your organization, the more effort and energy it will take, and you'll need to sustain that effort and energy for a longer period of time. None of this should shock you. As one of my colleagues notes, it will take you four times longer and cost four times as much as you estimate. Just know that it will be worth it.

    Begin with an audit. Where are we today on each of the RIGHT elements? I suggest going one step behind the RIGHT elements and asking, "Is our fundamental worldview relational or technical?" It's harder to instill the RIGHT elements where a technical orientation carries the day because elements like respect and humility have a harder time getting traction in a highly technical environment. The goal of an audit is twofold. First, an audit creates a baseline from which you can measure progress. Second, most audits reveal differential progress. You'll likely find that some RIGHT elements already permeate the organization's perspective. Your audit will identify the strongest platform to build on.

2. *Begin at the beginning*, and the beginning is respect. True respect, the type grounded in the fundamental dignity of the planet and all its inhabitants, living and nonliving, as innately valuable and worthwhile, enables progress on the remaining RIGHT elements. Respect colors and frames how the other elements are perceived. For example,

an attitude of integration forms differently with the self at the center than with others there. Respect also frames what type of growth you'll seek, it encourages humility, and bounds and constrains technology. Respect must be first among equals.

3. *Top-down matters.* Without the support of top management, a weltanschauung can't and won't change. The CEO doesn't have to initiate the change toward a sustainable, RIGHT worldview, but she has to establish buy-in herself. People throughout the organization will have different takes on any attempt to change fundamental perspectives, some positive and others decidedly negative. Everyone will, however, have the same question: "Is it real?" The CEO, and others in the C-suite, provide the only answer that matters to that question. If they support moving to RIGHT in word, you've got a prayer; if they support it in deed, then you've got a good chance. If they continue to support it over time and take the final two steps, then you'll succeed.

4. *Overcommunicate* and do more than just talk about moving to RIGHT. Common wisdom tells us that people remember 10% of what they hear, 20% of what they read, and 80% of what they see. I've seen organizations make changes just as deep and lasting as a change to RIGHT when they began to take safety seriously. Real change happened when people saw leaders acting safely, when they read signs, memos, and paystubs that carried messages about safety, and when they heard safety messages at the beginning of each meeting. Help people understand what the RIGHT elements are, and how they can put them into practice, and then repeat that message multiple times in multiple ways.

5. *Embed* the desired worldview into your systems, particularly those systems that impact and shape the human capital in your organization. One key lesson from Ecolab is that it's the second generation of leadership that yarn-dyes the worldview. EB Osborn, and those who followed him, yarn-dyed the culture as they continued to employ the RIGHT view. You begin to think about the next generation when you ask, "How do respect and the other core elements factor into hiring decisions in our organization? Does our team hire based on behavioral criteria that give us a chance to see respect in action?" A RIGHT view does not come from an Ivy League pedigree or a high GPA. Go beyond just hiring and think about how onboarding, training, and performance review processes all provide an opportunity to share and embed a RIGHT perspective.

CONCLUSION

I hope you've enjoyed this chapter for the window it opened into Ecolab's history. I also hope you've underlined passages that speak to you and your needs. I've discussed the base level of the pyramid of sustainable advantage; what follows in Chapters 5–9 will link that base to strategic process and triple-bottom-line performance. Movement up the pyramid does not happen by capillary action – a property of water that allows it to flow upward in small amounts. Chapter 3 chronicles that movement upward from perspective, through purpose and priorities and to processes. As you'll see in Chapter 4, that movement relies on the active involvement of senior leaders, and those leaders have to lead.

EMILIO'S THOUGHTS
Making an Impact Through Actions Large and Small

Over the past five years, I've attended many sustainability leadership conferences and roundtables to gain a better understanding of how companies are adopting sustainability practices and to learn about the relevance of sustainability to major brands. At these events, chief sustainability officers describe their company's mission and how they plan to operationalize sustainability and circularity in their companies. I recall one instance where I was asked how Ecolab embeds sustainability into its new technology pipeline. I paused for a moment and said: "We find the customer need and fill it."

I'm not sure what the more than 70 sustainability leaders from a range of global brands expected, but it changed the tone of the meeting. At Ecolab, our worldview is shaped by our customers. Our values, capabilities, and priorities are designed to address customer needs through innovative technology, deep customer knowledge, and outstanding service. The other sustainability leaders in the room were focused on the impact and risks to their enterprises. Don't get me wrong, that's important. But Ecolab also looks outward because our greatest sustainability impact is through our customers.

Trust, credibility, and respect are the foundation of Ecolab's customer relationships. Our highly trained field teams work side-by-side with customers to solve problems, enhance operations and help grow their businesses. We quantify the value of business performance while reducing the use of natural resources. It's that bird's-eye view of customer challenges that informs our innovation and technology portfolio. We do this for companies ranging from high-tech to small Mom-and-Pop operations. No matter who the customer is, we know we can make a difference.

Take Jonathan Butwinick, for example. He's an engineer at Ecolab. He gave up a job in the aerospace industry to work for us because he wanted to make a bigger impact in the world. And do you know what he's working on? Dishwashers. Jonathan was part of a team that developed our new Ecolab High Temperature (EHT) professional dishwasher. I know dishwashers might not seem all that exciting. But this machine does in 60 seconds what your dishwasher at home does in 60 minutes. We think that's pretty exciting. And what's even more exciting is this: It uses half as much water and half as much energy as the previous generation of restaurant dishwashers. For every new EHT dishwasher we install, we save enough water to fill two backyard swimming pools every year and enough energy to drive a Toyota Prius 200 miles every day.

In the US alone there are 660,000 restaurants, and almost every single one of them has at least one dishwasher. Imagine the water and energy savings if all of those restaurants replaced their dishwashers with newer, more efficient models. Then consider the savings if we applied this solution globally.

The same is true for automotive companies, dairies, microchip makers, lodging, steelmakers, and so on. In each case, we provide smart technology and services that enable them to reduce, reuse, and recycle water. The bottom line: If you do big and small things at enough places, you start making a real impact on the world. That's what we do at Ecolab. Through relationships, insights, and customer-driven solutions, we are making a positive impact each and every day all across the world.

Chapter 3

FROM PERSPECTIVE TO PURPOSE: eROI AND THE THREE PHASES OF SUSTAINABILITY

If you don't know where you're going, any road will get you there.
—The Cheshire Cat (Lewis Carroll, *Alice's Adventures in Wonderland*)

Las Vegas is a land of paradox. Let's begin with its name, which literally means "the meadows." Few to none of its 32 million visitors in 2021 would have described Vegas as anything like meadows as they peered over a parched land of sand and rock and wiped the sweat from their brows. The city got its name from the early-nineteenth-century explorers who found a grass-filled valley fed by local springs.[1] In 1905, those springs would entice the San Pedro, Los Angeles, and Salt Lake railroad to choose Vegas as a water stop for its steam engines. A town was born and Las Vegas became a haven for gambling, drinking, and the sex trade from its earliest days. The city's population exploded, and the core of modern Las Vegas took shape in 1931 when the US government completed the hydroelectric Hoover Dam.

Cheap electricity fueled the growth of the famous Strip over the decades, which currently features at least 12 *million* lights and costs casino operators a half-*billion* dollars a year to operate. And those 32 million guests (it was 42 million before the pandemic in 2020), make the Las Vegas Strip the third most visited site in the United States.[2] Those visitors stay in one of 150,000 hotel rooms (the city has 14 of the 20 largest hotels in the world!), dine at one of 4,337 restaurants, or 1 per 150 full-time residents, gamble at one of 200,000 slot machines or 31 casinos on the Strip itself, and consume lots of alcohol. The Mandalay Bay hotel reportedly spends about $6 million per year on spirits, and if you multiply that over the 30 properties on the Strip, drinking alone is a $180 million business. One side of the Vegas paradox is the tremendous economic success the city and region have enjoyed; the city operates at a scale of entertainment and tourism that boggles the mind.

That scale creates equally boggling problems for a sustainable economy, the other side of the paradox. The economic success that seems so stable builds on incredibly shaky, risky human and ecological foundations. Each of those 42 million visitors, for example, represents a disease vector (inbound and outbound) with global reach, and casino operators must manage the risks of hotel-acquired illnesses such as legionella, foodborne illnesses, or the lack of sanitation in hotel and casino restrooms. All of this economic activity takes place in a valley where the average daily temperature in July is 107°F, 42°C. A single one-hundred-acre lot on the Strip consumes 350 million gallons of water each year just to keep its 13 properties cool. That 25 city-block area consumes enough to meet the yearly drinking water needs of one in six Vegas residents.

Vegas prospered on the premise of stable electricity and a water supply from nearby Lake Mead – created by the Hoover Dam. The lake is fed by natural springs, but years-long drought means that as of 2022, the lake sits at less than 30% of its capacity.[3] Below a certain level, the dam won't generate any electricity and the city will go dark. The desert mirage generates huge economic profits and equally huge sustainability challenges in terms of human health and environmental stability.

When it comes to water services for the restaurant and hospitality industry, Ecolab owns the Las Vegas Strip. Of the 30 properties on Las Vegas Boulevard, all but a handful have service contracts with Ecolab's institutional business, for restaurant and hospitality cleaning, sanitizing, and warewashing operations, with Nalco Water's institutional division for air conditioning water tower maintenance, boiler/ steam room applications, and potable water management for tens of thousands of individual hotel rooms, or with Ecolab's pest control division to maintain a bug-free and clean environment. Ecolab's business benefits from this concentration as several of its field representatives have most of their routes in a single hotel. The Mandalay Bay, for example, has 21 restaurants onsite and many of those are serviced by a single territory manager.

The hotels benefit as Ecolab reps learn their businesses tremendously well. Territory manager Jose Prado services Ecolab equipment at the Mandalay Bay and routinely checks on and troubleshoots problems with equipment from other vendors. He'll train new staff on overall restaurant health, safety, and machine maintenance, and he'll connect his customers with other Ecolab products they need to maintain a high level of hygiene. Regarding water, Nalco's expertise helps customers improve their overall water management strategy. That 100-acre, 13-property plot mentioned above is a Nalco customer. Michael Sawlsville, the district manager, helps the property owner preserve equipment life by rotating production through different generators and cooling fans to avoid excessive scaling and corrosion. He's also working on a plan to help the owner reduce their annual water usage by 30%, which is no small impact in a desert where water is the scarcest of resources.

Las Vegas illustrates the integrated nature of Ecolab's businesses, and it provides a great setting to see how the RIGHT perspective of MJ's original core values continues to guide what its associates do on a daily basis. Jose

Prado and Michael Sawlsville employ each of the RIGHT elements as they help their customers run smooth operations and solve the unique challenges of serving millions of people each year in a very hostile natural environment. My goal in this chapter is to link that RIGHT perspective to the processes that drive both business and sustainability success for Ecolab. After laying that foundation, I'll describe how one key process, eROI, ties Ecolab's fundamental purpose and priorities to measurable results, and how the foundational logic of eROI can help your company work through the three phases of business sustainability.

FROM PERSPECTIVE TO PRIORITIES

Figure 3.1 shows the movement up the pyramid I introduced in Chapter 1. The basic structure remains the same, but I've added the core Ecolab priorities at the next level as well as the processes the company uses to bring those priorities to fruition in its markets and activities. The change in shade as you move up the pyramid (loosely) signals a change in effort from the work of leadership to management. Leaders constantly reinforce perspective and tie actions back to purpose. Managers orient people around the priorities that underlie an organization's most critical resource allocation decisions: budgeting, especially capital budgeting, and human capital management, or hiring, training, and compensation.

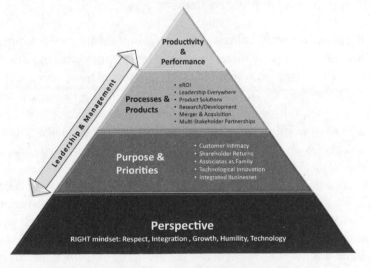

Figure 3.1   Sustainable Advantage at Ecolab

I'll talk more about the difference between leadership and management in the next two chapters.

Perspective and Purpose

Ecolab's 2022 purpose and values allow us to see the clear and explicit connections between the RIGHT perspective and its purpose:

> *Our purpose:* We partner to make the world cleaner, safer, and healthier – helping customers succeed while protecting people and the resources vital to life.
>
> *Our values:* Our values are internal driving principles that guide how we work:
> - We reach our goals.
> - We do what's right.
> - We challenge ourselves.
> - We work together with diverse perspectives.
> - We make a difference.
> - And we do this all with care, putting safety first.[4]

The company's purpose targets each of the 3Ps of sustainability: people, the planet, and profit. As you read the purpose and values, you may not see the RIGHT perspective at work, so let me link the company's public purpose with its private paradigm:

- *Respect.* Respect builds on the fundamental premise of dignity for those the company interacts with. The purpose talks of partnership, and successful partnerships build on a foundation of respect. I also see respect in the phrase "vital for life," which puts business activity in an overarching context of protecting and enhancing life. Respect powers the internal values of incorporating diversity and people working with care and concern for safety, another manifestation of the respect for life.
- *Integration.* MJ saw the world as an integrated whole with the pieces inseparable and reinforcing each other. The purpose considers people, planet, and profit as interconnected, as it does cleanliness, safety, and health. These are all "and" statements, not "or" ones, no trade-offs allowed. Note that the values of reaching goals and doing so ethically (doing what's right) appear next to each other. Too many

business leaders see goal achievement and ethical action as mutually exclusive and willingly cut corners. Ecolab people see the two as connected and integrated.

- *Growth*. The internal values reflect the reality and worth of growth. Ecolab people challenge themselves in many ways: growing their individual routes or market areas, deepening their knowledge base, and helping customers solve vexing problems. The purpose notes that customers should also succeed through the relationship, and one metric of customer success is growth of revenue, profit, or 3P impact.

- *Humility*. Humility is an accurate sense of self, including both strengths and weaknesses, which I see reflected in the key word *partner*. Ecolab isn't just bringing products to market, selling superior solutions, or providing great service to its customers. Ecolab partners with them to achieve their own goals and those of the larger world. When Jose Prado teaches workers at Mandalay Bay how to keep a kitchen clean, he helps his customer reach their own profitability goals; he also helps each hotel visitor have a cleaner, healthier, and safer visit.

- *Technology*. Ecolab is a chemistry company, a technical field. The importance of technology does not get explicit recognition in the purpose statement or the values; however, it lies just below the surface. "Protecting people and the resources vital to life" comes through the technical solutions of better chemistry. Ecolab makes the world better for each stakeholder through its technical expertise on display in its various products, solutions, and management services; indeed, each of the four pillars that ground the value proposition entail technical solutions for complex and technical problems.

Strategy scholar Ed Freeman wrote his groundbreaking book *Strategic Management: A Stakeholder Approach* in 1984.[5] Over the next 35 years, others would build on his insights and usher in the *stakeholder revolution*, culminating in the Business Roundtable's declaration that the purpose of business is to serve the interests of all stakeholders, not merely shareholders.[6] Note that when Freeman brought this idea to our collective attention, Ecolab had been practicing stakeholder management for five decades, and Nalco for four and a half; by the time the business community came on board, stakeholder principles and priorities had guided six generations of Ecolab CEOs.

Purpose and Priorities

CEOs throughout the years offered different flavors of priorities. MJ spoke about meeting customer needs, making associates feel like family, and providing a great shareholder return. Fred Lanners identified four key priorities that guided the company through its first half century: "First, products must fill an existing need. . . . Second, we would lead the way in developing new products and technology; third, . . . we would know more about the cleaning process of that industry than anyone else, including our customers; fourth, customer service is the key to success."[7] Al Schuman would collapse that into two simple priorities still active today: circle the customer, circle the globe.

My interactions with people across both companies revealed five "in-practice" or lived priorities that guide action and decision-making at Ecolab:

- *Customer intimacy.* MJ focused his efforts on understanding real needs and Nalco's Herb Kern used a simple phrase: "Find the customer need and fill it." Ecolab builds its business on what modern strategists refer to as customer intimacy, developing close and rich relationships of value. Customer intimacy includes Lanners' ideas about deep knowledge of a customer's business and providing outstanding service. It takes Michael Sawlsville years to develop the level of customer intimacy that makes him a trusted advisor on water management. Customer intimacy grows out of a respect for all and a recognition of their dignity.
- *Shareholder return.* I put shareholder return as the second priority because as I speak with associates across the company, making sales, growing the business, and earning solid returns for investors permeates every conversation. As Emilio noted in his comments in Chapter 1, the Ecolab people just don't buy into the assumption that it's all about profits *or* people *or* planet. Replace *or* with *and*. Providing a great return for shareholders ensures that Ecolab's businesses create real value, and those returns generate the cash flows needed to fuel further investments in planet and people enhancing solutions.
- *Associates as family.* Every company talks the talk about the importance of people. Ecolab walks the walk. As you'll learn in Chapter 5, the company invests real money and time in training its new associates. It continues to invest in its growth and development over

time. Both Ecolab and Nalco have long histories of providing good wages and excellent benefits packages, and both adopted employee stock purchase programs early in their history. Beyond that, however, Ecolab offers employees the satisfaction – not arrogance – of working for a market leader. Everyone wants to be on a winning team.

- *Technological innovation.* MJ hired his first director of research, Robert G. Murray, in 1927 and his first PhD, Dr. John Wilson in 1931. Later, as the Great Depression rolled on, MJ considered a proposal to cut the size of the research lab. He recounts his conversation with Wilson about each member of the staff and concluded:

> It seems to me that we would cripple our effort out of all proportions [to] the gain if we dispense with anyone now on the laboratory staff. To consider doing so would be even more ill-advised in the light of the increasing number of problems with which we are faced and which the laboratory is being asked to work on.

That commitment to science and technology as the core of the business remains today.

- *Integrated businesses.* From the *Soilax* dispenser in 1927 through the development of *Finish* and *Jet Dry* to complement *Electrasol* to today's efforts by people like Jose Prado to help sell pest control services and other products to his restaurants, the Ecolab portfolio truly centers on the concept of circling the customer. Integrating business units does not mean, however, creating an organization where everyone knows everything about every Ecolab service. Each business remains separate so that field associates, support staff, and executive leaders remain laser-focused on the complex and specialized knowledge and skill to meet each customer's need.

The five priorities appear to map cleanly onto each element of the RIGHT perspective, but my brief description has omitted the reality that *every value permeates every priority*. Take integration for example. Respect for the customer, particularly the knowledge to meet deep customer needs, limits integration between business units. Humility also plays a role; excessive integration – creating one uber-division where each associate sold every product – assumes an unrealistic human ability to gain and retain the technical skill needed in each specific business unit. Each priority becomes stronger and more resilient because each weaves together multiple facets of the RIGHT perspective. You'll see this in the next section where we move from intangible priorities and goals to the tangible processes that bring them to life.

FROM PRIORITY TO PROCESS: THE EXAMPLE eROI

Processes are where the rubber hits the road, the behaviors that make priorities real. They include the sequences of behaviors or checklists. They define and support organizational structures such as product divisions (think institutional, industrial, and pest control) and market organizations such as sales territories. The three key processes in any organization are budgeting, training, and reporting. The process of calculating the *exponential return on investment* (eROI) clearly falls into the latter category, but as I'll describe, it also includes elements of budgeting and training. In many ways, eROI captures Ecolab's current business model and value proposition.

eROI: The Basics

eROI is a measurable tool that each Ecolab team uses to prove the value the company's products and services bring to a customer's operations. Emilio created eROI in 2009 while working at Nalco, and I'll leave it to him to describe its origin. I can trace the logic of eROI, a tool to measure and report customer and societal value, to Herb Kern's idea that Nalco would be "honest and offer something good to society." It's also consistent with MJ's original vision that EL's products would result in the "saving of time – the lightening of labor – and the reduction of cost." eROI captures and synthesizes multiple measures of customer value across different aspects of the business.

A simple formula captures eROI:

Total dollar value delivered – Incremental dollar invesment /
Incremental dollar invesment.

Total dollar value delivered breaks into three categories, which represent investment returns to customers from using Ecolab products and services. Figure 3.2 describes the dimensions of each category. eROI measures three types of impacts: First, those that directly impact business outcomes, their customers, and their investors; second, the underlying

SUSTAINABILITY AT HIGHEST RETURN

Figure 3.2 The Components of eROI

drivers of those direct impacts, such as productivity and longer asset life; and third, the impact that extends beyond the four walls of the customer's operations and impacts local, regional, national, and global communities.

The other element of eROI is the incremental investment a customer pays for Ecolab products and services. That's not always the same as the total Ecolab bill. Where customers have a clear competitive choice – such as a competing provider of pest control or cooling tower management, the incremental cost represents the difference between Ecolab and that competitor. In some instances, such as using 3D TRASAR™ technology or developing a global water management strategy, customers can't choose from a competitive offering, and so the incremental cost would be the total cost of the service.

eROI and Its Links to Perspective and Priorities

eROI manifests respect in two important ways: first that customers deserve a positive return for their investment in Ecolab products and services, and second, that they should know what that return is. eROI goes beyond metrics such as Net Promoter Score (how likely are you to recommend Ecolab services to someone you know?) or qualitative measures such as customer satisfaction: eROI comes as a hard number, based on observed measures of performance.

eROI fosters the strategic priority of customer intimacy. To calculate eROI, Ecolab associates must have enough knowledge of the customer business to quantify gains in health, safety, brand protection, asset life, productivity, and actual energy savings. To be intimate with a customer is to know that customer, and to know the business well enough to spot areas where new value can be created in a relationship. eROI, provided periodically to every customer, makes the abstract strategy of customer intimacy tangible and tactical through a hard number.

The measure integrates value created at different levels for each customer: transactional, operational, and societal, and because each business at Ecolab generates its own eROI for customers, the tool helps customers see the value of doing business with an integrated partner. That integration facilitates growth for both parties. Ecolab reps can introduce more products and services – they can circle the customer – based on hard data that deepening the relationship creates more value. Individualized eROI reports allow customers to see how each Ecolab product or service drives greater sales growth or customer satisfaction through brand protection and improved safety. The final component of eROI, environmental impact, contributes to another form of growth – the growth of a green society.

The very nature of eROI, a return on investment, enhances customer intimacy as it puts on display the reality that shareholder (economic) returns matter to both the company and its customer. It fosters true win-win relationships. Rather than seeing sales as a mere transaction where money moves from customer to Ecolab, eROI puts the relationship on a more solid footing of joint value creation. eROI extends the notion of joint value creation to the societal level. Although eROI may only measure the impact of energy savings on the customer's bottom line, the measure could easily expand to include the monetized social value of a gallon of water saved, an infection prevented, or a thermal BTU saved.

In terms of technology, eROI helps customers understand and see the value of advanced technology solutions. The bedrock of any Ecolab product portfolio is a technical solution – cleaning, water purification chemicals, pest control solutions, or technical consulting, and eROI clarifies the payback on the purchase. For me, eROI manifests humility. I've studied and consulted with dozens of companies over the years and Ecolab is one of a very few who are willing to proactively disclose their value to customers. The cadence of eROI means that Ecolab will regularly report the value it creates or destroys for customers, which exposes both Ecolab's strengths and weaknesses. That's the essence of humility.

I'll close this discussion of eROI by showing one final way that it links perspective and priorities and makes them real through processes. eROI impacts budgeting processes for both Ecolab and its customers. The concept adds a layer of rigor for product development and pricing for Ecolab as it keeps development teams and pricing specialists focused on the three different levels of return. eROI is just as likely to encourage the company to charge more rather than less, consistent with MJ's original vision, price at a premium and still improve a customer's bottom line. That customer can also use eROI in improving its own budget processes; indeed, why not require other suppliers to quantify the value of their products and services?

eROI infuses training and professional development among Ecolab associates. First, everyone must have enough business knowledge to understand the concept – pretty straightforward – and how the company's offerings generate savings along each dimension. This transforms technicians and installers into business advisors, but it also makes sales and service professionals knowledgeable about the technical particulars that generate savings. Second, and most importantly to me, eROI helps develop the broad and integrated perspective that underlies both customer intimacy and the goal to circle the customer.

Jose Prado told me that Ecolab trained him, in multiple ways over multiple times, to look at his customer's operations more broadly. To see beyond the Ecolab systems is to look at the kitchen as a whole and look for ways to create value. That's the essence of the circle the customer philosophy, but it's also the foundation of eROI – a broader and more extended look at overall business performance.

eROI AND SUSTAINABILITY

eROI has proven to be a powerful tool for keeping associates and customers centered on the ultimate mission of the company around the four pillars of clean water, safe food, healthy environments, and renewable climates. eROI is not a sustainability strategy, just a measure of performance. However, we can see the core elements of a dynamic process to create a sustainable organization when we rearrange the elements of each eROI category: business outcomes, operational drivers, and environmental impact into a set of internal (asset life, productivity, cost), customer value (brand protection, product quality), and societal (water, energy, greenhouse gas emissions) elements.

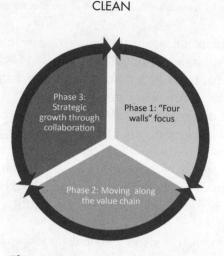

Figure 3.3 The Three Phases of Sustainability

When recast in this way, the core logic of eROI helps us see how a company can think about its journey to sustainability. Figure 3.3 illustrates the three phases, or generations, of actions that every company should take: a focus on becoming more sustainable within the "four walls" of the firm; creating customer benefit all along the value chain; and finally, strategic growth and societal level impacts through collaboration with others, including customers but also governments and civil society organizations.

I'll describe each of these three phases in a little more detail.

Phase 1: Internal Operations

The four walls focus looks at environmental issues such as energy and water use at production facilities, designing office and/or retail spaces to reduce energy use and vehicle fuel efficiency and, in a post-COVID world, the transmission of bacteria, molds, and viruses. That's on the planet P, and those things could feed into an internal eROI metric. On the people P, internal metrics include measures such as ethnic, gender, or racial composition of the workforce. Does the company's staff represent the communities where it does business?

I'd include compensation, benefits, and work hours as other key human metrics on this list. It does little good for a company to build sustainable products for its customers at the expense of its internal staff. Fair wages, opportunities for promotion, professional development, and adequate time for personal and family pursuits create a sustainable organization for the people inside. MJ's vision of his associates as his family, and treating them as such, gave Ecolab an early advantage in this area. An organization that treats its people well enables and encourages them to create sustainable outcomes for their customers.

Phase II: Sustainability Along the Value Chain

The company now turns its focus from its internal operations to creating business and social value for its customers. I use the QKS (pronounced Q-Kus) questions to help clients and students think about enhancing sustainability for clients and customers: What should we Quit doing? What should we Keep doing? And what should we Start doing?

Everyone wants to start new things and innovate, and it's too easy to overlook the substantial contributions that come from stopping. In 1935, EL acted as a distributor for another company's product that contained a caustic and dangerous chemical formulation. EL settled a lawsuit related to an injury that they could have fought, and MJ "repossessed, destroyed, and [discontinued] the sale of the item."[8]

Over the years, the company moved away from supplying chemicals in disposable drums and has replaced liquid with powder or cake formulations to enhance safety. Sometimes stopping creates a more sustainable world more quickly than starting something new. That doesn't discount the value of innovation – stopping complements starting – and when a company ceases an unsustainable practice, it usually has to figure out something new to replace it with.

Phase III: Collaborating for Societal Value

Chapter 9 will take up this topic in greater detail, but the core idea here is to extend the drive for sustainability from the business-centered relationships with customers to focusing on impacts that transcend transactions. That's easier said than done and so you can begin by looking for societal value opportunities that directly or indirectly link to the business. EL trained people with disabilities back in the 1960s less because it needed more office workers than because it offered a way for them to open up avenues for groups of people who had been marginalized and excluded from the types of work EL offered. The same was true of EL's move to train Laotian refugees. These seemingly small actions had very large effects.

At some point, however, collaboration must extend beyond the firm and work to extend the value chain beyond business partners, customers, and suppliers. One mechanism to do this is through a foundation. Ecolab has two quasi-internal vehicles for philanthropic engagement: the Ecolab foundation, launched in 1980, and the Ida C. Koran Trust, founded in 1967. Ida was MJ's first employee and rose to be a corporate director; she had a habit from the earliest days of loaning money to associates facing hardship. The foundation operates like most traditional corporate foundations, with dedicated giving areas and impact goals. The Koran Trust provides emergency financial assistance and scholarships to Ecolab associates. Both the trust and the foundation have given the company valuable experience and reputation in this sector that benefits other collaborations and partnerships the company engages in.

The Phases over Time

Figure 3.3 contains one other element worth calling out: the arrows. You'll see that the arrows are bidirectional for each phase or generation. That means two things. First, it doesn't matter where you begin. The ideal might be to move sequentially through the phases, but companies can enter at any point and begin the journey. If a foundation catches the vision of building sustainable communities, that energy will naturally flow into the customer value chain and inside the organization itself. Opportunities to extend that learning into customer relationships may become apparent, or you may see areas within your organization to work. What matters is that you begin somewhere. If political concerns prevent you from cleaning your own house, or if you have no clear product offerings to bring to customers, begin with community and social engagement. The same logic applies to each area. Momentum matters, and acting anywhere provides it.

Second, the arrows signify that you're never completely done with any phase. A timely example highlights this point. Ecolab has 25,000 field representatives spread across the globe, and many use a company vehicle. As of 2022, Jose Prado has been driving the most fuel-efficient truck of its kind, but it's not electric. Ford Motor Company has begun producing electric pickup trucks, but an order of 25,000 from Ecolab would overwhelm production and take years to fill. Electrification represents an important next step in Ecolab's four walls focus, and there are others that are emerging. My point is simple: A company never completes a phase for all time and moves on. Your journey always toggles between phases.

LESSONS FOR LEADERS

I close this chapter with some key lessons for your organization:

1. *Weave perspective into priorities, and processes will take care of themselves.* I've employed the metaphor of creating a yarn-dyed set of principles and practices to fuel and guide sustainability efforts. This chapter shows you how to yarn-dye, and Figure 3.1 serves as your roadmap. You saw in the last chapter that a worldview or perspective lays the foundation for everything else. Good leaders, like MJ, tend to be explicit about their view of the world; it becomes the dye that colors everything else. In this chapter, you saw how senior leaders from MJ onward have used language and metaphors consistent with that worldview, and they developed a mission and vision to reflect and enliven that view in goals and objectives. Those goals and objectives then encourage people like Emilio to develop tools like eROI.

   This chapter showed you how that transition can take place, but there's another valuable lesson about yarn-dyeing: it doesn't take 100 years to do it. If you follow the sequence of *clarifying perspective before creating priorities*, you're going to be injecting a powerful and consistent dye into the resulting purpose, objectives, and goals. It won't happen overnight, but as people come to share your perspective, they'll share your goals and they'll build out the core processes that translate those into tangible organizational behaviors. Those processes, like eROI, find their way into budgets and resource allocation decisions, they inform the type, breadth, and frequency of training, and they suggest what measures make sense. Follow this sequence and the results will come far sooner than a century down the road.

   The structure of Figure 3.1 reinforces this logic. Leadership motivates action and change by helping people adopt a coherent view of the world, including the causal chains I wrote about in Chapter 2, and then using that view to inform a purpose and priorities that naturally flow from that view. Good leaders, the ones who move the dial, help their people see the world from a clear and correct vantage point. Everything else flows by extension. For example, if we believe that respect and dignity are the correct ways to think about other people, then helping those people becomes the natural purpose and customer intimacy a logical strategy.

2. *Processes commit your organization, for better or worse.* Think of the risk inherent in a notion like eROI. What if it turns out that, by objective measures, Ecolab doesn't really add value to a customer's operation? The contract gets canceled, the business is lost, and Ecolab searches for replacement revenue. That's obvious, but there's another piece that includes the sad realization that products are mundane and the service an unnecessary overlay that adds no real value. That's a deep hit to an organization's identity and tends to demotivate people. These two very real risks drive most businesses to eschew formally and objectively providing something like eROI and focus on abstract, intangible measures such as customer satisfaction.

The willingness to quantify your value and to do so regularly reflects a fundamental humility and strong sense of self, as I've argued earlier. It has two other very positive effects. First, it prepares an organization for wider quantification and reporting requirements that a commitment to environmental, social, and governance (ESG) performance requires. The goal of ESG reporting isn't to shame companies, it's to hold their feet to the fire. If you already have a process like eROI, ESG reporting will not present an existential challenge.

The second effect of a commitment to measurable outcomes like eROI has an even more powerful effect on the organization: It forces, not merely invites, people to live in the real world. One of our worst capabilities as humans is our ability to explain away any poor performance and attribute it to some unmeasurable force or something out of our control. Living in a world where objective data and measurement rule counters this terrible tendency. A single instance may be a random event, but when measured over time, poor performance helps uncover the deep causes, and that's usually something we've done or not done. A culture of measurement *forces*, not invites, us to live in the real world, and living in the real world means that for performance to change, we have to change. And for the world we live in to become more sustainable, we have to change, individually and collectively.

CONCLUSION

This chapter moved our discussion from the base of the pyramid, and worldview, through purpose and priorities and on to concrete, actionable business processes. Ecolab has five other key processes that drive its success: leadership at every level of the organization (Chapter 5), a method for focusing on product solutions, excellent work in research and development (Chapter 6), an uncanny ability to create value through mergers and acquisitions (Chapter 7), divestitures (Chapter 8), and the ability to create and nurture multi-stakeholder partnerships, which I'll take up in Chapter 9. In the next chapter, I'll move outside the pyramid in Figure 3.1 and talk about the arrow and the role of leadership and management in creating movement along the pyramid.

I'll close where I began, with Ecolab in Las Vegas. Ecolab owns its market in Vegas, but the company has not bought into the two things that make Vegas what it is today. A popular marketing slogan for the city exclaimed that "what happens in Vegas stays in Vegas." Ecolab operates from a diametrically opposed view: in terms of sustainability, what happens in Vegas doesn't stay in Vegas, its effects move across the globe. Second, Vegas sells illusion – a fast life of hedonic pleasure. Other than winning at the tables, guests are encouraged to measure nothing and just relax. Ecolab measures everything, and it doesn't relax. The people at Ecolab work hard at what they do, and that ethic of hard work originated with MJ and carries on with his current successor Christophe Beck.

EMILIO'S THOUGHTS

eROI: Engine for Growth

As I reflected on this chapter, I had to ask myself to consider the word *value*. What is it, and why does it matter? While the dictionary definition is focused on monetary worth, to me it's more than that. Value is not simply the relative worth or utility of something. It is also how intrinsically desirable something is. Value creation is the primary aim of any business because value creation drives growth. And creating value means supporting a positive, meaningful impact on customers, employees, and stakeholders.

For a century, Ecolab has worked with our customers to solve their most challenging business, operational, and environmental problems. To deliver on that promise, we measure the impact of our solutions. We help customers quantify their return on investment and track operational improvements and progress across a range of performance goals. We are a customer intimate company and personal service is paramount to our success. And measuring and delivering customer value is at the heart of our business strategy. It's inherent in our DNA, or, in Professor Godfrey's words, it's about creating a yarn-dyed set of principles and practices to guide our sustainability efforts.

In 2009, as director of sustainability for Nalco Water, I had just completed several listening sessions with global leaders on the role of sustainability in their businesses. Back then, many companies viewed the growing sustainability movement as purely altruistic. This was despite the fact that customers were already experiencing operational resource challenges, increased environmental regulations, and issues related to climate change, such as droughts and extreme weather events, that impacted their operations and supply chains. But at that time, sustainability and the movement we now call environmental, social, and governance (ESG) were not mainstream.

Through my listening tour, I learned that our commercial teams worked tirelessly to capture the business and operational performance benefits of our solutions, including those related to regulatory compliance, health and safety, and cost reductions. I experienced this myself working in the automotive industry as an application engineer, where we helped the Big Three automakers at that time drive asset life performance of their critical assembly-line welding operations. Little did the public know that water and energy are the lifeblood of manufacturing the family minivan. With vehicles rolling off the assembly line every few minutes, uptime and productivity are a production manager's dream and what they value most of all. Our unique cooling water chemistry and automation technology enabled welders to operate without disruption while increasing asset life and reducing overall costs.

What we didn't share with the production managers back then were the millions of gallons of water savings and water quality improvements that resulted from our efforts. You could argue that this wasn't really relevant to a production manager unless the water supply was disrupting operations. However, the automotive company's corporate functions did care. Corporate environmental teams were beginning to track water and energy intensity per vehicle, and that information was being reported in annual corporate sustainability and responsibility reports.

So, I reported my findings to the Nalco Water executive leadership team. What I told them, essentially, was that our commercial teams needed to communicate the holistic benefits of our approach to an increasing set of customers for whom sustainability was a growing and relevant business driver. At that time, I was also working with our CEO, Erik Frywald, and Mary Kay Kaufmann, chief marketing officer (CMO), to reposition the brand of the company from a chemical services provider to the essential experts for water, energy, and air. This made it even more crucial to substantiate the business, environmental, and resource efficiency benefits of our technologies from individual sites and roll them up to the corporate level. And doing it consistently so large multinationals could depend on Nalco Water to deliver systemwide reliability and operational performance at the lowest total delivered cost was crucial.

We needed a simple, business-relevant moniker to demonstrate the full breadth of our impact and the value we delivered to our customers. So, we developed a concept known as eROI. At that time, it stood for *environmental* return on investment. But early on, Christophe Beck understood that eROI was a point of differentiation for our company. It enabled us to provide customers with an outcome-based approach that would not only demonstrate the operational and environmental benefits of partnering with Ecolab, but also the monetary returns – in essence, the total value delivered. Today, eROI refers to the *exponential* return on investment because it truly accelerates benefits for customers across three dimensions:

- Business outcomes – such as increased brand recognition, reputation, customer satisfaction, health, safety, and profitability.
- Operational efficiency – or doing more with less to increase productivity, reduce labor, extend asset life, and improve product quality.
- Environmental impact – which includes water, energy, greenhouse gas, and waste reduction.

Implementing the process at the local level requires our commercial teams to monetize and aggregate the benefits across all three dimensions. The financial sum leads to the total value delivered (TVD) of our solutions. Based on the customers' incremental investment in Ecolab our teams will then calculate and communicate the eROI (our universal value metric) of the project or solution to the customer. Typically, our customers will see a greater than 25% eROI in working with Ecolab. In many ways, eROI enables the business case for why they should do business with Ecolab on several business, sustainability, and social impact priorities. The concept of customers receiving a return on their investment with Ecolab has been a fundamental part of our history since 1923. Ecolab has always had a strategy that included the use of value-added programs to improve a customer's profitability.

We have built capabilities and tools to help local Ecolab managers deliver on our holistic value at the local level. That also includes creating a library of over one thousand eROI customer impact case histories across different sectors, leveraging these testimonials with customers all over the world as measurable proof points of Ecolab's performance and return on the customers' investment in Ecolab. Our first eROI case history, back in 2009, was about our partnership with a Dow facility in Freeport, Texas. Dow implemented the 3D TRASAR™ smart technology to manage over 80 critical cooling systems to further advance operational reliability. These efforts resulted in 1 billion gallons of water savings and $4 million in total cost savings. That's enough water to supply nearly 40,000 people in the United States for one year. This

Table 3.1 The Elements of eROI

Business Outcomes		Operational Drivers		Environmental Impact	
Human Health & Safety (Reduced workers' comp payments)		Assets (Lengthened life)		Water Savings (Monetized)	
Food Safety (Reduced costs of food waste, customer illnesses)	+	Productivity (More dishes washed/hour)	+	Energy (Lower energy bills)	= Total Value Delivered
Brand Protection (Fewer negative incidents)		Product Quality (Appearance, freshness)		Greenhouse gases (Monetized)	
Profitability (Bottom-line impact)		Costs (Lower labor or maintenance costs)		Waste (Monetized and disposal costs)	

is a great example of how our work with customers also impacts the community and the social benefits of water stewardship. We have had scores of other eROI success stories since then, and there will be more to come in our future.

We *know* that addressing water use and advancing ambitious sustainability goals need not come at the expense of growth. For 100 years, Ecolab has led with purpose and has focused on making a positive impact, knowing that innovation and growth will inevitably follow. Ecolab eROI enables our value proposition for customers to come to life. It's the tangible proof, not promises, that helps us keep customers for life (Table 3.1). Using our execution excellence, we work to drive this critical "value journey" forward – with every customer, at every location, on every day. That's the firm belief and goal of Christophe Beck, our president, chairman, and CEO. It holds true today and will hold true tomorrow as well.

Chapter 4

THE TONE AT THE TOP: EXECUTIVE LEADERSHIP AND MANAGEMENT

The work of cooperation is not a work of leadership, but of organization as a whole . . . but leadership is the indispensable fulminator of its forces.

—Chester Barnard

Ecolab purchased the Kay Chemical Company in November 1994, paying $90 million for the privately held, Greensboro, North Carolina, leader in cleaning and sanitation supplies for the fast-food industry. Ascendant CEO Al Schuman noted that the combined total available restaurant market, Ecolab's full-service and Kay's quick-service businesses, now totaled $1 billion. Not bad for a company with total sales at the time just south of $1.3 billion. Early in 1995, Schuman offered the job of running Kay to a relative newcomer to Ecolab, Procter & Gamble-trained Doug Baker. Baker jumped at the opportunity.[1]

Over the next few months, Baker found plenty of opportunities, just not the type he anticipated. Kay's 1994 revenue of $65 million relied on one primary customer – McDonald's Golden Arches, with its thousands of US locations – that constituted two-thirds of Kay's business. As he adjusted to life in Greensboro and to leading a team that was going through the roller coaster of "being bought" by a much larger company, Baker headed to New Orleans for a McDonald's supplier convention. At a reception the evening before the meetings, he ran into a former colleague at P&G. The colleague offered his hearty congratulations on Doug's promotion. Then he offered his condolences as he gave Doug a heads-up: the next day McDonald's would announce an "alternative sourcing" policy for all suppliers.

Alternative sourcing meant that McDonald's would shift about $20 million from Kay to P&G, enough to destroy Kay. At that moment, Baker realized just how unstable Kay was – he described it to me as "tippy" – and his competitive nature made him try and keep the entire McDonald's account. That became central to the company's purpose. Baker also realized that $20 million in sales, vital to Kay, represented little more than a rounding error at P&G, with $33 billion in 1995 revenue. To retain the whole McDonald's account, he set out to turn the competition with P&G from a marathon, where P&G's staying power and deep pockets gave it the advantage, to a decathlon, a number of shorter sprints that would give Kay the advantage. Although a relative neophyte at Ecolab, Baker employed the classic playbook: Win through innovation and service in the short term and make the long-term business far less "tippy."

Drawing on the 70-year-old *Soilax* example, Kay pioneered a new dispensing system that made it easier for McDonald's employees to use Kay products correctly and effectively. As Baker went to his superiors in St. Paul with a request for $17 million for new equipment, he knew that such a large expenditure would significantly impact the payback horizon for a $90 million outlay. He reasoned that a longer payback on the acquisition beat the alternative: the loss of the whole $90 million. Kay dramatically improved the level of service it provided the Golden Arches and other customers. Its fast action raised the cost for P&G to service a small account, and P&G's slow-moving culture allowed Kay to show McDonald's that second-sourcing cleaning products was a bad move.

Stabilizing the Mc-Revenue helped, but left Kay just as tippy as, if not more than, before. Baker and his team worked to expand Kay's business base across the quick-service food industry. They expanded to retailers like Sam's Club, and, borrowing another page from the Ecolab playbook, they took Kay's product line global. Baker learned valuable lessons through this experience, and his leadership and actions laid the foundation for Kay to grow from $65 million in 1994 to $1.2 billion in 2021, a CAGR of 11.87%. He took many of those lessons with him to St. Paul when he left Kay in 2000.

Joel Johnson, the former Hormel CEO and Ecolab board member, noted that the Kay experience played a significant role in Baker's promotion to CEO four years later. "Doug had demonstrated great confidence in running the Kay acquisition, . . . He not only generated excellent results, but he [ran] them with some more degree of autonomy than you'd have if you were operating out of headquarters. . . . He also demonstrated a lot of strategic foresight."[2]

Doug Baker exhibited great leadership at Kay and would go on to transform Ecolab into a leader in corporate sustainability. You'll recall from Chapter 1 that I defined leadership in terms of what leaders do, they mobilize people to act, learn, and change to improve the long-term viability and vitality of the organization in three ways: purpose, people, and productivity. *Purpose* is realized more effectively, *people* experience increased personal growth, meaning, and purpose in their work and lives, and *productivity* is strengthened. They do so by using the traditional tools of management: allocating resources, controlling and coordinating action, and measuring/reporting results. Leadership is the engine that powers the creation and maintenance of a sustainable advantage. In this chapter, we'll focus on the six CEOs who have led Ecolab and in the next chapter, we'll look at the way the company develops and deploys almost 50,000 leaders worldwide.

UNDERSTANDING LEADERSHIP

I build a model of leadership with inspiration from a contemporary of MJ Osborn's, Chester Irving Barnard. Barnard was born in 1886 in Malden, New York, and spent his life in New England and the mid-Atlantic states. In 1927, Barnard accepted one of the most stable leadership positions in America: President of New Jersey Bell, the government-sanctioned telephone monopoly. During the Great Depression, he ran the New Jersey state relief effort and spent most of World War II running the United Service Organization. Barnard died in New York City in June 1961.

In November and December of 1937, Barnard gave a series of eight lectures at the Lowell Institute in Boston which he later worked into one of the first books on management and leadership, *The Functions of the Executive*. Barnard held that organizations formed to allow people to coordinate their efforts to produce a commonly shared purpose; the distinct work of the executive lay in ensuring the viability and vitality of an organization. In our terms, organizations are people working productively to attain a purpose. Leaders enable that collective to work by focusing their efforts on two factors Barnard referred to as *strategic* and *moral*. Table 4.1 outlines how these factors impact the three foci of leadership: purpose, people, and productivity.

"The limiting (strategic) factor is the one whose control, in the right form, at the right place and time," will allow people to accomplish the current purpose."[3] Strategic factors tend to be technical in nature and

Table 4.1 The Role of Leaders

Organizational Element	Strategic Factors	Moral Factors
Purpose	Clarify through resource allocation	Create through mission/goals
People	Direct through coordination/control	Empower through vision and mindset
Productivity	Realize through measurement	Define what's worth measuring
Key Questions	How?, When?, and Where?	What?, Who?, and Why?
Outcome	Viability	Vitality

they shift over time. You can think of the strategic factor as the constraint or roadblock that impedes people from realizing the organization's purpose; one year it might be a supply chain bottleneck, the next year an attack on the brand. Leaders allocate financial and human resources to break through those roadblocks and allow people to get the critical work of the organization done. Managing the strategic factor determines whether the organization will survive from year to year. The strategic factor focuses on the high-level questions of how, when, and where money is spent and people work.

Barnard described the moral factor as the "necessity of leadership, the power of individuals to inspire cooperative personal decision by creating faith: faith in common understanding, faith in the probability of success, faith in the ultimate satisfaction of personal motives, faith in the integrity of objective authority, faith in the superiority of common purpose as a personal aim of those who partake in it." The moral factor builds on a relational *weltanschauung*; it aligns different departments, functions, and silos around a unified and overarching purpose.

The moral factor defines who should join the organization, why, and what each must do to reach that overarching why. As leaders do this moral work, they align individual and organizational purposes and empower people – through faith and hope – to realize those goals. The moral factor helps leaders define key actions and how to measure them. The "faith in the probability of success" generates vitality – a sense of liveliness and energy – that allows an organization to thrive over time.

Organizational success and survival depend on the ability of leaders and leadership teams to attend to *both* strategic and moral factors and incorporate both technical and relational perspectives. Strategic factor management ensures that the work of the organization gets done, that products move, services get rendered, revenue gets collected, and bills get paid. All of these combine to create a viable, living organization. Moral factor management provides members with meaning and a feeling of being connected to something larger than just the mundane exchange of labor for wages or cash for products, services, or shares of stock. Moral leadership spawns a vital organization, one that's alive.

EXECUTIVE LEADERSHIP AT ECOLAB

How have Ecolab's executive leaders performed along the dimensions of strategic and moral leadership? There have only been six CEOs at the company. The two with the last name of Osborn sat in that chair for over half of the company's life; the other four averaged just over a decade each, ranging from 4 to 16 years. Three CEOs spent their entire career at the firm; of the other three one founded the company, one became CEO after 15 years at the company, and one was a pure outside hire with no Ecolab experience.

I attempted to quantify the performance of each CEO along the dimensions of strategic and moral leadership. The annual reports and other written materials, some from outsiders, gave me a strong sense of what each CEO accomplished in terms of financial, strategic, and cultural performance. I wanted to supplement those fine-grained insights with something more quantitative. Could I find data that served as a proxy for performance along the strategic and moral dimension of leadership?

I measured the performance of strategic and moral leadership through the stated financial goals of the organization: sales growth, return on sales, and return on beginning shareholders' equity. I excluded debt/equity for two reasons. First, norms in business about the value of debt changed over the last century; EB Osborn realized a goal of no-debt in the 1970s while in Doug Baker's world that would be seen as an irresponsible limit to growth. Second, each CEO kept debt/equity within the investment grade benchmark during his tenure. I substituted return on assets for additional insight into how efficiently each managed the balance sheet.

For each of the four measures (sales growth, return on sales, return on shareholder starting equity, and return on assets), I calculated the CEO's average score. This represents, to me at least, their ability to maintain a viable and growing organization, or management of the strategic factors. I also calculated the standard deviation for each measure, or the dispersion of yearly performance around the average. Standard deviation is an accepted measure of risk, and I believe that the willingness of a CEO to accept risk acts as one measure of the moral factor, instilling purpose and inspiring action through change. Change is always risky and uncertain. I then plotted the six CEOs along both dimensions. Figure 4.1 presents these results.

The dotted line in Figure 4.1 represents an ideal, balanced leader, one who excels at both strategic and moral factors. As you see, leaders who balance both factors are rare birds. For most of its history, the CEO leaned either toward defining and redefining Ecolab's core purpose or to turning that purpose into productive performance. Let's take a brief look at what each CEO did along each dimension.

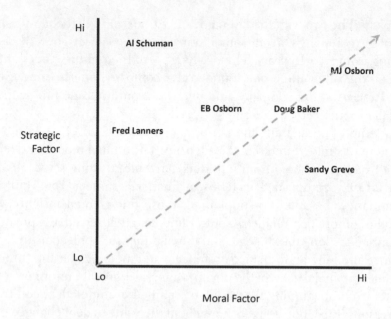

Figure 4.1 Executive Leadership at Ecolab

MJ Osborn

MJ founded the company and led it from 1923 until turning operational management over to his son EB in 1951. MJ ranked second in strategic leadership and first in moral leadership. I find a perfect example of strategic factor management in the 1925 annual report, where he chastises his investors for constraining the growth of the company by not providing more working capital: "No marked progress can be made on the inadequate capital [with] which we are attempting to operate . . . Your management feels it has justified your confidence in the progress it has already shown, but must have additional tools (capital) if it is to take advantage of its opportunities – if it is to show any marked progress."[4]

As a moral leader, MJ articulated the purpose of the company, "the saving of time, the lightening of labor, and the reduction of costs" for customers, and the creation of a "business family" for associates. These founding principles energize the company today; today's value proposition focuses on saving water, labor, energy, and cost. Leaders still try to cultivate and maintain a "family-style" culture.

EB Osborn

EB began his tenure at Economics Laboratory in 1928, shortly after receiving his degree at Dartmouth. He became president in 1951 and created the CEO position a decade later. EB ties with Doug Baker for the third place on the strategic factor ranking, and is fourth in terms of the moral factor. During his tenure, EL grew up. The company went public and grew both organically and through acquisition. He initiated formal strategic planning and centralized research and development, purchasing, operations consulting, and acquisitions at the corporate center. EL became a major corporation, one that would join the Fortune 500 toward the end of EB's career.

As a moral factor leader, he laid out his contribution at the death of his father and mentor. He wrote upon his father's passing, "[MJ's] influence will continue to guide the organization, to which he dedicated a life-time of effort, and as President, it will be my single objective to carry on his work." EB carried forward MJ's core purpose, and he expanded that purpose in two ways. First, he moved the company beyond dishwashing to an expanded view of cleanliness and hygiene. Second, he articulated environmental responsibility in the early 1970s as the energy crises of the day highlighted the need for ecological sustainability and energy conservation.

Fred Lanners

Lanners joined EL in 1947 and spent much of his career growing and managing the international division of the company. Lanners assumed the CEO's role upon the death of EB Osborn in 1978 and served through 1982. Lanners ranks fourth on my strategic factor and sixth on the moral factor. Financial performance was good but not great; however, Lanners led EL through the difficult era of stagflation – low economic growth and high inflation – of the late 1970s and early 1980s. In the early 1980s, he reorganized the company to better match products and services with customer groups.

Lanners did not change the core of EL's moral mission, nor did he make changes around the periphery. He helped EL adapt to tumultuous times. Under his watch, the company rolled out a benefits program to help employees with chemical dependency and mental health issues, problems that became crises over the ensuing decades. Lanners felt that free enterprise offered the best way to a better society and worked to counter the general competitive malaise and antipathy toward business that characterized the late 1970s and early 1980s. He spearheaded the acquisition of Apollo Technologies in 1980 in an attempt to move the company into a new market, pollution control products and services for the utilities industry.

Sandy Greve

Pierson "Sandy" Greve came to Ecolab after a very successful career at consumer goods company Questor. He served as CEO from 1983 to 1995 and ranks last on my measure of strategic factor management and second on my ranking of managing the moral factor. Even though he came in last, Greve still averaged a return on beginning equity of 16%, the envy of many firms then and now. His averages look so bad, in part, because he brought EL out of competitive somnambulism and laid a foundation for future growth. He renamed the company Ecolab in order to bring brand consistency to the company around the world.

Greve refined Ecolab's core purpose and value proposition. Within a week of taking office, he sold off Apollo and took a $42 million loss as the market the acquisition hoped to exploit vanished. He closed down the company's Magnus division, which sold specialty chemicals to the marine and pulp and paper industries, and he sold EL's valuable consumer business, built on strong brands such as *Electrasol*, *Finish*, and *Lime Away*. Known as a tough boss, he worked to instill a more competitive culture and spirit in the company. When he sold Apollo, Greve hoped to grow the company without "crapshoot acquisitions." Finally, Greve articulated the core of Ecolab's strategy: Circle the Customer, Circle the Globe.

Al Schuman

Al Schuman began his career as a sales representative for EL in New York City. The year was 1957; 49 years later he would retire as chairman of the board, having served as CEO from 1995 to 2004. Schuman managed the strategic factor better than any other CEO, ranking first. He ranked fifth on moral leadership and risk-taking. Return on beginning equity soared to a 25% average over the almost decade he led the company. Al realized the goal of return on sales above 7%, averaging 7.8% over his tenure. Sandy

Greve made a small acquisition in the pest elimination space in 1985, and Al grew that small acquisition into a nationwide leader by selling pest control services to Ecolab's primary customers.

Schuman employed the moral factor rarely, his major contribution was driving the circle the customer, circle the globe strategy deeply into the architecture, systems, and processes of Ecolab. Schuman also moved the company toward leadership in corporate sustainability. Under his watch, the company took a technical statement of environmental principles developed in 1993 and expanded that into 21 principles that emphasized a sustainable relationship with the planet.

Doug Baker

Baker came to Ecolab in 1989 after attending "business school" at Procter & Gamble. Baker is the most balanced of Ecolab's CEOs, tied for third place with EB Osborn on the strategic dimension and third in his management of the moral factor. Return on sales peaked during his 16 years at Ecolab's helm, averaging 8.1%. The average return on beginning equity stood at 19.73%, barely missing the 20% target the company had long held. Baker reorganized Ecolab into business units that maximized both closeness to the customer and potential synergies across Ecolab businesses.

Baker fundamentally shifted the course of Ecolab with the 2011 purchase of Nalco. Company sales recorded their highest ever gain at 74% growth (sales in 1935 grew by 71.5%), but more importantly, Ecolab redefined itself as the world's leader in water management as well as cleanliness and hygiene, and the company deepened its commitment to helping customers save water, energy, and money. When he turned the reins over to Christophe Beck in 2021, Ecolab had become a recognized global leader in sustainability.

THE DYNAMICS OF LEADERSHIP

The individual histories of Ecolab's outstanding CEOs provide leaders everywhere with templates of how to grow from a small startup to a Fortune 500 company without losing the entrepreneurial spirit. I highlight another important leadership lesson from Ecolab's first century: its success depended on great leaders *in* each period, but shifting the balance between strategic and moral factor management *over* time. Figure 4.2 illustrates the dynamics of these transitions.

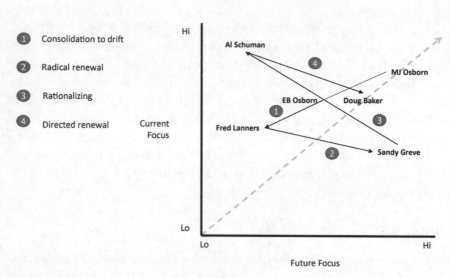

Figure 4.2 Executive Performance at Ecolab

The most apparent lesson from both Figures 4.1 and 4.2 is that few leaders perfectly balance the strategic (technical) and moral (relational) dimensions of leadership. This should surprise no one, most of our default leadership strengths and styles tilt us toward either strategic or moral factor management, just as most of us have a default worldview that tends toward the technical or relational. Al Schuman inspired faith in Ecolab, and Sandy Greve was no slouch when it came to managing strategic factors for operational results. It's just that Schuman was much better at the strategic element and Greve at the moral one.

A close study of the four lines in Figure 4.2 reveals another lesson: the pendulum needs to swing between defining/refining purpose and consolidating/implementing that purpose. EB Osborn certainly loved his father, but EL didn't need more vision in 1951, it needed to mature into a large company, rationalize its business systems, and go public in order to grow at the rate it desired. In 1983, Ecolab's original mission had stagnated; the company needed, and the board recognized this, the outside perspective and tough style of Sandy Greve to perform the radical surgery needed to arrest its drift and refine its core purpose.

As Greve sold some businesses and closed others, sales, earnings, and equity all took a hit. Morally, he worked to change a collective mindset. Greve disposed of Apollo within a week, but it took another decade to cement a new mindset inside the company. Greve noted in 1984 that much of his radical surgery was cognitive: "Our people have worked hard, and they've done the hardest thing of all – changed their perspectives, their standards of excellence, and their productivity while preparing themselves for new beginnings. Because of that, an exciting tomorrow for our shareholders and employees is much closer."[5] He renamed the company Ecolab in 1986. That brought strategic coherence but also the moral realization that Ecolab had refined, but not fundamentally changed, its mission.

LEADERSHIP AND SUSTAINABILITY

How do leaders create a sustainable advantage, and in Ecolab's case an advantage around sustainability? Morally, they define and refine the company's core mission, which rests on the footings of a coherent perspective and the foundation of core priorities. Strategically, they employ the tools of management – resource allocation, coordination/control, and reporting structures – to build a set of processes that fuel the company's activity set. You might recall from Figures 1.1 and 2.1 (from Chapters 1 and 2) that processes act as the bridge between priorities and performance; processes move values from abstract to action, they connect the moral to the strategic factor.

Operating and Dynamic Processes

Processes coordinate and control the ongoing activities of the firm by defining a sequence of human behaviors and connections to tangible and intangible assets that enable and shape the activities of the business. *Operating processes* will be repeated time and again each day, week, and month and provide the fuel for performance. Over time, these processes become sedimented into the memory of the business. People become so familiar with operating processes, they become taken for granted. When Emilio wrote in Chapter 1 that the way he works today is the same way he worked when he started at Nalco in the 1980s, he's referring to the stable operating processes that run in the background and guide his workday. The tasks he performs have evolved, but the rules of engagement remain the same: Does my action help discover and meet a customer's need? Will the results lead to comprehensive solutions and growth? Do my actions follow the principles of humility and build on strengths while acknowledging weaknesses?

Leaders define and organize operating processes that mobilize people in productive, purpose-driven ways. Processes must develop and become perfected over time; they don't spring fully formed like Athena from the forehead of Zeus in Greek mythology. They arise from multiple trials and errors, and analysis and reflection of what worked and why. Leaders leverage their position and exert their authority to repeat those processes enough times that they "yarn-dye" the fabric of the organization. Once dyed, those processes spread throughout the organization. Leaders drive that process by allocating resources for training and professional development, for example. They also insert processes, and the priorities that underlay them, into and across the human capital architecture of the firm through the systems that guide hiring, performance review/promotion, and incentives. Operating processes provide a solid platform of action that stabilizes the firm and drives performance.

Great leaders do more than design operating processes, they also develop what strategists refer to as *dynamic capabilities*, or procedures and routines that facilitate changing, updating, and freshening processes as markets and societies change.[6] The annual budget cycle and the allocation of funds represent continuous investments that maintain current capabilities. Dynamic capabilities help leaders look for signals of internal drift or external changes manifest in measurement and reporting systems. Internal drift occurs when processes move from sequences that animate behavior to checklists for half-hearted compliance. External changes arise from the unsettled and evolutionary worlds of technology, regulation, macroeconomic movement, and shifting customer preferences. Dynamic processes keep stability from ossifying and help the business change.

Like operating processes, the growth of dynamic processes – learning how to learn – take time and energy. They require the same purpose-based resource allocations and budgets, coordination, and measurement – and the willingness to accept those measurements that signal the need for change – to generate learning and change processes that permeate the organization. Ecolab's worldview of the role of technology, the need for growth, and a humble approach have helped it define and refine the dynamic processes that fuel change, development, and innovation that all keep the company driven to look for emerging customer needs.

Leadership and Sustainability

Leadership matters for sustainability, not just for a sustainable advantage, for at least two reasons. First, sustainability, the 3Ps (profit, people, and planet) at whatever level we talk about them, requires the coordinated, purpose-driven activity of many people. *Sustainability is an organizational problem, and will only be solved by well-led organizations.* Organizations provide individuals with the moral and strategic tools they need to lead a more sustainable life, from a moral case for recycling, to actual bins and recycling plants and on to couches made out of old bottles. Families, firms, schools, community groups, and governments at all levels must share a vision and coordinate their actions in productive ways to realize that vision.

That vision has two distinct moral components, moral in the ethical sense of ultimate distinctions between right and wrong, and moral in the Barnardian sense of requiring collective vision and faith in our ability to reach that purpose. Leaders at all levels must employ and manage the moral factor if we hope to realize ambitious goals for protecting the planet and helping all its people prosper. Given the complex nature of sustainability, and ongoing contention about what a sustainable world should look like, leaders must constantly articulate their vision and inspire those they lead to engage in meaningful action over time.

Second, leadership matters because the long-term nature of sustainability requires the same constant and continuous attention to the strategic constraints that so easily distract our focus and disrupt progress in building a sustainable society and world. Lasting carbon footprint reduction requires more than just driving to work one fewer day, and reducing waterborne illnesses won't happen if water is clean only half the time. We'll need strong and easily replicable operating processes that over time evoke and facilitate the deep behavioral changes upon which sustainability depends. The operating tools of management, budgets, tracking systems, and holding people accountable represent our best hope to encode and then sediment routines in our businesses, churches, homes, and workplaces.

Operating tools will do the heavy lifting, but leaders who hope to give birth to a truly sustainable world must attend to dynamic capabilities as well. We need processes that allow us to learn over time and to solve new challenges and problems as they arise. What defined sustainable best-practices a decade ago has changed as we discover more about the complex challenges of sustainability for people and the planet. A constantly visible purpose becomes central to this process because so often learning becomes an end in itself and in our rush to do what's new we fail to ask the fundamental cost and benefit questions that purpose illuminates. Good leaders instill dynamic processes with checkpoints that force learners to put new lessons into larger contexts and goals.

So, yes, leadership matters for creating a truly sustainable world. Leaders must do far more than motivate their followers with grand speeches or idyllic visions of a pollution- or poverty-free world. They must mobilize action by creating faith in our collective ability to do hard things and build a better world. They must also provide those they lead with the tools to loosen constraints and break through barriers.

LESSONS FOR LEADERS

As I draw my discussion of leadership to a close, I'll highlight four action items you should pay attention to in order to improve your own leadership skills and deepen the leadership bench of your organization. Your ability to move the dial on the 3Ps depends on how well you and others lead. Organizational size doesn't matter. It may change how you implement these items and how much time you spend on each of them, but these lessons apply to the Fortune 500 or the smallest startup.

1. *Leadership is the critical "strategic factor"* in your organization, and leadership development needs to be job one of every leader in the company, from the board chair on down. From the mid-1970s on, Ecolab has paid conscious attention to leadership development, both through cognitive training and experience in leadership positions. A practice from another company highlights the point. I consulted with an organization some years ago that wanted to improve its service capability and reputation in its market. Marriott's service levels were legendary at the time, and I had a friend who worked for Marriott at the corporate level. We invited him in, and my client began to probe about how to improve service. My friend began by noting that CEO and Board Chair Bill Marriott spent one day a week in one of his hotels to determine if he had the right leader running the right hotel. Bill Marriott knew that great service was an operating process and the work of

leadership. Leader-driven processes mobilized and motivated people, rather than merely directed them. Leadership was the key to great service.

Leadership ability, both moral and strategic, turns out to be the biggest and most durable strategic constraint that either drives or limits growth. Growing your own organization, let alone getting it to move the dial on internal or market sustainability, depends on the depth of leadership. My experiences have taught me that a leader's effective sphere of influence is about 25 people. After that, her personal ability to mobilize and create a thriving, vital organization begins to wane. Leadership signals from the top of the organization are relatively weak and need a boost from local leaders who can translate the vision and clarify how the general purpose and vision, not to mention budgets and organizational structure, should adapt to best fit the needs of their particular unit.

2. *Leadership can be learned, and you have to develop leaders.* Bill Marriott didn't just visit hotels, assess the quality of leadership, and then move leaders around like pieces on a chess board to ensure the right fit. Even a company like Marriott didn't have that deep of a bench. Those visits highlighted the symbolic importance of great leadership but the substantive requirement of 40 hours (one whole week) of training each year for each manager/leader in the organization created leaders at every level. Playing musical chairs with leaders at different levels costs little, but you'll get what you pay for. Leadership is a learned skill, and both emerging and experienced leaders need ongoing exposure to timeless principles and timely trends.

How much energy, money, and time do you put into leadership development? As I noted above, this is one area where what you'll reap is in direct proportion to what you sow. If training focuses on compliance issues or other mandated training, you won't see much development from your leaders. They'll be better managers, but not better leaders. I'm biased toward executive education, but more sophisticated and principle-driven training gives your leaders more to think through and more to work on. Active leadership development also occurs when you have your leadership team work with community organizations, from youth soccer to answering phones at a suicide hotline. In each of these roles, your team learns and masters leadership through real practice.

3. *Leadership can be a team sport.* Leaders like Doug Baker who balance attention to moral and strategic factors are hard to find. Leadership may take a team approach that blends leaders who build faith with those who bust barriers. Another illustration of this point comes from the leadership team of Michael Eisner and Frank Wells at the Walt Disney company, leaders recruited by the board after an attempted hostile takeover in 1984. Eisner exhibited great moral leadership. He pushed the company into the emerging videocassette market, and he revived the company's moribund animation unit and cranked out hit feature films like the *Lion King* and the *Little Mermaid*. He was also known to be aloof, arrogant, and agonizing to work with.

   Frank Wells, Eisner's COO, complemented Eisner's visionary moral leadership. He was a consummate strategic leader. Wells excelled at working with people, knowing how and where to allocate resources, and creating an overall environment where people did great work. Wells tempered Eisner's worst impulses and his ability to manage Eisner as well as the corporation played a significant role in Disney's great run from 1984 to 1994. Wells died in a helicopter crash in 1994, and after his death the company struggled to find a replacement.

4. Finally, *the ideal type of leader changes over time.* When MJ Osborn moved away from the day-to-day at Economics Laboratory in 1951, his company didn't need more vision. It needed to grow up, act like a big, mature company, and provide consistent and reliable products and services to a rapidly growing customer base. It *needed* a leader who made the train move in the right direction and run on time. In 1983, Economics Laboratory didn't need someone to make the trains run more on time, it needed a leader to redefine and re-envision why people should catch that train and where it would take them. The company needed Sandy Greve; a leader willing to risk current performance to build value for the long term.

   The same holds true for your organization. Inspiring moral leaders make work exciting and fun, they imbue the organization with real vitality. We feel alive and energized. When the next leader comes along, however, the organization may not need a new vision or mission but just attention to day-to-day details. I always chuckle when a new CEO rolls out a new mission when the strategic direction is already clear but tactical performance needs improvement.

Organizations need a leader that matches the moment, and good organizations have dynamic processes that find new leaders who will meet the current need. If you are the leader on the way out, avoid the strong and inevitable temptation to choose someone just like you. Success may depend on someone with a different set of skills than you have.

CONCLUSION

We've covered a lot of ground so far. I've made the case for the foundational role that a coherent perspective – a weltanschauung – plays in building a sustainable company and one that leads toward a sustainable future and then showed how that perspective energizes purpose, priorities, and processes. Founding leaders lay that first foundation and then translate that perspective into a set of priorities. In the next chapter, I'll expand on the advice I offered about developing leaders at all levels and we'll look at how Ecolab encourages leadership in each of its 48,000 employees.

EMILIO'S THOUGHTS

"Winning as One" with Sustainability at the Core

> If your actions inspire others to dream more, learn more, do more and become more, **you are a leader.**
> —John Quincy Adams (sixth US president)

On December 1, 2011, Ecolab acquired Naperville, Illinois-based Nalco for $8 billion. The merger instantly transformed Ecolab into the global leader in water management in the industrial, institutional, and energy sectors and positioned us to serve more customers with a more comprehensive portfolio of solutions. Then Chairman and CEO Doug Baker appointed Christophe Beck, current chairman and CEO, to lead the effort to combine two massive companies into one new Ecolab. "Winning as One" was Christophe's rallying cry the following week to a full event hall at the Marriott Depot in downtown Minneapolis, which brought the new company's full integration team together for the first time.

Doug Baker opened the session with some very meaningful remarks. He talked about how the merger was driven by outstanding top-line opportunities that would enable the combined companies to more effectively succeed as one. And that together we would be stronger, with more consistent long-term growth opportunities and with the people, business, and financial resources to capture that growth. And then he said something that was music to my ears. He said that sustainability would be core to the purpose of the new company.

He went on to highlight the following points to instill greater confidence in the anxious group listening at the Depot, emphasizing what the merger would do:

- *Produce a market leader, serving megatrends.* A common focus would be on safe, efficient, sustainable results, and the new company would be well-equipped to address shifting economic trends, increased food and energy demands, water scarcity, and the health-care needs of an aging population.
- *Create a winning combination, poised to capitalize on these trends.* We would drive even faster growth through a unique "circle the customer" approach, innovation and process synergies, increased scale and participation in emerging markets, a strong management team and financial resources.
- *Enable a strong business model, technology, and culture fit.* The new company would value a shared customer service mindset, unique yet similar service and technology models, and highly compatible, leverageable technology knowhow.

He concluded by saying that through this combination, we would continue to invest in and expand products and services for existing customers while adding new opportunities for enhanced customer service. He said he looked forward to bringing our two great companies together to develop new and improved solutions for critical customer needs and, in turn, deliver even better shareholder returns. As we left the Depot in Minneapolis, the integration team had a clearer picture of why we were coming together, where we were going, and what we needed to do to get there.

Embedding Sustainability into Everything We Do

At the time of the merger, I was leading the sustainability workstream for the combined companies. Think about the importance placed on it in 2011 when sustainability didn't command the attention that it does today. Sustainability was one of the 20 critical workstreams because Doug Baker and Christophe Beck had a shared vision of doing well by doing good in partnership with our customers.

As the integration progressed, Christophe Beck was then Ecolab's executive vice president and integration leader. He saw the tremendous opportunities that would result from bringing Ecolab and Nalco together. Good leaders instill dynamic processes with checkpoints that force others to put new lessons into larger contexts and goals. I spent many meetings with Christophe at the integration offices creating our "Winning as One" sustainability blueprint for the new company, which established how we would operationalize sustainability into the day-to-day operations of the company.

The company vision also reflected the importance of sustainability:

> **"Ecolab will be a global leader in providing clean water, safe food, abundant energy, and healthy environments."**

By emphasizing sustainability in both purpose and vision, the company's leadership gave added meaning to the day-to-day work of the merged company's then-40,000 employees and provided them with the inspiration to make a difference.

In developing a corporate sustainability approach, it's important first to determine the greatest opportunity for positive impact. Many organizations achieve the greatest environmental impact upstream, by setting high standards for suppliers, or internally, by improving their own operations. Both Ecolab and Nalco knew their greatest impact was downstream, helping their customers conserve natural resources.

With that core understanding, the challenge was to develop a shared approach for delivering sustainability benefits to customers. During the integration period, senior leaders from both companies agreed on a *total impact approach*, a holistic view of the environmental, economic, and social impacts of the company's products and services on customers. Going forward, each of the company's businesses would need to consider how its solutions would increase customer efficiency, optimize costs, minimize the use of natural resources, and improve safety – from sourcing, manufacturing, and use to disposal.

Doug Baker's commitment to developing an inclusive, purpose-driven company – with a culture centered on making a positive impact on the world – has helped enable growth. Today, Ecolab is a global leader in sustainability and is highly regarded for its ethical practices. That reputation was earned in no small part because of his leadership.

The journey continues, but the leadership lessons learned thus far continue to resonate across Ecolab today with Christophe Beck at the helm.

Chapter 5

LEADERSHIP THROUGHOUT THE ORGANIZATION: 48,000 STRONG AND COUNTING

Leadership is an action, not a position.

—Donald McGannon[1]

Paul Langlois (pronounced Lang-Loy) grew up in St. Paul, Minnesota, and had one of those high school teachers who propels a student toward a particular career. His French teacher at Humboldt High School lit a fire in him for the French language and teaching. Paul received his degree from St. Paul's Macalester College in 1990, where he majored in French and earned a secondary education teaching certificate. His career as a French teacher lasted a year. He discovered that the teaching profession was a lot of administration and babysitting but very little teaching. For the next decade, he worked a number of jobs until he landed at Best Buy in 2002 on their continuous improvement team. Over the next eight years, he had the opportunity to coach, teach, and train adults. He loved it, and it reignited his passion for teaching.

Paul came to Ecolab in 2010 as training director and Master Black Belt for the company's Lean & Six Sigma corporate program. He soon connected with Ros Tsai, who lead training for the institutional division, and the two began to build a learning community by bringing together what was then a set of very siloed training operations at Ecolab. As they began their work, Ecolab doubled in size with the Nalco acquisition. That meant building a community that spanned different businesses, cultures, and global locations. They brought leaders from the units together and thought about what a truly global training organization should look like.

By 2014, their efforts focused on creating a common online platform and repository of Ecolab and Nalco training materials – with room to expand the platform as new companies joined the Ecolab family. That took three years to put together. When implemented in 2017, the new learning platform provided a centralized online repository of training and development content from each business unit. Langlois and his leaders, including Executive Vice President of Human Resources Laurie Marsh, envisioned the site as a place where trainers, line managers, and Ecolab employees could go to deepen their skills base in one or multiple areas.

With a strong community of training leaders now well established and the virtual resources in place, the team took the next step of developing a common leadership development program for the company's then-45,000-plus employees around the globe. CEO Doug Baker provided direction and motivation as he told the group that if they didn't "get first-line managers right," the company wouldn't win in current or future markets.[2] The customer intimacy strategy required highly motivated, well-trained employees who took the initiative. In other words, strategic success depended on creating a cadre of leaders at every level of the organization.

Langlois became an Ecolab vice president in 2019, as the program rolled out across the organization. Every 18 weeks, 30–50 new first-line supervisors, defined as anyone with a direct report, create a new cohort for the "manager essentials" course. Cohorts span roles and business units; a new Nalco field supervisor working in the mining industry would be in a group with research supervisors running a life-science lab and a pest elimination sales director. These mixed cohorts learn a common set of skills; they also become part of Ecolab and not just their functional business unit. As in every successful organization, training helps establish and reinforce cultural norms and goals.

That cohort spends the first eight weeks doing an online, self-paced introduction to the core concepts of leadership. They learn concepts and skills, reflect on their past performance using – or not – that skill, and face a number of scenarios where the new skill could, and often should, be employed. Armed with that new knowledge, the cohort comes together for two "virtual practice together" modules, where line leaders throughout the company engage them in cases studies, practice sessions, and reflection exercises that help them apply what they've learned. The final eight weeks constitutes mentored learning and more practice. Each participant's mentor is that person's supervisor, who has completed both the same course and a follow-on "leader coaching" course.

Langlois and his team designed a program that leveraged the best technology had to offer; the cohorts only meet during the online, virtual "practice together" sessions. This allows the training to operate at global scale, and the wisdom of this approach showed during the coronavirus pandemic of 2020–2021. Indeed, the company created an emergency course on virtual selling that helped Ecolab's then-48,000 employees survive and thrive in a very challenging environment. Paul Langlois loves what he does; he's taken the passion he felt for teaching while in high school and used it to prepare Ecolab for a new, digital future.

The previous chapter treated leadership in a very traditional way: the great individual theory of leadership. I focused on the important role of those at the top and the overall strategic direction they set for the company. You could easily get the impression that Ecolab's success depended on six CEOs. That's just not true. The company's success depends on the leadership capabilities manifest in each of its 48,000+ employees. It's always been that way and will continue to be that way during the company's second century. This chapter describes the why, what, when, and how of leadership development at every level, something I encouraged you to think about in the final section of the previous chapter.

As you read this chapter, you should see three core themes coming through. First, leadership is about relationships first and technical skill second. Chester Barnard, who I introduced in the previous chapter, argued that the authority held by leaders comes not through position but as a relationship-based grant from followers. Second, you should also see the yarn-dyed RIGHT (Respect, Integration, Growth, Humility, and Technology) perspective infusing training and development. That tight linkage connects people to the company and culture, and it ensures that training aligns with other core processes outlined earlier in Figure 3.1. Finally, you should keep in mind that Ecolab's vision of a sustainable world relies much more on the individual actions of its 48,000 people and their daily work than on the work of the six, or even sixty, top leaders in St. Paul.

LEADERSHIP AT EVERY LEVEL: SELECTING GOOD PEOPLE

Creating a pool of leaders throughout a company depends on two core processes, hiring the right people and then training and developing them. It takes both to succeed; if you hire people with the attributes you are looking for, then training becomes a tailwind that pushes them along to become their very best and most productive. If those people lack a core set of personality traits and attributes, they'll act as a headwind that slows the process of training and limits its results. Put simply, the quality of human capital outputs depends on the quality of human capital inputs.

Ecolab defines quality inputs in terms of six deep traits they screen for in every hire: A desire for autonomy, business acumen, the ability to collaborate and network, a penchant for entrepreneurship, skill in managing complexity, and a strategic mindset. I'll describe how each one contributes to leadership:

- *Autonomy* is defined as the condition of "self-government."[3] People with high levels of autonomy do three things well. First, they initiate action without instructions. They see what needs to be done and do it. Second, they accept and even demand responsibility for outcomes.

They accurately emphasize their role in success or failure and don't blame others. Third, they adopt high standards of what constitutes "good" work; they act as their own toughest critics and judges. People with high degrees of autonomy require little supervision and openly and proactively report their performance. Autonomy is considered a personality trait that draws from conscientiousness, one of the big five personality traits. It comes as a part of a person and proves very difficult to inculcate or teach.

- *Business acumen* refers to an individual's ability to see and understand how a business runs and how it makes money. The lesser part of business acumen rests in the ability to understand the traditional accounting metrics of how a business runs, like a profit/loss statement or balance sheet. The greater part of the skill involves seeing the deep causal drivers of how a business generates revenue and turns it into profits. That may come from producing at scale or providing a highly customized service, acumen is the ability to understand how the company creates and then captures customer value. People with business acumen do more than just perform a service for their customers. They see how that service contributes to the success of the business and they make sure they contribute. They also act as consultants with an outside perspective that sees misalignments that insiders don't.

- *Collaboration and networking* are touted as critical skills for a knowledge-based economy; however, Herb Kern at Nalco and MJ Osborn at Ecolab realized the value of their salespeople being able to work with, not just for, customers. And that was 100 years ago. Collaboration proves vital in the twenty-first century because of the complex and interrelated nature of most businesses. So much detailed knowledge exists behind and inside processes, products, and organizational roles that no one individual can know it all. Working together builds strong networks, and networks allow people to access financial, knowledge, and physical resources they don't have on their own. Ecolab's success depends on its people's ability to work together with multiple stakeholders – competitors, customers, regulators, suppliers – to create win-win situations for each of the 3Ps (people, planet, and profits).

- *Entrepreneurship* can be a very fuzzy term and mean lots of things. For Ecolab it means two things: innovation and ownership. Innovation happens when someone sees a problem without a solution and then works to find or create a new solution. Ecolab depends on innovation throughout the organization to fill its mission as a growth company. Autonomy captures an essential part of ownership, the willingness to hold oneself accountable for success or failure. Ownership also means seeing a territory or business problem as "my own," and growing the number of accounts and seeking new business. Owners also invest their own resources into business success. Those investments include the time and energy devoted to learning new skills, and teaching and training customers about how to run their business.

- *Managing complexity* manifests itself in multiple ways. Ecolab's customers run complex businesses with lots of moving parts and high levels of interdependence between those parts. One aspect of managing complexity is the ability to keep all of those moving pieces moving. Complexity also arises around data. Ecolab measures everything and it expects associates at every level to understand and respond to signals that data provide about the health of its, and its customers, business. Think of the data needed for field reps and managers to accurately compute eROI, which relies on data at three levels of impact, customer business outcomes, customer operational drivers, and societal environmental impact. As the digitization of its business moves forward, the amount of data and the level of complexity will only increase. It's not just the ability to do math or collect data, those who manage complexity put that data to work in the service of profit, people, and the planet.

- A *strategic mindset* can be traced to the origin of the word strategy, *strategos*. It's a Greek word that means, broadly, "the general," and to have a strategic mindset is to take the general's view.[4] Those with a strategic mindset can do two things. First, they look broadly at the context of any business issue, understand the larger goals of any operation, and act to meet those goals. They see the forest from the trees. More accurately, they see the forest *and* the trees and coordinate their actions to meet multiple goals. Second, people with a strategic mindset look toward the future. They predict what's likely to happen next, based on the combination of past performance and its confluence with current contexts. Then they act, which includes innovation, to prepare for that expected future. People with a strategic vision may not always get the future right, but they are rarely caught flat-footed.

You can see how being very clear and explicit about the base traits and capabilities of people they hire aids Ecolab in its quest to create leaders at every level. Laurie Marsh and others will tell you that finding these people takes work, it takes time, and they don't always get it right. You take the time to hire smart, because if you don't, you have to manage tough, and that's always harder.[5] Ecolab leaders will also tell you that good inputs determine the ultimate quality of those who they hire, train, and deploy in the field. As Doug Baker noted, it's hard to win without the right people.

LEADERSHIP AT EVERY LEVEL: MAKING GOOD PEOPLE BETTER

MJ hoped to create a company where associates would feel like family and want to invest in the company. In the pre-publicly traded EL, that meant buying company shares. As it begins its second century, Ecolab encourages people to invest something far more valuable than money; the company wants their time, their minds, their energy, and their undivided attention. The company invests its time, its energy, and its collective intelligence in creating programs that develop the skills and knowledge its associates possess. Everyone reaps the dividends and a cadre of leaders at every level allows Ecolab to pursue customer intimacy, sophisticated innovation, and a commitment to sustainability. Associates win as they enjoy meaningful work with ample opportunities to grow. When I asked Laurie Marsh how important these development investments are, her response was both simple and telling: "Training is oxygen."[6]

That oxygen comes in an extremely pure form because the goal lies in helping people leverage what they brought with them; to enhance their autonomy, deepen their business acumen, develop richer and more meaningful collaborations, fuel their entrepreneurial desires, manage complexity more effectively, and extend their strategic vision. In short, Ecolab's palette of training helps employees enrich their jobs. That they succeed is no surprise because for over a half century, management scholars and theorists have validated the value that job enrichment brings in increasing motivation and performance.

I obliquely mentioned the author of job enrichment theory in Chapter 1. Fred Herzberg was born in April 1923, just a month after MJ started Economics Laboratory.[7] Herzberg studied psychology and did his tour in the US Army as a guard at the recently liberated Dachau concentration camp. This cemented for him a desire to learn about and improve mental health. He went on to found the Department of Industrial Mental Health at Case Western Reserve University in Cleveland. By the mid-1950s, his attention turned to motivation, and he developed an innovative and powerful model of motivation based on a simple question: What really motivates people and increases both their productivity and satisfaction?

Herzberg observed that many of the motivational tools employed by organizations reflected the motivation of the manager, not the employee. Employees who were satisfied with their jobs exhibited higher levels of motivation and performance; employees who weren't had lower motivation and performed much worse. As Herzberg dug deeper, he had a keen insight: Satisfaction and dissatisfaction were both active psychological states, and the opposite of satisfaction was not active dissatisfaction, but rather, a *passive* state of indifference. Ditto for dissatisfaction; it's opposite was also indifference.

With this insight, he modeled each as a separate end state, and each was subject to its own set of forces. His most important insight came from the natural conclusion of this logic: removing factors that led to dissatisfaction would not lead to satisfaction, something else was needed. Figure 5.1 captures his core insight and identifies what he labeled "hygiene factors," or things that would remove dissatisfaction, and "motivating factors" that enhanced satisfaction.[8]

Four things stand out to me in Figure 5.1. First, notice that the most traditional and popular managerial levers such as salary, security, and

| Dissatisfaction | ← | Satisfaction |

Hygiene Factors	Motivating Factors	Ecolab Core Perspective
Company policies	Achievement	Respect
Supervision	Recognition	Respect, Humility
Relationship with supervisors	The work itself	Integration, Growth, Technology
Work conditions	Responsibility	Respect, Growth
Salary and compensation	Advancement	Respect, Growth
Personal issues	Growth	Growth, Humility
Relationships with subordinates		
Status		
Job security		

Figure 5.1   The Herzberg Model and Its Application at Ecolab

status don't actually satisfy or motivate people. The best you get by throwing money at people is that they won't be unhappy. That matters, but it will never generate the positive energy that creates a winning organization. Second, as the third column in Figure 5.1 shows, each motivating factor ties directly to an Ecolab core perspective. MJ and his successors up and down the organization see the world in a way that encourages motivation and job satisfaction. Third, as you'll see later, these same motivators apply to customers, suppliers, and other stakeholders who benefit from Ecolab's extensive knowledge base and training programs. Finally, what you'll read that follows describes a very deliberate and intentional effort by Ecolab to enrich the job of every employee – from the most senior executive to the most junior field representative.

The Strategic Foundation: The Medical School Model

Ecolab operates across a range of diverse business, from heavy industries such as mining and oil & gas to the fine, technologically complex life science field. With such diversity, a one-size-fits-all development approach would mix apples and oranges and eviscerate Ecolab's hallmark technical expertise that brings so much value to clients. There are, however, commonalities of leadership, selling, and customer service principles and standards that apply across the organization. To cut at the joint between the corporate center and the business units, Paul Langlois and the training team employ a medical school analogy.

The first three years of medical school transmit knowledge, competencies, and cultural norms that span the medical profession. Future allergists study side-by-side with future anesthesiologists and one important learning of medical school entails an identity and set of behaviors that define what it means to be a doctor. In the fourth year, students begin to specialize within a proctored or mentored environment. Upon graduation, newly minted MDs begin their intensive practical training, which lasts another 4 to 10 years. Medical students move from generally useful knowledge to highly specialized skills.

Universal Training

The medical school analogy guides training and development at Ecolab. Almost every new employee – exceptions are few and far between – learns about the 3Cs (creating, communicating, and capturing value). The 3Cs training provides each Ecolab associate with a framework and set of skills to maximize the total value delivered by the company, particularly as measured by eROI. The tool in use is only as good as the associate using it in the field.

New associates learn how to *create* value for their customers, in terms of identifying needs, their division's products, and how to use the menu of Ecolab and Nalco solutions to "circle the customer" and create more business value. They learn how to *communicate* that value to the customer, including using tools such as informal and structured reporting, and eROI. My experiences with people in the field confirm the importance of this; the value added through training, cross-selling, and nurturing relationships to learn about other customer needs can easily get lost because there's no physical product delivered. The final C is to *capture* value. That includes making sure that all services and solutions get paid for, and helps customers see that value delivered vastly exceeds prices paid. Capturing value means earning anew each day Ecolab's premium brand position in the market place and customer's mind.

The High-Wide-Deep logic helps associates understand how and where the 3Cs play out at a customer site. *High* means taking a strategic look at the customer's business and applying acumen to generate a mental model of strategic success for the customer. *Wide* entails looking at each relevant stakeholder at a customer site and understanding their needs. *Deep* focuses on creating unique solutions to meet each customer's need. Ecolab's 3Cs model complements another core framework that I'll describe in the next chapter: Nalco's Six Service Standards. *High*, *Wide*, and *Deep* invites an integrative, strategic approach to every job that centers on three questions: How do our customers make money? What are their sustainability challenges in terms of people, planet, and profit? How can Ecolab create value for customers and help them build a more sustainable world?

All customer-facing associates also receive training around consultative selling. Consultative selling means creating customer relationships that go far beyond mere schmoozing, golf outings, or personal friendships with customers; it entails developing trust around competence and character that provides a window into the real, and usually unmet, needs of the customer. Field reps and sales managers don't really "sell" in the traditional way of pigeon-holing a customer need into the closest product or service that solves *some* of the customer's problem but meets *all or most* of the salesperson's objectives. Sales reps and field personnel serve as consultants who help customers identify, define, and refine deep needs and then tailor a customized, or semi-customized solution that solves the real problem. Moving from "I'm here to make a sale" to "I'm here to solve your biggest problems" doesn't just happen; it comes because of explicit training.

Managerial Training

As I described at the beginning of the chapter, every first-line supervisor or manager – defined as anyone with a direct report – receives the "manager essentials" training, and when they get promoted again and manage managers they learn the "leader coach" method. The first course prepares people for the enriched job of leading others within Ecolab as well as consulting customers. The second course moves to the next level of helping those they mentor along their own path of personal development. Both courses have detailed frameworks that guide learning, and both focus on behavioral outcomes; it's not enough to think differently, a manager should act differently after completing the module. Manager Essentials focuses on 12 behavioral competencies and Leader Coach on five. Modules enhance personal and professional development, autonomy, and achievement, and as participants do more than just know more, they become more.

Advanced Customer Support Training

Two other general courses exist for associates working in customer facing roles, Negotiations, for those actually working with customers to capture the value created through the Ecolab relationship, and a course on Corporate Story Telling. Ecolab is a complex business that creates value through so many different vehicles, many of which you'll read about as you move forward.

These six courses (the 3Cs, Consultative Selling, Manager Essentials, Leader Coach, Negotiations, Corporate Story Telling) constitute the "medical school" portion of training and originate at the corporate center. Note that each course has an application and practice component that happens within the participant's business unit. After completing these general courses, most training is run by the business units and focuses on detailed technical knowledge that sells particular solutions. Pest Elimination associates learn about effective chemicals and their careful application, and Nalco associates master the art of clean water management and how to reduce, reuse, and recycle water. Ecolab institutional teams go deep on hygiene solutions in their businesses.

The Tactical Model: The Structure of Development

Paul Langlois spent his college career learning about pedagogy, or how to teach children and teens. Their biological, cognitive, emotional, and social stage frames what type of learning works best, from the rote learning of the multiplication tables in elementary school to the basics of critical thinking in a typical Advanced Placement high school course. Pedagogy doesn't work for adults, however. Their biological, cognitive, emotional, and social developmental stages present different opportunities for and constraints on learning. Most corporate training programs fail because they build on pedagogy. They try and teach adults as if they were still children.

Ecolab's developmental programs build on solid foundations of adult learning, which Langlois and his team deftly employ.[9] Successful adult learning requires that students see the *relevance* of the content for the work they currently do or will likely do in the near future. Adult brains are primed to focus on current needs; training that clearly helps them do their job better is almost always welcome. Adult learners have different styles and effective andragogy (the technical name for adult learning models) presents materials in *multiple ways, multiple times*.

Relevant content and multiple learning methods provide the best setting for learning new conceptual material; after that, adult learners need opportunities to *practice* and eventually *master* knowledge and skills. The "manager essentials" course follows this protocol. The first section, self-study, allows for students to learn new concepts and apply those in generic, abstract settings. The second section brings them together for more intense, socially monitored and mediated practice. The final section enables mastery through continued concrete practice within their current role.

Ecolab also employs technology consistent with a RIGHT outlook. Langlois and Tsai's first task was to create a unified community out of a siloed, global, and intellectually diverse company. It didn't take long to realize that such a broad community could only emerge using digital technology and online interactions. Those digital platforms, once developed, laid the foundation for the medical school portion of training. The only way to make it work for a global organization is online, and it fosters a global sense of belonging and commonality. A digital foundation gave Ecolab a leg up during the pandemic and they just created new, pandemic-relevant content such as the module on virtual selling; they could push new content through an already robust pipeline.

The laddered structure of the training allows managers and others to develop in systematic and connected ways. New first-line managers gain a common core of essential skills. With the next promotion comes the next logical set of needed development, becoming an effective teacher and "proctor" (to keep the medical school analogy) within each business unit. These second-line leaders, and everyone above them, focus on five discrete behaviors that assist first-line supervisors in their quest for leadership mastery, including maintaining an attitude of helpfulness, creating receptivity with their mentees, asking great questions, developing actionable and focused plans for improvement, and helping mentees commit to measurable results. After completing these two courses, managers can access the digital learning platform for content that allows them to continue to grow.

The common training curriculum and the medical school model foster an identity as a member of the Ecolab business family. Just as pediatricians and geriatricians all receive a common core shoulder to shoulder, restaurant specialists rub (virtual) shoulders with those working with sophisticated laboratories. This egalitarian basis of common training engenders a feeling of a common identity, but it does more than that. These mixed cohorts learn first-hand respect for those in other units, they may establish relationships that will later help them circle the customer, and the group setting encourages and reinforces a humility that comes from seeing the technical prowess and sophistication across different business units and functions. Like any good educational system, Ecolab's development programs inculcate a common set of values that guide the next generation of leaders.

Paul Langlois chairs the Ecolab Learning Counsel. This group brings together the 10 members of the corporate training staff and the business unit training leaders. The council comes together to discuss common needs and emerging issues, to share best practices, and to coordinate efforts and schedules across a global organization. These people represent the core development community, and they will engage what Paul refers to as "champions" to deal with special challenges. They have talent champions to help with selection and talent acquisition, engagement champions who run employee engagement surveys and monitor results within each business unit, and the company designates learning leaders or champions to lead large, one-off or new development initiatives. The learning council exemplifies the RIGHT perspective: they respect each other as leaders, integrate their work, help grow the talent pool at the company, humbly learn best practices from each other, and use the latest technology to make their work as effective and efficient as possible.

Ecolab has built a sophisticated, intentional, and well-integrated program to attract and develop human capital. I asked Paul Langlois how his program stacked up to competitors. He didn't know about competitors directly, but he told me he presents to several organizations at the level of the Conference Board. At those meetings, he fields questions from people wishing they could build and sustain something like Ecolab's program. His team has created a great program, and going on the road reminds him of just how good it is. MJ would be proud that his company still hopes to create a "business family" among associates.

LESSONS FOR LEADERS

This chapter differs from the others in an important respect: I've chosen not to discuss the direct impact of having skilled people engaged in creating a more sustainable world. Put simply, they're essential. What I'll do now is highlight three questions you should ask as you evaluate your own human capital development program. I hope you've noted other things in the margin, but here are my key lessons:

1. *Are you hiring smart?* I share the notion about hiring smart with every student group I teach and every executive team I work with. Hiring smart turns out to be hard work. It means that hiring teams need to define the core dispositions, relationship capabilities, and technical skill sets of people they hope to hire *before* beginning the process. That often means the candidate with the best technical package won't get the job. Hiring smart also means taking time. Sometimes a position will be vacant for several months before you find the right candidate and the rest of the team does the work. That's a sacrifice, but well worth it.

   The second part of the phrase, the alternative, is managing tough. That means active supervision, detailed job assignments and reporting, and constant follow-up to make sure the job gets done right. At the end of the day, the financial, time, and emotional cost vastly exceeds the short-term pain required to hire smart.

   The quality of inputs drives the quality of outputs; the best training and development programs hit the ceiling created by the dispositions and traits of the people being trained. Do you have a list like the six traits Ecolab looks for (autonomy, business acumen, ability to collaborate and network, entrepreneurship, skill in managing complexity, and strategic mindset)?

Note that none of those core traits have anything to do with technical background. They each focus on relationships, with the self, the work, and others. PhD-level chemistry takes a long time to teach, for example, but you can't teach autonomy. Finally, Ecolab's six traits all link to the core strategy of the company; they all enhance its ability to create exceptional value through customer intimacy.

So, lesson number one is hire smart. It makes everything else easier.

2. *How tightly does your training and development program link to the core perspective and culture?* Ecolab's development program rests on well-grounded business principles – what we've learned from a half-century of job enrichment theory and motivation – and it sinks its roots deeply into the core RIGHT perspective that frames the Ecolab world. I repeated myself to highlight a point, and the third time is the charm: one big component of the Ecolab system is enculturation into the core perspective, purpose, and identity of the company. People pick up technical skills, but they refine their professional identities.

Company training programs often build on a "flavor of the month" mentality and focus on the newest technical findings and innovations or the latest management fad. These may be worth incorporating into your program, but only if they are consistent with who you are and who you want to be as a company. Smarter people don't always generate strategic success; people grounded in your core perspective and infused with your mission will. Whether your focus is on people, planet, or profits, development programs and knowledge only help when they align with and reinforce your core identity.

Look forward as well and make sure that your developmental content fits your business model and strategy. During the pandemic, Ecolab saw a clear threat to its business model – personalized service and selling – when personal contact no longer took place. Their training program was immediately relevant for everyone in the organization. What did you do during the pandemic? Contract with a new content vendor to help your people expand their skill set? Ecolab maintained its share through the pandemic because it featured new content that advanced the strategy.

3. *How well do training and development integrate across your organization? What's your model?* Most businesses of any size face a problem similar to Ecolab: They operate in a variety of product and market segments, each with its own knowledge base and skill demands. Executives in these organizations face a Goldilocks problem around general versus specialized training. Organizational inertia drives most companies into a siloed selection and training model, and they hire experts for each business and give them the skills they need. After a while, however, these organizations find that technical depth has come at the expense of general skills.

The other default is to control training at the corporate center and use a mix of in-house and off-the-shelf development tools to provide people with a generalized set of skills. In the off-the-rack case, skill development happens with no attention to cultural consistency. This model trades breadth for depth and produces apprentices of all trades and masters of none.

The medical school model works for Ecolab, a broadly diversified, global corporation that has clear needs for both specialized and generalized training, and helps them produce people with both breadth and depth of knowledge. This is a good model, but may not be right for your organization; however, your organization needs an overarching framework for training and development that helps those at the center and those in the hinterlands understand their roles and which content areas belong to which group. That model will define how much, what type, and when coordination needs to occur. Without a model that answers these key strategic questions, your organization will never get close to a "bed" that truly fits your own Goldilocks.

CONCLUSION

For all of the nineteenth and most of the twentieth century, the Great Person theory of leadership dominated and framed our collective discussion about leadership. This idea isn't without merit; indeed, Ecolab has flourished under the executive leadership of six individuals, some of them larger than life in their contributions to the company. So, yes, it takes great leadership at the top, *and* it takes great leadership throughout the organization. The challenge of our day is to create a sustainable world, and that will require active leadership at all levels of every organization, business, government, nonprofit, and religious. Ecolab provides a great example of how to create leaders at every level.

In my last conversation with Laurie Marsh, I asked her how she made sure that training and development in the business units garnered all the funding they needed. She told me that my question made no sense to her; "training is oxygen" is not just a slogan used by corporate HR or those working in business units. It's a deep belief held by every line manager at every level of the corporation. Training budgets have a sacred quality to them, and they would be the last, rather than the first, cut during a business downturn. Laurie Marsh, Paul Langlois, and the team at Ecolab understand the value of one of my favorite Zig Ziglar quips: "The only thing worse than training people and having them leave is not training them and having them stay."

When trained people stay, they do marvelous things. One of which is create world-class products and solutions that meet the real needs of their customers. The next chapter will provide you some insight into the product and research processes at Ecolab and their role in fostering a sustainable world.

EMILIO'S THOUGHTS

Wisdom is not a product of schooling but of the lifelong attempt to acquire it.

—Albert Einstein

A Nalco territory manager gets a call from the general manager at a major full-service hotel about a problem. It seems that the copper piping installed in the hotel's domestic water system is leaking and causing damage to the ceilings, walls, and carpeting. The territory manager investigates and analyzes the corrosive material on the inside of the pipe. The analysis reveals that the incoming water source is soft – a perfect environment to accelerate corrosion in copper piping. To protect the replacement pipe, the territory manager recommends pretreating the water to minimize its corrosive nature. The leak disappears.

This is a familiar story for our commercial teams, who are called into action by our customers to support the day-to-day challenges that impact their operations. These relationships are built over time, with Ecolab serving as both problem solver and partner. Understanding our customers' operations, processes, and businesses as well as they do is one of the most important ways that Ecolab creates value for our customers. But this level of customer trust just doesn't happen. Our onsite representatives earn that trust through positive intent, credibility and capability. They convey an "I'm here to solve your biggest problems" mindset from Day One. Across Ecolab, this process and philosophy leads to deep customer relationships. It's part of our culture and our values, and it's inextricably linked with performance. These values and beliefs are the internal driving principles that guide how we work with customers. Simply stated:

- We reach our goals.
- We do what's right.
- We challenge ourselves.
- We work together with diverse perspectives.
- We make a difference.
- And we do this all with care, putting safety first.

Having frontline managers who can balance the performance and core values of their field teams helps sustain our company's winning value proposition and success. The concept of smart hiring that Professor Godfrey shared is about hiring capable candidates who share our view of the world and our core values. That's really important because time and time again, we see that sustained performance is linked to internalizing our values. When it all comes together, our personal customer service is a true differentiator versus our competition. It's vitally important to delivering on our company's purpose – partnering to make the world cleaner, safer, and healthier – and helping customers succeed while protecting people and the resources essential to life.

This book outlines a number of elements that make us successful, including our integrated approach to delivering unique programs, personal service and digital insights. But leadership and initiative are as, if not more, important. Without this, all the technical knowledge in the world won't move the dial on success.

Building on Professor Godfrey's commentary in this chapter, I'd like to focus on what Ecolab delivers to our customers through our onsite experts. Rooted in science, the leadership of our innovative and determined problem solvers is the secret sauce behind our deep customer relationships.

Creating onsite experts who demonstrate stewardship and ingenuity requires intense technical and industry training in the first year. Many of our customer-facing team members come to us with a strong educational foundation. For example, we hire paper engineers to support our large paper and pulp customers and food safety and quality engineers for the food and beverage industry. We deliver comprehensive programs and solutions, with focused, data-driven insights and unmatched service to advance food safety, maintain clean and safe environments, optimize water and energy use, and improve operational efficiencies and sustainability for our customers.

Throughout our 100-year history of helping customers improve their operations, our associates have remained committed to our core values. They're approachable, dependable, and trusted advisors who connect with customers on a personal level. We have accomplished this by taking these steps:

- *Support and champion our customers' success.* Our onsite experts have a deep understanding of customer realities, and they deliver tailored solutions to maximize customer performance with less dependency on natural and human resources. Our customers rely increasingly on digital solutions and automation to power their businesses. While modernization can improve productivity and profitability, it has reduced the size of the workforce, with manufacturing's share of employment declining from a peak of 25% in the 1950s to 10% today.[10] This sometimes leads to gaps in decision-making, problem-solving, and analysis that are not easily replaced by automation and smart manufacturing. In these situations, our value to our customers continues to grow because our integrated solutions and personal service ensure that they have a reliable partner to support them.
- *Bring the power of science, insights, and technology to anticipate what's next.* We know we need to be focused and agile, to stay ahead of the curve and optimize our solutions for an ever-changing world. Industry 4.0 has led to tremendous benefits for manufacturers including Ecolab's smart water management solutions such as 3D TRASAR™ and the ECOLAB3D™ cloud. These solutions deliver data and insights to our customers to help them make informed decisions 24 hours a day, 7 days a week. But that's not enough. Why? Like many things in life, there are interdependencies in customer operations that require a fresh set of eyes to diagnose and resolve problems. For example, in a brewery, cleaning and sanitizing

Merritt J. (MJ) Osborn at his desk, circa 1934. EL had grown from $4,000 in sales in 1924 to $160,000 in 1934. MJ served as President until 1951 and as board chair until his death in 1960. Photo courtesy of Ecolab.

Above: MJ and Edward Bartlett (EB) Osborn, 1946. In 1946, EL's revenue was $3.4 million. EB took Ecolab public in 1957 and spent his career helping the company mature and expand. At the time of EB's death in 1978, EL's sales stood at $398 million, a 50-fold increase under his leadership. Photo courtesy of Ecolab.

Above: EB Osborn and Fred Lanners, 1978. Lanners served as the first non-family CEO. Photo courtesy of Ecolab.

Above: Pierson "Sandy" Grieve is the only executive appointed to the CEO role from outside the company. Grieve's time at Ecolab marked an important shift in strategic direction with a focus on business-to-business sales. In 1983 he divested Apollo Technologies and in 1987 he divested the consumer brands business. Grieve also adopted the company's current name in 1986. Photo Courtesy of Ecolab.

Above: Al Shuman was Ecolab's CEO from 1994-2004. During his tenure, the company expanded its product and service lines to better circle the customer and circle the globe. Shuman started at Ecolab in 1957 as a sales representative. Photo courtesy of Ecolab.

Above: Doug Baker succeeded Al Shuman as CEO in 2004. Baker successfully integrated Nalco and 120 other acquisitions and pivoted the strategy to a focus on sustainability and water management. Photo courtesy of Ecolab.

Above: Christophe Beck was appointed Ecolab's CEO in January 2020. He continued the company's high growth, guiding it through the COVID-19 pandemic and the development of Ecolab Science Certified™ program. His leadership also placed water and climate at the center of the company's future growth strategy. Photo courtesy of Ecolab.

Above: Ida C. Koran was the first employee hired by MJ Osborn in 1923. She became corporate secretary in 1925 and a director in the mid-1930's, at a time when few women reached the upper echelons of corporations. Photo courtesy of Ecolab.

Above: EL warehouse worker, early 1930s. The highly successful Soilax product was purchased by hardware stores and others who sold the product in bulk. Photo courtesy of Ecolab.

Above: An Ecolab Clean-in-Place system. In the 1960s, CIP changed production in the dairy, and food/ beverage industries. Today's CIP incorporates Ecolab's extensive data collecting and reporting technology. Photo courtesy of Ecolab.

Above: Herbert A. Kern and P. Wilson Evans merged their companies in 1928 to form the National Aluminate Corporation, later changed to Nalco. Kern and MJ shared several values, and when Nalco joined the Ecolab family in late 2011, those shared values made the integration successful. Photo courtesy of Ecolab.

Above: 3D TRASAR™, introduced in 2004, is the technical backbone of Ecolab's water, food and beverage, and energy businesses. Measuring water quality every 6 seconds, 3DT provides rich data for analysis. Photo courtesy of Ecolab.

Above: Nalco Water's 21st Century solutions include advanced membrane solutions. Nalco Water's combination of technology, data analytics and consulting provides unmatched water management capabilities. Photo courtesy of Ecolab.

FORM 411 REV. 7-59

EL **SOILAX SERVICE REPORT** **EL**

PRINTED IN U. S. A.

ECONOMICS LABORATORY, INC.
SPECIALISTS IN FOOD UTENSIL SANITATION

CHAIN NO. 39

ACCOUNT **STATE OFFICE BLDG.** TIME **8:30 AM.**

ADDRESS **300 WEST PRESTON ST.** DATE **10/15/50**

CITY **BALTIMORE, MARYLAND** ROUTE NO. **9**

MACHINE MAKE **TOLEDO** MODEL **TW4** LOCATION **KITCHEN**

	DISHES	GLASSES	SILVER	POTS	
• RESULTS •	GOOD	GOOD	GOOD	GOOD	GOOD
Product Used	SAW	G/M	ASSW	P/D	R/D
Stock on Hand	2 BBLS	1½ BBL	4 CS	1½ BBL	5 CS

• OPERATION •	ACTIVE	IDLE	• EQUIPMENT •	
Alkalinity	.22		Fill Valve	OK
Wash Temp.	140°		Wash Arms	CLEANED
Rinse Tank Temp.	160°		Wash Valve	—
Final Rinse Temp.	185°		Rinse Arms	CLEANED
Rinse Period	AUTO		Final Rinse	CLEANED
Scrapping	GOOD		Rinse Valve	OK
Racking	FAIR		Overflow	OK
			Drain	OK
			Pump	OK

INJECTOR **OK** MODEL **DRI-VAC** DISPENSER **OK** MODEL **SOL 20E**

MEMO TO: MR. **MANAGER.**

REMOVED UPPER AND LOWER WASH TUBES AND END CAPS AND FLUSHED OUT.

REMOVED UPPER AND LOWER RINSE TUBES AND FLUSHED OUT.

REMOVED UPPER AND LOWER FINAL RINSE TIPS AND CLEANED OUT.

INSTRUCTED NEW OPERATOR ON PROCEDURES FOR PROPER RACKING & CLEANING OF DISH MACHINE.

CUSTOMER'S SIGNATURE

SALESMAN'S SIGNATURE **Joe Salesman. 416**

REORDER DATA

Above: The company's commitment to great service goes back to 1923. This service report, from 1950, illustrates how EL reps did a thorough inspection during every visit and recommended changes and improvements. Photo Courtesy of Ecolab.

ECONOMICS LABORATORY, INC.

SERVICE POLICY

The purpose and objective of Economics Laboratory service is to assure food service operators of a properly operating warewashing function. EL service is a safeguard measure—its true value lies in knowing that your dishroom will operate correctly at the present and that it is designed to avoid breakdowns in the future.

1. **We will advise the Manager, at all times, of the situation existing in his Dishwashing Operation.**
   In effect, act as his assistant in charge of dishwashing advising him both of conditions which are extremely good and those extremely bad, requiring his attention, and relieve him of the remaining common or "usual" problems. This information, including all of the items which follow, are submitted both verbally and in writing.

2. **We will regularly inspect samples of all types of eating utensils.**
   The results of those in storage indicate conditions prevalent since our Warewashing Specialist's last call and those coming out of the dishmachine represent conditions at that moment.

3. **We will check all equipment.**
   We will perform minor adjustments of all heavy repairs needed. We will, on request, put management in contact with qualified agencies to do heavy repair work.

4. **We will measure the concentration of the detergent wash solution by chemical analysis.**
   We will maintain this concentration at all times within the range of proper dishwashing. We will take steps to remedy conditions which allow this concentration to go too high, resulting in over consumption, or too low, resulting in poor results.

5. **We will check and regulate the temperature of all the wash and rinse solutions in the dishmachine tanks and the temperature of the final fresh water rinse, with an accurate thermometer, thereby checking the machine thermometers.**

6. **We will check time, in seconds, each item is washed and rinsed.**
   We will obtain the proper rinsing period for proper dishwashing, and the proper combination of washing time and detergent strength for washing.

7. **We will check steam and fill valves for leaks.**
   We will report major valve trouble to management immediately to eliminate the high cost of faulty valve operation.

8. **We will check wash manifold arms and sprays, rinse arms and sprays for efficient operation. If they are clogged, the EL Warewashing Specialist will instruct operators on the proper daily cleaning method. He will check rotating wash arms for proper pitch and pressure and check wash and rinse arm bearings to see that arms are revolving freely.**

9. **We will inspect the by-pass action, the over-flow action, and the balance of the machine.**
   A dishmachine's effectiveness is totally dependent upon this by-pass and over-flow action. Good results are impossible if it is not operating properly.

10. **We will check the drain valve and plumbing.**
    Improper plumbing and drain valve trouble destroys the over-flow action, giving poor results.

11. **We will check the pump and motor.**
    We will check pumps for leaks, the motor, shaft, and universal joints for excess vibration, poor alignment, and wear. We will check pump impellors for wear, buildup, and foreign objects. The pump delivery in gallons per minute must be in accordance with proper dishwashing conditions or NSF Standards. These items, as well as low line voltage, reversed motors, clogged or improper strainer screens may all affect wash pressure.

12. **We will check all other equipment in the dishwashing operation according to manufacturer's recommendations and specifications.**
    This includes over-head and fountain type pre-scraping equipment, special glass and silverware equipment, etc.

13. **We will check all accessory equipment to the dishmachine, such as detergent dispensers and drying agent injectors.**

14. **We will check over-all operation of the Dishwashing Department.**
    The EL Warewashing Specialist, with his knowledge and experience, must coordinate the type of operation, available equipment; personnel; traffic flow, volume of dishes, including peaks and lulls; and other factors in order to obtain maximum efficiency at lowest cost. The savings he effects, both tangible and intangible, can be astounding, many times actually exceeding the net profit of the organization.

We will supply management with the following:

15. **Written Service Reports on each Service Call.**
    These reports can be filed by Management for review regularly. These Service Reports supply Management with a picture of the over-all dishwashing operation. They indicate factors requiring its attention regarding manpower, costly waste areas, and data for future purchases or changes.

16. **Special Surveys, when needed, analyzing operation and equipment conditions for special study.**

17. **Operating Charts for dishmachine operators regarding the care and use of the dishmachine (available in English and Spanish).**

18. **Training Instruction**
    We will train dishmachine operators in:
    a. Proper racking of dishes
    b. Pre-scraping procedures
    c. Specialized handling procedures
    d. Daily machine cleanup procedures.
    We will make recommendations to the Manager on all phases of the dishwashing operation and advise him of the latest ideas and equipment in the dishwashing field. We will provide special training films—"Flying Saucers", "Spotlight on Breakage", and a slide training program to instruct new personnel.

The ECONOMICS LABORATORY Warewashing Specialist is qualified in all phases of warewashing sanitation because he is a graduate of the standardized EL training program. He trains for up to two years under a senior salesman in the field until he is fully qualified. In addition to his dishwashing knowledge, he is backed by the most advanced dishwashing products modern research has developed and the best sold. Only this combination can give you true service.

C. B. Osborn
President

Above: EB Osborn formalized and extended EL's service policy. The value proposition for customers included high quality products supported by EL associates who knew as much, if not more, than they did about their business. Photo courtesy of Ecolab.

Above: Ecolab technicians help customers clean water to reduce costs and increase asset life. Some Ecolab employees work full time at customer sites. Photo courtesy of Ecolab.

Above: Sales-and-service associates use site visits to inspect equipment. Ecolab's extensive training encourages reps to learn about their customers' entire operation. They can easily recommend other Ecolab products/services that circle the customer. Photo courtesy of Ecolab.

Above: Warewashing was Ecolab's first growth business. Today, the company offers a range of integrated solutions to meet the needs of large and small restaurant owners. Photo courtesy of Ecolab.

Above: A hallmark of customer service includes in-depth trainings sessions with people at all levels to share best practices and improve performance. Photo courtesy of Ecolab.

Above: Ecolab's Healthcare business operated within the Institutional unit until 2020, when it grew into its own business unit. Healthcare's exacting product standards became important inputs into the Ecolab Science Certified™ program. Photo courtesy of Ecolab.

Above: Nalco Water brings customers to its site for extensive training on water stewardship. Water Stewardship is Ecolab's strategic focus as it begins its second century. Photo courtesy of Ecolab.

Above: Ecolab's efforts around water stewardship took a giant leap forward with the Water Risk Monetizer 3.0 in 2017. Ecolab contributed its expertise and partnered with Microsoft and S&P Global Sustainable1 to build out the interactive, Publicly available web-based tool. Photo courtesy of Ecolab.

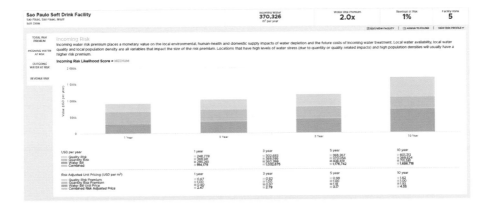

Above: The Water Risk Monetizer helps industry understand the full value of water at the facility level and monetize it in business terms so site managers can act. In 2021 the tool became the Smart Water Navigator™ to focus on broader water stewardship issues.

Above: During the COVID-19 pandemic, Ecolab scientists developed the Ecolab Science Certified™ program to support customers and calm consumer fears about hygiene in businesses they frequent. Photo courtesy of Ecolab.

Above: Ecolab Science Certified™ marks the company's return to highly-visible consumer branded activities. The program's seal can be found in grocery, restaurant, and retail locations. Photo courtesy of Ecolab.

Below: To raise awareness of the Ecolab Science Certified™ program, Ecolab returned to television advertising, raising consumer awareness of the company and its solutions. Photo courtesy of Ecolab.

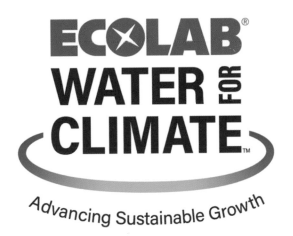

Above: As it deepens its commitment to sustainability over the next 100 years, Ecolab rolled out a new integrated product solution to help customers meet their water and energy use goals. Logo courtesy of Ecolab.

Above: Experts at Ecolab's Global Intelligence Center (EGIC) analyze data from IoT-connected systems to provide real-time monitoring and measurable results. The EGIC operates at six locations around the world: The base in Pune, India, and additional centers in Brazil, China, North America, Saudi Arabia and The Netherlands. Photo courtesy of Ecolab.

practices impact everything from the packaging and filler lines to the proper operation and compliance of the onsite wastewater treatment plant downstream. Ecolab teams monitor the practices and cleaning chemistry being discharged to the waste treatment plant to mitigate risks and reduce operational costs.

- *Deliver meaningful impact.* We achieve real and measurable business results through responsible solutions that advance business *and* sustainability goals. Doug Baker would often say you can set ambitious goals but at the end of the day all that Mother Nature cares about is the impact to the planet. Professor Godfrey entitled this chapter "48,000 Strong and Counting." Our people are responsible for our strength and the reason Ecolab is a trusted sustainability partner to our customers. We deliver on their business and sustainability goals but we also translate that into meaningful and measurable impact. In 2021, Ecolab helped our customers collectively deliver on the following performance:

  - 215 billion gallons of water conserved, equivalent to the drinking water needs of 734 million people.
  - 3.6 million metric tons of CO_2 avoided, preventing almost 5.9 million pollution-related illnesses.
  - 1.4 billion people fed safely.
  - 60 billion hands cleaned.

We'll talk more about our 2030 impact goals in Chapter 9, but these goals showcase our global team's dedication to helping our customers thrive and make a positive impact on water, climate, food, and health.

Success for Ecolab and our customers depends on leadership. And we know that leadership is all about relationships. Our people are demonstrated leaders in terms of the level of service they provide to customers. That, in turn, creates long-lasting relationships that can transcend change. No matter the challenges that come our way, our leadership and our commitment to our customers will continue. It's the bedrock of our success.

Chapter 6

CREATING A SUSTAINABLE PRODUCT PIPELINE

The ideals I had in mind in forming the Company were to develop products in the field of chemistry of such high quality and efficiency as would win his approval, loyalty, and continued use of them, and to serve his interests in every way possible.

—MJ Osborn

We go to hospitals to heal, but, ironically, far too many of us get sicker while there. Healthcare acquired infections (HAIs) have nasty names such as *Staphylococcus aureus, Pseudomonas aeruginosa,* and *E. coli,* each leading to pain, suffering, and, too often, early mortality. Perhaps the most famous is *Clostridioides difficile,* also known as *C-diff,* the leading cause of antibiotic-associated diarrhea and one of the most common HAIs around the world.[1] *C-diff* alone infects over a half-million patients in US hospitals each year, and almost 30,000 (6%) will die. For comparison, the mortality rate for COVID-19 came in at 1.1%.[2] For those over 65, *C-diff* will kill 1 out of 11, or 9%, who contract the disease. *C-diff* adds 2.4 million patient days in US hospitals per year at a cost of an additional $6.3 billion; the total for all HAIs runs to almost $29 billion annually.[3]

C-diff preys on those who have recently taken antibiotics that wipe out healthy probiotics in the digestive and intestinal track, and the bacteria thrives in the fecal matter of those infected. The most common vector for spread is unwashed hands, whether a healthcare worker, family member, or other visitor. *C-diff* should be easy to control, but proper hand hygiene in healthcare settings turns out to be problematic; only 40% of healthcare workers comply with best-practice standards for hand hygiene. Those dirty hands contaminate patients and surfaces, which increases the risk of transmission and infection. Ecolab knows a thing or two about hand hygiene and sanitizing surfaces.

The tip of the spear in Ecolab's *C-diff* arsenal is a sophisticated collection of chemicals, sensors, and digital reports that focus on patient room hand hygiene. The chemicals include high-quality hand sanitizers and soaps, along with dispensers. Workers wear a lightweight (less than 1 oz), sensor-equipped badge. When they enter a patient room, the badge flashes red to indicate the need to sanitize hands. As the dispenser doses sanitizer, it also emits a wireless signal that updates the badge status. The patient bed has its own set of monitors that create a digital "safe zone" that turns the badge light to green when a sanitized employee enters the safe zone. After leaving the patient zone, the badge's red light flashes on.

Employees must wash their hands in order for their badge to return to neutral, "safe" status. The badge records hygiene performance for later review, and the process repeats itself in the next patient room. The impact of the complex system? Proper hand hygiene compliance moves from 40% to greater than 80%, and the risk of *C-diff* and other HAI transmission drops significantly.

This sophisticated hand hygiene solution is only one weapon in a much larger Ecolab arsenal. The company also provides environmental hygiene products for hard surface cleaning and disinfecting, along with monitoring devices including fluorescent gel markers that improve the thoroughness of patient room cleaning. The chemical solutions kill germs faster, help maintain a cleaner overall environment, and create a safer space for patient healing. Ecolab solutions extend beyond patient rooms to the operating theater, where a similar combination of chemicals and sensors allow staff to quickly clean the theater and prepare for the next surgical patient. The surgeon's tools have also been cleaned and sanitized by another Ecolab sterile room cleaning solution. If that's not enough touch points, Nalco Water teams help ensure overall water cleanliness and quality.

A fully serviced healthcare facility employs five unique (patient programs, Operating Room programs, central sterile department, hand hygiene, and water solutions) but interrelated product and service suites that minimize *C-diff* and other HAIs. Those systems focus on eight unique touch points, each of which is a potential vector: hands, surfaces, surgical instruments, pre-op patient skin, endoscopy equipment, medical devices in the operating theater, patient temperature monitoring systems, and water.

Those eight touchpoints involve three different Ecolab businesses: infection prevention (the first five), surgical (the next two), and Nalco water (the last one). Each business brings products, operational efficiency that saves time and resources, outstanding service, customer training, and analytics on performance and trends. That represents a significant investment by Ecolab in coordinating products and services at a healthcare facility. Is it all worth it?

While the savings vary by hospital and number of systems employed, the full suite of Ecolab solutions result in direct annual incremental savings – in excess of costs – of hundreds of thousands of dollars from the "lightening of labor," improved compliance, reductions in unnecessary patient stays, and lengthened asset life. That doesn't include the true eROI benefits of patients who avoid an HAI, the physical and emotional stresses of an additional illness and delayed healing, and the economic costs of a longer hospital stay or missed days or weeks at work.

I hope you see the traces of MJ Osborn at work here; you should see each of the RIGHT elements in play. *Integration* across business units and customer needs almost leaps off the page, as do *technology* (from core chemicals to digital analytics), and *growth* (HAIs continue to grow and so does a business that fights them). *Respect* is embedded in the integrated nature of the complete solution set that tracks a typical patient journey throughout a facility and honors that journey with attention to every step. Hand hygiene embodies *humility*; we've known about the value of clean hands for a couple of centuries now, but we still – collectively – struggle, and it takes a detailed analysis of where and how to intervene that makes a difference.

In this chapter I'll more fully describe the principles behind Ecolab's product development and research, development & engineering processes, and how those principles drive overall sustainability for the company, its customers, and the larger community.

CUSTOMER INTIMACY AS THE CORE STRATEGY

I noted back in Chapter 3 that Ecolab's strategy since 1923 would be described today as customer intimacy, or deep relationships between the company and its customers that both meets existing needs and enables discovery of new ways to create value through the business relationship. I also noted that respect plays a foundational role in these deep, interactive, and long-term customer relationships. In this section, I'll employ a different framework for thinking about products and services as jobs-to-be-done for customers. Ecolab's Nalco subsidiary developed a customer service process that uncovers customer jobs-to-be-done, which I'll analyze.

The Job-to-Be-Done Framework

In 2006, management guru Clayton Christensen described value creation in a job-to-be-done framework. It turns out that customers don't care all that much about products themselves; what they do is "hire" products or services to do jobs they really care about. As marketing guru Theodore Levitt noted almost a half-century before Christensen, "People don't want to buy a quarter-inch drill. They want a quarter-inch hole!"[4] When companies understand and respond to their customers' job-to-be-done, they can create a lasting competitive advantage.

Nalco's Herb Kern had said the same thing three decades earlier: Find the customer need and fill it. Whether we call it "job-to-be-done" or "find a customer need," both ways of thinking about customer intimacy as a strategy emerge from the core perspective of respect. Without respect for customer needs, and their ability to know and describe their own needs, a company, from sales reps to researchers, won't develop the type of trust that uncovers current and emerging customer jobs-to-be-done.

MJ provided his original answer to the job-to-be-done question in the 1953 summary that I opened the chapter with:

> The ideals I had in mind in forming the Company were to develop products in the field of chemistry of such high quality and efficiency as would result in "The Saving of Time – The Lightening of Labor, and The Reduction of Costs" to the user of such products, as would win his approval, loyalty, and continued use of them, and to serve his interests in every way possible.[5]

EL's goal was not merely to clean dishes, hands, or other things; it was to help customers do the important job of turning a profit or, in the consumer business, running a household. Ecolab's products and services do more than just clean. At the level of strategy, that "doing more" happens in one of two ways: superior physical products and/or the services that accompany and provide the context for those products.

Superior Products

Superior products either do more jobs for customers or they do a single job better than alternative offerings. Nalco Water treats water, and water matters to most businesses – think about how important water is for the Coca-Cola Company, Marriott Hotels, or Rio Tinto's mining operations. With tools such as 3D TRASAR™ and digital analytics, Nalco Water treats water with more precision than competing products. When you add in water management services, Nalco Water helps customers solve more jobs, and solve them more completely, than its competitors. As it helps its customers plan and implement programs to reduce the total amount of input water used, reuse that water through several production cycles, and clean wastewater before release back into the ecosystem, Nalco Water does an important sustainability job for communities and societies as well.

Customers get more important jobs done, and those jobs get done better, and so they willingly pay more for Ecolab products, usually a 10–20% premium. Customers pay more because they get more, and Ecolab closes that loop as it provides customers with a periodic assessment of its total value created through eROI reporting. The combination of high-quality products, constant monitoring, high-touch service by Ecolab field representatives, and an extensive knowledge base that trains customers to do their jobs better represents a recipe for product suites that, in the words of Nalco's Herb Kern, constantly find customer needs and fill them.

Superior Service

After a half-century, Nalco Water expanded and codified Kern's dictum about finding value into the six service standards, displayed in Figure 6.1.

The standards play two critical, ongoing roles in executing a customer intimacy strategy. First, they outline a recurring and systematic process for identifying the customer job-to-be-done, or deep customer needs both *in* and *over* time. The process begins with data collection as an associate

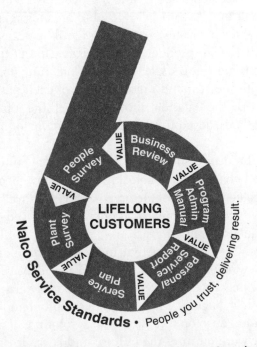

Figure 6.1 Nalco's Six Service Standards

identifies both the important people in the organization (those with needs) and the physical plant itself (where those needs become manifest). The next two elements involve deliberate and iterative planning of how the real customer needs will be met and codifying that plan to ensure accurate implementation. The last two steps ensure follow-up to verify that the expected value has been delivered.

The standards also define and develop a set of cultural norms around what customer intimacy really means. Take the first element, which too many corporate sales teams misinterpret. They view the people survey and relationship plan as a quick tactic to identify buyers and find their hot buttons. That drives a quick-buck sales culture that focuses on the most surface level of customer need or pain; indeed, taking the time to dig deeper means that another client's surface needs may not be met.

For the Ecolab and Nalco Water teams, the people survey goes deep into the organization. It begins by identifying *everyone* who benefits from the product and how they benefit, from the CFO who makes capital expenditure decisions to the plant engineer or restaurant owner who oversees the entire system each day, to the people who operate the water system or wash dishes. As associates develop ongoing relationships, both surface-level and deep jobs-to-be-done emerge. The next service standard identifies which Ecolab products and services will get those jobs done. It's not about turning a quick sale, it's about matching products, services, and training with the real and unique needs of each customer, and the courage to provide the data that shows how well the job was done. The six service standards develop an external standard for what customers can expect.

The standards nurture and perpetuate an internal culture of customer intimacy as the behaviors that each standard requires become ingrained and communicated throughout the organization. As I walked through the Nalco Water cafeteria with Emilio on one visit, he asked colleagues he'd known for decades to recite the six service standards, and everyone did.[6] That represents a cultural perpetual motion machine as the standards form a fundamental element of the Nalco Water identity. It's not just for show, however, because when problems arise in a relationship, the six standards provide a diagnostic to see where the problem lies, understand the job-to-be-done, develop a value creating solution, and report results. That day-to-day work nurtures the culture and keeps it vibrant and vital. I hope you see the similarities between Nalco's six service standards and today's 3Cs training I described in the previous chapter.

CUSTOMER INTIMACY AND SUSTAINABILITY

I've made a consistent point throughout the book: the RIGHT perspective (Respect, Integration, Growth, Humility, and Technology) provides the best foundation for any company hoping to engage in the three phases of sustainability. You've now seen how RIGHT defines and dictates how Ecolab thinks about products and solutions. The six service standards, or their Ecolab equivalent the 3Cs, drive RIGHT deep into the cultural DNA and across the operating units of the company. In what follows, I'll outline why that same chain, from RIGHT to the six service standards, represents the *best way forward* for advancing a sustainable business agenda.

First, job-to-be-done logic naturally integrates each of the 3Ps (profit, people, and planet). Every executive needs to turn a profit, and Ecolab's history shows that a focus on making sustainability a profitable activity advances the cause in and over time. Emilio noted in his commentary to Chapter 1 that the company sees no trade-off between the jobs-to-be-done in each of the 3Ps. Customers have several jobs, from cleaning dishes and human hands (social sustainability) to managing industrial water flows (environmental sustainability) in addition to making a profit (economic sustainability); job-to-be-done thinking recognizes each of those jobs as important and that recognition forces both customer and company to think through how to best do multiple jobs well.

Second, when anyone and everyone in the organization employs the six service standards – the pathway to uncovering and meeting jobs-to-be-done – they deploy a system designed to discover customized and deep needs regularly and iteratively. Those needs exist within the company, customer organizations, and larger communities. Both Ecolab and Nalco learned early that water is more than just H_2O, and each geographic region had its own unique blend of minerals and microbes that could thwart how well a detergent worked and required custom chemical mixes to purify it. No two customers are exactly alike, and even competitors in the same geography have different ecological histories and profiles.

Jobs-to-be-done have a custom element for each community and each of the 3Ps; the six service standards mark the path to finding what must be uniquely adapted to meet each stakeholder need. Real progress in creating sustainable businesses and a sustainable world requires a level of customization deeper than a generic "carbon footprint" or "net zero emissions" goal. That customization only emerges in the context of real and intimate relationships of trust that foster the communication that unearths critical jobs-to-be-done. The six service standards create a behavioral roadmap to customize sustainability to each customer.

Third, the iterative nature of the standards invites everyone to actually measure outcomes and adjust along the way. Progress reporting shows meaningful movement against benchmarks. Reporting protocols also invite a hard look at outcomes that may be less than meaningful, or even retrogression in performance. The end of one performance cycle invites real analysis and reflection about why goals weren't achieved, which jobs were not done, and what mistakes were made, even when those mistakes reveal unintended or unforeseen consequences of attempting to do a particular job. Reporting always involves healthy doses of humility and courage; we all know it's easier and less painful to believe we did well rather than measure whether or not we did well.

Finally, and perhaps most importantly, job-to-be-done logic turns the focus of products and services away from the technical and toward the relational. Sustainability, at its core, is a set of relationships between humans, economies, and the natural environment. Building a sustainable future won't happen without technology and technical solutions; it also won't happen unless and until our economic and social relations with each other help all of us accomplish our individual and collective jobs-to-be-done. Asking about those jobs through a systematic process of understanding-planning-reporting allows us to uncover the real jobs to be done. Then progress can happen.

CUSTOMER INTIMACY AND RESEARCH, DEVELOPMENT, & ENGINEERING

Technology, more specifically the belief that technology can provide sustainable and valuable customer solutions, has been a bedrock principle at Ecolab for a hundred years. *Absorbit* and *Soilax* came from scientific research, and as I noted in Chapter 4, MJ gave great deference to the people running the research lab because he recognized its central role in EL's success. In fact, in 1969, the company wanted to highlight the role of technology and they introduced a unique logo to embody their commitment to technology. I've reproduced that logo as Figure 6.2.

Larry Berger holds the title of executive vice president and chief technology officer at Ecolab. He's eminently qualified for the post – a bachelor of science degree in chemical engineering from SUNY–Stony Brook and master's and PhD degrees in materials science and engineering from Cornell. Berger spent two decades at DuPont, so when I asked

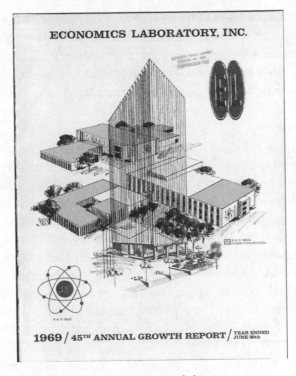

ECONOMICS LABORATORY, INC.

1969 / 45ᵀᴴ ANNUAL GROWTH REPORT / YEAR ENDED JUNE 30th

Figure 6.2 A Unique Ecolab Logo

him about what makes research, development, and engineering (RD&E) unique at Ecolab, he's got a great base of comparison. Berger identified two overarching themes – without being prompted by the earlier Figure 3.1, my analysis of the RIGHT perspective, the purposes, priorities, and processes that drive the company. Those two themes are first, RD&E at Ecolab operates with a customer-centric view, and second, the unit focuses on the future – of the company, its customers, and the planet.

Customer-Centric Research

When MJ gave up his Ford dealership and turned back to his first love of chemistry, he realized that his $5,000 (around $90,000 in 2023) precluded a full line of pharmaceuticals so he focused on finding a single formulation that would meet a customer need and provide revenue. *Absorbit* met the customer need too well, but MJ repeated the process with *Soilax*, and the goal was to save time, labor, and overall expense for customers. That spirit still infuses the 1,600 people who work at the company's RD&E campuses around the globe. Three organizational practices keep that spirit alive and front and center in the company's efforts: a clear value proposition, tight integration between researchers and field reps, and an emphasis on integrated solutions.

Value Proposition

The causal arrow for RD&E at Ecolab runs from technology to customer and organization, not the other way around. In other words, technology works to serve the organization and customer. The clear and explicit goal is to create "outsized customer value by [products that act] faster, better, and at the lowest total cost – including waste and labor savings."[7] Simple thought, you say! Yes, but harder to do in practice than you'd think. I did some work for a large technology company to help them understand what made effective R&D, and I interviewed people who managed or interfaced with R&D at nine leading technology companies – names you'd easily recognize. How did the top companies run their research labs?

Far too many of those companies compartmentalized RD&E. Operating units did D&E if they could cobble together the resources (product development and engineering often exist as separate silos). Basic research occurred at some kind of centralized lab. Most of these labs operated with high degrees of autonomy and worked separately from the main organization. What did they work on? Common answers were "out-of-the-box thinking," "futuristic projects," and "who knows?"

Research at some companies follows a slot machine model, where researchers pursue a diverse set of projects and hope that one hits the jackpot. In these companies, the causal arrow runs from company to technology. Customers don't even enter the equation. The organization serves technology. This is not the Ecolab model; RD&E is fully integrated with the core strategic value creation process of the organization.

Field Team and RD&E Integration

Back in the 1960s and 1970s, EL reported on its unique approach to RD&E. Field sales reps had free access to and regular contact with the labs in Minnesota. The lab learned about customer challenges, issues, and new jobs-to-be-done and researchers could get quick, market-based feedback on their work. That saved both time and money because it quickly shot down solutions that worked in the lab but not in the field.

That same setup exists today. Berger noted that "one of the reasons we've been able to sustain our pace of innovation is due to how closely our field teams and RD&E teams work together. Our field sales reps are our eyes and ears to the challenges and opportunities to help our customers. . . . Additionally, our [RD&E] people spend substantial time at customer sites. This ensures they, too, can foster a rich understanding of our customers' businesses and challenges."

Two things are worth noting about this setup. First, we have here another example of yarn-dying the RIGHT perspective into operating processes. Integration is clear, but you should also see respect, humility, and growth. The type of continued, value-added interactions between the technician in the laundry and the chemist in the lab requires a level of respect for the value that each brings and the humility to admit the deep knowledge that each party holds. Second, these relationships help Ecolab grow as they help technology be more effective in meeting customer needs and more efficient, in terms of time and funds expended.

Note that Larry talked about sustaining a "pace of innovation" at Ecolab. Research that focuses on market-driven challenges and gets rapid feedback from that market speeds development cycles. All of this feeds the core priority of technology-fueled growth.

Integrated Solutions
You saw earlier in the chapter how customers benefit from integrated product solutions, both in terms of discrete areas such as hand hygiene and at the level of the entire facility, but how does an integrated approach help the RD&E group? It helps research teams maintain a broad focus. Put simply, integration creates T's not I's, and that benefits the team, the customer, and the organization.[8] "I's" are specialists, people with deep knowledge and expertise in a narrow area, while "T's" have an area of deep experience but also knowledge that spans areas and domains.

I's are great in stable environments, and the types of research labs I learned about at some technology leaders have created a stable environment where researchers can deepen their knowledge in their core domain. T's become extremely valuable in worlds that feature uncertainty, change, and lots of connections between domains. You might think of hygiene, sanitation, and water treatment as stable businesses that favor I's, but think for a moment about the COVID-19 pandemic and all the uncertainty around its long-term fallout, or climate change and the unknown ecological, political, and social challenges that places on global water supplies. T's excel in such a world; from MJ to Larry Berger, Ecolab has always fostered an environment where T-shaped people could prosper.

Future Focused

As he reported on EL's 1927 performance, MJ Osborn made two observations. First, he noted the establishment of an in-house research laboratory, "The accomplishments of our research and development laboratory, established in April 1927, are of such an outstanding character as to leave no doubt that the investment in equipment, services, and council have been fully warranted, and that *the later returns on our investment will be large.*" To corroborate the investment he had just made, MJ attached to his shareholder letter a report by management consultants Arthur D. Little explaining that nineteenth-century profits came from owning natural resources but the twentieth century belonged to chemistry. A bet on chemical businesses was one that would pay off handsomely within the next 5 to 10 years.[9]

MJ was future focused, and the company remains so today. Its work in RD&E reflects that in three ways: a relentless push to improve current products, looking at the broad impacts of innovation on the planet and its people, which includes a lifecycle view of new product development, and measuring success through a vitality index.

Push to Improve

EL introduced its first line of Ecotemp dishwashers in 1970. The concern at that time was energy usage, and the Ecotemp line, with its associated detergents, aimed to provide the same level of cleaning at lower temperatures, resulting in energy savings. That product line has continued to evolve over the last half-century to become more energy efficient and less water intensive and the machines and dispensers more durable. Annual reports from 1970 on are replete with the latest upgrades to Ecotemp and every other Ecolab product or solution.

As Emilio noted in his comments in Chapter 2, Ecolab also changes the trajectory of development when it makes sense. After 50 years of perfecting low-temperature dishwashing, the company is rolling out its Ecolab High Temperature machine. The value lies in speed – the machine cleans in 60 seconds what used to take 60 minutes and cuts water and energy usage in half. Sustainability is an iterative process, as we see with the Ecotemp line; it's also a process that requires pivots to move to the next level, as we see with the new High Temp line.

Broad View

For Berger's R&D teams, the research process involves more than just a technical solution; teams also look at how relationships will change due to the innovation. First and easiest to see is the impact of chemicals and technology on the natural environment, but the company also looks at impacts on social and community impacts. That analysis includes safety, efficacy, and product usability. There are dozens of hand hygiene products, but Ecolab's solution moved beyond just the sanitizer itself and created a sensing system that fits how healthcare workers do their jobs. A broad view that included the social system doubles compliance and dramatically reduces the risk of HAIs.

Looking broadly at the current context improves innovation performance, and Ecolab supplements that with a lifecycle analysis of products and solutions. This assessment looks at the relationship between the product and planet over time and along the value chain. What raw materials will be needed? Can more sustainable alternatives be used? How can Ecolab minimize resource use, inputs and energy in sourcing, production, and at customer sites? How will the product be disposed of at the end of its life? Can elements of the product, particularly dispensers and housings, be designed for disassembly and reuse? Each of these questions, and others like them, help Ecolab work toward Phase I (four walls) and Phase II (customer value chain) sustainability.

The Vitality Index

I noted in Chapter 2 that Ecolab uses R&D dollars very efficiently, and it generates new patents at about a third the cost of competitor P&G. Berger and his team use another measure they refer to as the vitality index: What percentage of Ecolab revenue comes from products less than five years old? This is not a new measure. Annual reports of EL back in the 1950s contained extensive sections on the development and business impact of new products. Today's goal is that 30% of revenue should come from products introduced within the last five years. That's a high bar.

The vitality index also serves as an internal filter of which innovations to focus on. Very small and very incremental investments may be cheap to produce, but they come at a high opportunity cost – the cost of RD&E time and dollars that could be spent on higher-value contributions.

The vitality index helps Larry Berger and his team focus on major projects, ones that will move the dials of sales growth. As of 2022, the projected annual revenue of the current pipeline is more than $1 billion. Ecolab's total revenue for 2021 was just shy of $13 billion, and if each year's innovation contributes $1 billion, that's $5 billion over five years – mission accomplished.

The logic and process of product development, a solution-focus, and intensive and thoughtful RD&E allow Ecolab to constantly renew itself. As the challenges and metrics of sustainability change, the company has the RIGHT focus that allows it to identify and meet new challenges, and constantly improve its ability to help it achieve its sustainability outcomes.

LESSONS FOR LEADERS

By this time, you know the question: How can I implement what Ecolab has taken a century to perfect? There are a lot of things to learn, but I'll suggest three areas that will pay great dividends:

1. *Adopt the job-to-be-done framework and develop your own six service standards.* The deep power of the job-to-be-done framework comes as it changes your perspective about what your own products do. You realize that everything, yes everything, is a service, and that invites you to think about your products more broadly. That's a huge payoff for most companies in and of itself, as they see their products from a customer perspective. That's the minor gain; the major win comes as job-to-be-done thinking invites/forces you to rethink your whole relationship with your customer. The framework naturally invites respect because your team begins to see the importance of the jobs they need done. Clayton Christensen used a core question: "What job is the customer hiring your product to do for them?" That turns the focus from you to them, and that's where it needs to be.

   Creating your own six service standards, tailored to your organization, provides your team with a behavioral roadmap to discover and complete the job-to-be-done. You need the two to complete the package. As I described above, your version of the six service standards helps with customers, and it yarn-dyes a customer- and sustainability-focus deep into the organizational fabric. If you couple your six standards with financial and promotion incentives, they will become a part of your core operating culture much quicker.

2. *Design the fit between technology and the rest of the company.* What I hope you saw earlier is how a company effectively harnesses research and technology to create strategic wins. Remember those autonomous and strategically distant research labs I wrote about earlier? My client at the time had one of those labs and wanted to know how to make technology serve the organization, not the other way around. The first step here, as always, is to look to your core perspective and purpose. Where do R&D and technology fit into your view of the world? You can't put guardrails or guideposts around innovation if you have an extreme view of tech in your perspective. If technology reigns supreme, or is seen as irrelevant, in your world-view and resulting culture, no policy can help; in the former, technology becomes the overarching objective of the company, and in the latter, it can't get a toehold.

Putting appropriate bounds around technology in your organization matters for two reasons. First, technology matters for sustainability. Creating a more sustainable world will not come by turning the clock back to a preindustrial age; technological innovation will play a critical role. When technology aligns with other organizational purposes, the likelihood of appropriate technological solutions – that consider broad impacts – increases. Second, *technology*, as the word implies, is all about technical solutions. As it integrates with the rest of the organization, those relationships, with field people to strategic planners, knock the hard edges off a purely technical focus.

3. *What's your vitality index?* I've mentioned the importance of measurement in earlier chapters, and products and services should be no exception. I'd suggest the two metrics that Ecolab uses, percentage of revenue driven by new products and the projected dollar impact of the pipeline, but I'd suggest two others. Part of Ecolab's success comes from bundling products and services into complete solutions, so I'd develop a metric for percentage of product sales that come through integrated solutions. Solutions usually earn greater margins than stand-alone products and so as this measure goes up, so should operating profit (one prong of a sustainable enterprise). Second, I'd add metrics around services levels and quality. The job-to-be-done framework teaches that customers buy services, not products, and so you'd be wise to measure the quality of the services that come through the product itself (quality, reliability, etc.) and also the supporting services offered by your firm.

CONCLUSION

Product development is a key process for Ecolab. As I've shown here, products and product development can trace their heritage back to the core RIGHT perspective that permeates the company. Respect for customers led MJ Osborn to instill quality in *Soilax*, his first product, and he quickly realized that the product would create more value in an integrated solution. Those integrated solutions, in 1923 and 2023, fuel growth and depend on technological innovation. They also invite and require a humble attitude of learning what jobs customers really want done. For HAIs, that job is a safe environment in which to heal, which is why Ecolab offers healthcare institutions a suite of products and services that span its entire business portfolio.

In the next chapter, I'll talk more about that portfolio and its construction. The core may have been internally developed, but the company uses mergers and acquisitions to create and enhance fully integrated product solutions for its customers.

EMILIO'S THOUGHTS

The whole is greater than the sum of the parts.

—Aristotle

In my second month as a new onsite Nalco field engineer in 1984, my area manager invited me to join him in a business review with one of our biggest customers, a General Motors assembly plant in Oklahoma City. I was thrilled but also apprehensive. I was a "newbie" who had just begun a six-month technical training program. Having spent most of my time servicing Nalco programs and troubleshooting critical cooling, steam, and process systems in manufacturing, I was much less familiar with the business aspects of the customer relationship. So, I was looking forward to the meeting with a bit of trepidation about how and where things would go.

A week later, I attended the Nalco business review with the GM team, which was held mid-afternoon at shift change and featured a distracted audience of plant engineering and production managers and their staff. They were all monitoring their radios as my area manager began the meeting. He started with a clear outline of the purpose, process, and payoff for the meeting. But what he said after that altered my view of the business world and my life's work at Ecolab.

His words were: "Our job is to prevent, anticipate, and solve customer problems," a statement that came from W. H. Clark, Nalco's then chairman and CEO. For me, this led to an epiphany. My manager's focus wasn't on selling Nalco's products and services. It was on how our solutions could deliver results, such as increased production time, improved asset life, and reduced risk of downtime.

As the meeting went on, there was a noticeable change in the room. In that moment, these busy automotive managers understood that we were there to help solve their problems, not just sell products and services to them. In what turned out to be a productive meeting, we uncovered this particular customer's key challenges and concerns by doing a deep dive into the organizational and personal motives behind their work. We then defined an approach (the "how") of inputs and activities to deliver the customer's desired goals.

I start with this story because it highlights our focus on providing integrated solutions versus simply selling products. As a new onsite engineer, I was focused on the ingredients of the offering – the technology and service – and not the big picture, namely integrated solutions, impacts, and outcomes. As an industry leader, Ecolab does offer unique technology. But our solutions go far beyond that. We're focused on systematizing processes with programs that deliver the best possible customer outcomes at the lowest total delivered cost.

Take, for example, a hotel. For this type of customer, the best possible outcome could be delivering guest satisfaction through our Smart Power™ dish machine technology. Or, to provide an example from a different industry, it could be reducing the amount of virgin fiber and increasing the fiber recycling rate for a paper mill through Nalco® Water Filler-TEK technology.

No matter who the customer is, our clear and explicit goal is to create "outsized customer value [through products that act] faster, better, and at the lowest total cost – including natural resource use and labor savings." Our integrated solutions approach is a result of our customer intimacy and problem-solving focus, which creates lasting customer partnerships. We work behind the scenes to partner with our customers to make the world cleaner, safer, and healthier – helping customers succeed by achieving their business objectives *and* their sustainability goals.

Our associates drive positive change, outcomes, and impact every day for our customers and society. It's built into our culture and business strategy. Professor Godfrey refers to our ability to learn, understand, and

ECOLAB		JOINT VALUE	CUSTOMER	
Inputs	Activities	Outputs/Impact Drivers	Impact (eROI)	Outcomes
Personalized service	Technical audits			Guest satisfaction
	Operator training			Reliability
	Six service standards	Business health	Profitable growth	Reduced enterprise risk
Chemistry & dispensing	Water/Climate/Food/ Health risk assessments	People health	Operational efficiency	System assurance
	Industry knowledge	Planet health	Environmental impact	Enhanced brand and reputation
Data-driven insights	System engineering			Environmental, social, & governance performance
	Real-time monitoring			
	Safety			

Figure 6.3 Creating Sustainable Value with Customers

deliver on the jobs our customers want done – going beyond a product to delivering customer outcomes. Figure 6.3 outlines our impact framework and how this is done.

That framework begins with the inputs and activities that catalyze the holistic approach that we refer to as an integrated solution. It also includes personal service, chemistry, and data-driven insights to address our customers' impact drivers of business, people, and planet health. And at the heart of our process is impact measurement that quantifies and monetizes the value delivered, something we refer to as the exponential return on investment, or eROI.

Our ultimate goal is achieving customer outcomes at the highest return. There is perhaps no better example of this than the launch of the Ecolab Science Certified™ (ESC) program in 2020. Rewind to early 2020 when the world was turned upside down by the coronavirus disease (COVID-19), which quickly became a global pandemic. Everything was unpredictable as the global economy began to shut down. To help protect our people, Ecolab enhanced our already stringent cleaning and sanitizing protocols, provided personal protective equipment (PPE) to our associates and implemented social distancing. We also supported our teams through pay protection and expanded healthcare coverage. Taking care of our own organization was a top priority.

We then pivoted to our customers. How could we ensure their ability to stay in business under such difficult and trying circumstances? We began by making sure we were able to safely serve customers and meet increased demand for our critical cleaning, disinfectant, and hygiene solutions, which rapidly rose 5 to 15 times above normal volumes. And we established the Ecolab Science Certified™ (ESC) program, a comprehensive, science-based program that helps deliver a higher level of cleanliness to help keep employees and customers safe.

Why did we do this? Because our customers needed our help to stay afloat. Many hotels, restaurants, commercial buildings, and other facilities had been temporarily shuttered. They needed a way to get back on their feet and bring customers back to their locations. To do so, they had to demonstrate a visible commitment to cleaner, safer practices – something that would provide peace of mind to a wary and frightened public.

Gail Peterson, Ecolab's chief marketing officer, was focused on partnering with the leaders in our institutional business to develop and deliver a holistic program based on science and customer and consumer research. We asked customers and consumers what would make them feel safer, and we learned that they wanted more hospital-grade products and the services of a third-party auditor with experience in hospital-level cleaning. In June 2020, Ecolab Science Certified was launched, with Ecolab's expertise in food safety and public health as the backbone of the program. The Ecolab Science Certified™ program offers a comprehensive system that promotes four key elements that help provide rigor and give our customers and their guests confidence:

1. *Creating clean* through hospital disinfectants, food-contact sanitizers, and cleaning and disinfecting protocols.
2. *Checking clean* through rigorous training and periodic auditing, performed by highly trained Ecolab specialists focused on public health and food safety.
3. *Seeing clean in action* through front-of-house procedures.
4. *Believing clean* through a visible sign of participation, with the Ecolab Science Certified™ seal displayed on businesses and storefronts.

Today more than ever, consumers are looking for visible evidence of hygiene and public health best practices when they are away from home.

With the Ecolab Science Certified seal, businesses can demonstrate their commitment to advancing cleaner, safer practices by meeting the program's rigorous criteria. And because Ecolab wasn't as well known to consumers as we were to our customers, we launched a multimedia advertising campaign to support the protocol and the program. This enhanced visibility helped establish Ecolab as a trusted brand, providing greater assurance to the people who matter most – our customers' customers. It also provided associates with a sense of pride, as a visible reminder of the important work we were doing to address the challenges of the pandemic.

Using the impact framework, our inputs and activities were shaped by our customers' customers. Consumer expectations for health and safety remain highly important. According to a study of consumer attitudes that Ecolab conducted in 2022:

- 95% want to see as much or more cleaning now and in the future (post-pandemic).
- 70% are concerned that businesses will reduce their health and safety practices in the future.
- 71% want to see employees visibly cleaning, and 64% want hospital products used.
- 47% want independent audits completed.
- 86% say a business's commitment to public health and safety factors into their decision to patronize that location.

The Ecolab Science Certified™ program is backed by insights from our global team of scientists and our Ecolab field team – all of whom are experts in advancing practices and protocols to achieve a higher level of cleanliness in the locations you frequent. The program's stringent training and auditing for frontline hospitality and foodservice employees help verify that effective cleaning and disinfecting practices are being implemented.

It's not that we don't have unique products. In fact, Ecolab was the first company to receive EPA approval for a proven and effective solution against SARS-CoV-2, the virus that causes COVID-19, in Electrostatic Spray Application. But we go far beyond products to offer much more.

The Ecolab Science Certified™ program is a strong example of Ecolab's commitment to innovation. It was developed in a matter of months to address unprecedented market needs and expectations. It was also an integrated solution that delivers on the joint impact drivers of people, planet, and business health. With increased expectations for cleaning and food safety and continuing labor challenges, the program helps businesses deliver a higher level of cleanliness and customer confidence through an integrated solution. And it leads to outcomes our customers are truly focused on – guest satisfaction, increased customer traffic, and operational efficiency.

Many things have changed since my first customer business meeting back in 1984. But one thing that hasn't is our commitment to solving – not selling – and addressing customer challenges through an integrated, holistic approach.

Chapter 7

ACQUISITIONS: SUSTAINABILITY THROUGH ADDITION

According to most studies, between 70 and 90 percent of acquisitions fail. Most explanations for this depressing number emphasize problems with integrating the two parties involved.

—Graham Kenny[1]

Sodium aluminate seemed destined to be an orphan. Some of America's early twentieth-century business titans knew this chemical could be the next big thing in an industrializing country; however, realizing it would never be central to what they did, they passed on building a new market. That job fell to two entrepreneurs. Herb Kern, a 30-year-old chemical engineer from Lake Elmo, Minnesota, founded the Chicago Chemical Company in 1920. Kern's introduction to sodium aluminate came from a war colleague, Frederick Salathe, who had discovered the compound's superior properties in softening water while working for Standard Oil of Indiana (#14 on Forbes list of largest companies in 1917). Standard granted Salathe rights to the chemical because its core business, pumping and refining oil, had little overlap with cleaning water.[2] At the same time, Wilson P. Evans noticed the value of sodium aluminate in cleaning the boilers of his employer, the Armour Meat company (#3 on that Forbes list). Like Standard Oil, Armour had little interest in moving into industrial chemicals and ceded commercial rights to Evans. A few Armour executives saw the overall potential and took stock in Evans's new company, the Aluminate Sales Corporation, when it formed in 1922.

Chicago Chemical and Aluminate Sales worked together from almost the beginning. One company targeted industrial plants, the other railroads and so they had little market overlap; however, they shared the production and shipping of the chemical and developed an excellent working relationship. Their largest bulk supplier, the giant Aluminum Corporation of America recognized the value of sodium aluminate but lacked the skill and expertise to sell it. (Alcoa, a huge monopoly, was privately held at that time and so not on the Forbes list.) Kern and Evans merged their company into the National Aluminate Corporation in 1928 with Alcoa as a major shareholder.

The new company grew over the ensuing decades and changed its name to the Nalco Chemical Company in 1959, a change that reflected a business that had moved well beyond industrial water softening into all types of industrial water treatment for the manufacturing, mining, nuclear energy, oil and gas, and pulp and paper industries.[3] The company operated with a simple philosophy of a commitment to science-based products and outstanding customer service, reflected in a growth philosophy of "find the customer need and fill it."

French water giant Suez Lyonnaise purchased Nalco in 1999 for $4.1 billion in its quest to become the world's largest water treatment company.[4] The acquisition failed to create the value it hoped for, and Suez unloaded Nalco to a consortium of private investors in September of 2003 for $4.35 billion.[5] Those investors led an IPO of Nalco in 2005 that saddled the company with $3.7 billion in debt. That debt constrained Nalco's ability to grow, an unfortunate situation for a company with a revolutionary new water management system, 3D TRASAR™.[6]

Patented and brought to market in 2004, the 3D TRASAR™ system commanded a significant price premium because customers lowered not only their operating costs through higher-quality recyclable water and less system downtime, but the new system also extended asset life due to reduced scaling and other impurities. 3D TRASAR™ opened the door to additional services, such as an electronic control and monitoring service that allowed Nalco to manage its customers' water. Nalco owned 28% of the fragmented industrial water market, and in 2004 earned the distinction of "water company of the year."

Shortly thereafter, customers came to Nalco with a new request: they wanted more than just treated water, they wanted Nalco to help them conserve water and operate more sustainably. Nalco developed systems to help customers improve water sustainability by reducing total use, reusing water as long as possible, and recycling it in preparation for disposal into water systems. The three Rs (reduce, reuse, and recycle) enhanced *both* sustainability and profitability by improving performance in five areas: safety concerns from impure water, conservation and quality, energy reduction, waste recycling and reuse, and longer asset life. By 2011, sustainability had become a central component of Nalco's value proposition, and Nalco helped a number of its clients land on prestigious indexes, such as the Dow Jones Sustainability Index.[7]

Ecolab purchased Nalco in December of 2011. The combined skills, resources, and processes of the two companies added momentum to each other's transition toward a sustainability-driven strategy. In this chapter, I'll do a deep dive into the Nalco acquisition to explain how the Wall Street activity of buying companies can propel your company forward in Main Street sustainability performance. Since many readers have little familiarity with acquisitions, I'll begin with a short primer on how acquisitions *should* create value; remember, however, that the rule of thumb is that about three-quarters of all acquisitions fail to create their expected value.[8]

ACQUISITIONS: A PRIMER

The business activity known as mergers and acquisitions (M&A) describes the process of buying and selling companies. I've seen precious few true mergers in my career because no matter what executives say, in reality, one company runs the show and buys the other. M&A is almost always just A. Acquirers fall into two categories, *conglomerates* (also known as holding companies) or *operating* companies. Conglomerates own a portfolio of companies and, other than extracting profits and redistributing them across the portfolio, they are hands-off owners. Ecolab, like most acquirers, employs an operating company model.

Two questions constitute an "acid test" to determine the potential value of an operating acquisition: Why will the *acquired* businesses be more valuable under new ownership? And why will the *acquiring* business be more valuable because it owns its target? You'd be surprised how few acquirers can articulate coherent answers to these two questions, given that only four real answers exist: The new entity can sell to new customers, sell more to existing customers, or do both, or it can service existing customers at lower overall costs. Hence the low success rate.

Just as acquirers fall into two neat groups, so do acquisitions: *related* and *unrelated*. Relatedness refers to the extent to which both companies share stakeholders like customers or suppliers, common knowledge bases, or use similar processes in manufacturing or distribution. Acquisitions get labeled as unrelated when the acquirer and acquired company have little to no overlap along the value chain. Related acquisitions help an acquirer either *expand* its capabilities and processes or *exploit* its existing advantage in new market segments.

For an operating company like Ecolab, acquisitions create value through one of four Ss; they either create synergies, share knowledge, provide a stepping stone to new markets, or leverage similar business models. *Synergies* arise when the combined companies create more value together than they would as separate entities. *Shared knowledge* creates value for the combined firms when each employs and can leverage the same knowledge base or core processes. Some acquisitions use shared knowledge to smooth the way for a company to enter a new market; knowledge and skill provide a *stepping stone* that speeds entry and reduces the need for the acquirer to come down steep learning curves.

Finally, acquisitions create value when both companies operate from a *similar business model* or have a dominant logic.[9] Newell company owns brands as diverse as Rubbermaid®, Calphalon®, Papermate®, Coleman®, and Yankee Candle®. These seemingly unrelated businesses sing from the same sheet of music; they all produce at high volume/low margin and all sell primarily through mass retailers. What works for one brand should work for all, and when one brand struggles, it portends trouble ahead of the others. If you can successfully sing that tune, you can assemble quite a diverse choir.

I've tried to keep it simple, but I know your head might be spinning with all those terms and categories. I took this detour, however, because these terms highlight four common elements that successful acquisitions all share: the buyer and seller know *their roles* (conglomerate or operating), they know *how they fit together* (related or unrelated), and they have a clear investment thesis – they know *where to expect value* (the four Ss) and as I'll discuss below, how to *manage integration* to realize that value.

In what follows, I'll mainly focus on the Ecolab/ Nalco acquisition to tell the story, but I'll look at other successes over the years. Ecolab has had its share of failures, and I'll look at those in the next chapter. In both cases, I'll describe how acquisition (or divestiture) helps with sustainability across the 3Ps (profit, people, and planet), and I'll point out lessons your company can apply as you think about using acquisitions to enhance your sustainability portfolio.

ACQUISITIONS AT ECOLAB

Role: An Operating Company

Ecolab buys other companies to operate them. It always has and always will because being an operating company is deeply embedded in Ecolab's identity and worldview. They do more than just buy companies, however. Angela Bush, executive vice president of Corporate Development explained that Ecolab doesn't just acquire a company, they adopt it into the family. Ecolab's RIGHT worldview guides how the company engages in M&A. They don't buy and absorb; they adopt and graft them in. For example, Bush described the Nalco opportunity as "finding our long-lost brother," and bringing him home would help the combined family grow and prosper.[10] The activities of M&A at Ecolab look the same as at any other company, on the surface at least. At a deeper level, each element of the RIGHT perspective lays the groundwork for later value creation.

Respect drives the process of adoption of employees into the Ecolab compensation and benefits system, and the perspectives of humility and integration dictate the structure and market presence of the post-acquisition company. Integration into Ecolab-named product lines and solution sets happens when and where that makes sense, otherwise the acquired company retains its brand name and runs its own operation. Klenzade had a great brand in the 1950s before being acquired and it retained its brand name until 1987, when Ecolab organized its Food and Beverage division. Nalco still sells under the Nalco Water® brand, with the subtitle "an Ecolab company." Branding decisions preserve and blend identity.

Doug Baker summarized Ecolab's four guiding assumptions. First, acquisition changes both companies, and a proactive stance toward change eases the pain associated with an acquisition. Second, Ecolab must act humbly and avoid the conqueror's mindset: "Our company bought yours and so we must be better than you." Nalco had probably forgotten more about water treatment than Ecolab might ever know, and a humble attitude supported the search for new value. Third, the best acquisitions employ a "best of" mentality, where the best practices of either company would be adopted going forward. Finally, synergies behave like an annuity. Wall Street forgives and forgets the costs of implementation as a one-off expense, and loves the recurring value of cost and revenue synergies.[11]

Fit: Growth and Relatedness of Products or Processes

Ecolab's weltanschauung invites growth, and the first question of fit becomes, "How will the acquisition help Ecolab grow?" Over its first four decades, EL had developed and refined a philosophy of growth, typified by the Klenzade acquisition in 1961. In the mid-1950s, EL began selling cleaning and sanitation products to dairy farmers in Minnesota and Wisconsin, and later in Illinois, Iowa, and Missouri. After a few years of learning and proving the business at a small scale, EL bought Klenzade, a market leader, to gain a national presence in the dairy market. A few years ago, some colleagues of mine came out with a "revolutionary" concept, "Nail it, then scale it."[12] Ecolab has been part of that revolution for seven decades. Table 7.1 summarizes some of the company's major, transformational acquisitions over the years; it is not an exhaustive list. Just during Doug Baker's tenure, Ecolab bought well over 100 companies.

Ecolab only buys related businesses, but sometimes relatedness is not apparent. Traditional relatedness looks for similar "front ends," customer groups or distribution channels, or "back ends," suppliers, financing mechanisms, etc. Ecolab uses these, and also another measure to judge fit: "While we are only a very small part of our customers' cost to operate,

Table 7.1 Major Successful Acquisitions at Ecolab

Year	Acquisition	Purpose	Notable
1935	License to sell Calgonite	Product expansion. Calgonite was a good product.	Cancels license in 1937 after developing own product
1955	The Moran Company	Market penetration into Southwest US	First major acquisition as a public company
1961	Klenzade	Market expansion into dairy business	Core of Food & Beverage today
1966	Magnus	Market expansion into industrial coatings, solvents	
1973	Fraser Laundry Service	Market expansion into laundry services	Core of Textile Care business today
1985	Steamship/ ESS	Market expansion into pest elimination	Core of pest control today, a $1 billion business
1991	Henkel KGaA	Consolidation of European operations	
1994	Kay and Company	Market expansion into quick service institutional	
1994	Industrial Maintenance Corporation	Market expansion into water management	Culminates in Nalco acquisition in 2011
1998	Blue Coral Systems	Market expansion into vehicle care	Becomes leader but later divests as noncore
2001	Henkel KGaA	Consolidation purchase of joint venture	
2011	Nalco Water	Market expansion into industrial water management	Significant synergies with other Ecolab businesses
2013	Champion Technologies	Market expansion into upstream oil and gas	Becomes Nalco Champion, divested as Champion X in 2020
2015	Swisher Inc. (US business)	Market penetration in institutional cleaning	
2017	Anios	Market expansion/ penetration in healthcare	
2019	Lobster Ink	Product expansion into training services	Adds significant digital resources and process
2021	Purolite	Market penetration into life sciences	

because we ensure their ability to operate and protect their brand equity, we impact a large part of their P & L."[13] Nalco fit this description, and so does the 2019 acquisition of Lobster Ink, an online training company. Both water and training aren't significant costs in themselves, but when managed well, they have a huge impact on a customer's income statement.

Cultural fit is nonnegotiable. Do the companies share a similar worldview? Priorities? Relatedness at this level provides not only a common worldview but a common language to describe that world, and what behaviors drive success. Angela Bush explained that when she's looking at a potential acquisition, culture comes up early, right after, "Hi, my name is Angela." This lesson looks obvious, but Ecolab learned this lesson through experiences of buying companies that didn't fit, both in terms of strategic relatedness and cultural consistency.

Expected Value: Synergies and Other Ss

Value creation is the *raison d'etre* of acquisitions, and Ecolab generates synergies that better allow it to circle the customer and circle the globe. While acquisitions usually operate with a similar business model, share knowledge, and often allow Ecolab to step into a new market, each of these other Ss help generate synergies. Two historical examples illustrate relatively simple synergies, and the Nalco acquisition reveals a more sophisticated set of synergies available to Ecolab and its acquirees.

Al Schuman built on Sandy Greve's investments in pest control to create global value in its institutional operations. Pest control, warewashing, and textile services all share the same commercial customers: hotels, hospitals, restaurants, and resorts. A newly acquired pest business received a customer list on day one and piggybacked on Ecolab's great reputation among those customers to quickly grow revenue; other Ecolab units won as they circled the customer more tightly. Ecolab's pest business stays out of the residential market because, while there's lots of potential revenue, there are no synergies. Klenzade offers another example. Klenzade had developed the equipment for a clean-in place (CIP) system; however, that system became far more valuable when EL cleaners and sanitizers coursed through that equipment. The result was a dramatic extension of milk's shelf life for dairies and drinkers and industry leadership for EL and Klenzade.

Ecolab announced its intention to purchase Nalco on July 20, 2011. Ecolab agreed to pay $38.80 per share for Nalco, a 32% premium over Nalco's trading price. Ecolab would also assume Nalco's $2.7 billion debt load. The premium and assumption of debt created significant doubt on Wall Street, and Ecolab saw the need to realize synergies sooner rather than later.

Ecolab's leadership team believed that the merger would create substantial value. On the financial side, their initial calculations showed the purchase as accretive to Ecolab shareholders – a core priority – and so they pressed ahead. Early due diligence projected initial run-rate cost synergies of $150 million a year; $50 million was savings in general and administrative costs, and $100 million from supply chain efficiencies.[14] As the acquisition and integration unfolded, those synergies multiplied to $250 million per year.

Doug Baker's experience at Kay, as I noted in Chapter 4, left him with a clear sense of what it meant to "be bought" by someone else, and many Nalco employees had lived through the failed Suez acquisition. Grounded in respect, humility, and the desire for both quick and lasting growth, Baker created an integration team that drew key people from each company. Half the team came from Ecolab, with Christophe Beck at the head, and half from Nalco, initially with Stewart McCutcheon and then with Mary Kay Kaufman, a senior vice president, representing Nalco.

Beck and Kaufman both saw the merger as more than just a financial deal; Ecolab and Nalco had a once-in-a-lifetime opportunity to transform two very similar companies into one that blended water expertise with sanitation and hygiene mastery, all motivated by the goal of improved sustainability. They went to work and spearheaded 28 separate project teams to identify and realize revenue or cost synergies throughout the business, from overall mission and vision through product and technology development to the most mundane back-end business operations.[15] Other teams focused on more immediate opportunities, and three became known as the Winning as One (WAO) projects that would surprise and delight customers and investors.

The first new WAO team integrated Nalco's 3D TRASAR™ system with Ecolab's CIP technology to improve performance in food and beverage processing plants. This project required significant innovation to combine 3D TRASAR™'s continuous monitoring system with CIP's batch processing logic. Product teams developed ways to use 3D TRASAR™ to monitor the cleaning system's performance so that the "right" chemistry (the proper amount to properly clean and sanitize, without waste) flowed through the CIP system. The improved system cleaned more effectively and cut waste out of the process.

The second project entailed transferring Ecolab's advanced chemical knowledge to 3D TRASAR™. Nalco used liquid chemicals in 3D TRASAR™, which created extra costs, difficulties of operations (space requirements, changeovers, maneuvering heavy containers of liquid to the application site in the plants or buildings), and safety issues (spills of hazardous materials). Ecolab's institutional business required concentrated, dry chemical bricks to deal with the challenges of its healthcare and hospitality customers. The WAO team developed hard brick versions of Nalco liquids, with a twist. Engineers created a "lock and key" feature, where the chemical bricks were formed into a shape (a key) that would only fit in the appropriate 3D TRASAR™ port (a lock). Customers would reduce cost (solids are cheaper to produce and transport than liquids) and space requirements, improve safety for their own employees, and eliminate a potential source of error in the process.

The third project worked to leverage Ecolab's competence in antimicrobial treatments for use in Nalco's oil field business. At the wellhead, both oil and water come to the surface, and that water often contains impurities, organic and inorganic, that foul pipelines and other collection equipment. Fouling impeded flow rates – which then required more energy to move the product through the pipeline – and degraded asset life through corrosion.[16] The WAO team added Ecolab-developed antimicrobials to Nalco's treatment systems for oil field hydration and water use; chemistry designed for healthcare customers would now be delivered in tanker trucks in oil fields around the world.

The three WAO products entered the market shortly after the acquisition closed on November 30, 2011, with the intended effect; skeptical customers and employees of both companies saw the value-creating potential of the combination. The projects brought in new revenue and provided a platform for further integration and synergy creation. Sales for the new Ecolab in the oil and gas industry, for example, grew 21% during fiscal 2012.

The company's 2019 purchase of Lobster Ink marked an evolution from creating physical to digital synergies. Lobster Ink provided app-based training for workers in the hospitality industry. Ecolab gained another way to circle its institutional customers with a new training platform, and Lobster had new content. Deeper synergies should arise as Ecolab and Lobster share knowledge and build a platform for real-time communication with customers – think notifications – that will allow the company to share real-time data from things like 3D TRASAR™ and generate predictive analytics about system performance.

Integration: Managing for Value

Post-acquisition integration comes in four flavors: bolt-on, bury, blend, or build. Conglomerates employ a *bolt-on* strategy, where the two entities remain deliberately separate and the only point of contact lies in the transfer of cash between units, either capital investment into the acquired unit or dividends to the acquirer. In a classic takeover, or *bury* acquisition, the target disappears, from branding to product lines, fully absorbed into the acquirer's operations. Mergers try to *build* a new organization, complete with a new identity, culture, and corporate brand. The logic of best-in-class determines how the company organizes backend processes.

Ecolab has tried each of these integration methods, but the experiences from Klenzade, Magnus, Fraser Laundry, Kay, Nalco, and more recently Lobster Ink suggest that the *blend* model creates the most value. Backend processes sift out on a best-of-breed basis but customer-facing activities may remain separate and distinct, based on expertise and needs at the time the deal closes. Evolution from blend to bury or build evolves as the business and markets change and may take decades.

Regardless of which B drives the strategy, high-profile, executive-led teams from both companies bring the credibility and authority that helps break down the natural resistance to integration that inhibits synergy. The primary decision, in terms of sequence and importance, involves which company culture will permeate the new entity. Nalco's deal team knew its first task was to win the hearts and minds of both companies' employees. Beck explained the wonderful cultural opportunity the merger presented:

> Culture is usually one of the top two or three reasons why mergers fail. In our case we had the chance to have a similar business model built around service, supported by technology, chemistry and information. . . . Ecolab was more of a Sales culture whereas Nalco was more of a Technical / Engineering one. I think we managed to combine the strength of both to create who we are today. A sales culture with solid technological expertise. We also leverage safety as a great Nalco strength that would not only make the company better but protect its most important assets, its people.[17]

ACQUISITIONS AND SUSTAINABILITY

Acquisitions, when done well, can enhance a company's sustainability around the P of profit through three mechanisms. First, acquisitions allow a firm to *deepen* its knowledge or technology base and the new business *expands* the combined company's ability to create value for its customers. Second, acquisitions allow the combined firm to *broaden* its reach and *exploit* new opportunities for product or market growth. Finally, whether a buyer hopes to expand or exploit, acquisitions do either at greater speed. Buying technology, tacit knowledge, or market knowhow can, under the right circumstances, shave years off product development cycles and millions or billions off the cost of market entry.

Table 7.1 categorized 7 of Baker's 100+ acquisitions as transformational. That would put well over 100 as "sustaining" acquisitions. That's over six per year, or one every other month. Most of these acquisitions helped the company expand its product line or deploy that line to new geographic regions. We picked one random year – turns out a slow one – during the Baker era to highlight the role of these sustaining acquisitions. In 2017, Ecolab acquired Cascade Water Services, a small company that "broadens the range of water treatment services we provide to commercial building, lodging and healthcare facilities in the eastern US." Holchem Group Limited broadened and deepened Ecolab's presence in the United Kingdom's food and beverage, foodservice, and hospitality industries. Finally, the company bought Bioquell PLC to bring its "hydrogen peroxide vapor bio-decontamination systems and services" to bolster Ecolab's growing life sciences business unit.[18]

Saving time, as well as broadening or deepening the portfolio of products and processes, works for the other 2Ps of sustainability (people and planet). Acquisitions that expand a company's internal technical core, either through new proprietary technology or a larger trove of patents, provide more tools to solve the very real physical, biological, and social issues that make our current world unsustainable. Your company, like many Ecolab businesses, possesses part of the technical solution for people or the planet, but not all. A well-designed and executed acquisition program brings more of those pieces of the technical puzzle together.

Similarly, smart acquisitions allow your team to deploy and exploit its expertise with greater breadth, and hopefully higher impact. Whether your products and services promote sustainability for people or the planet, it's a big, wide world out there. The North American Industrial Classification system divides the economy into 20 sectors, with each sector having up to 10 subsectors, each subsector with 10 industries, and each industry with up to 10 groups. We're already at 10,000 markets – you get the point. Lasting global sustainability requires that we impact all 10,000 of those markets. Acquisitions increase your reach.

Reach matters, as does speed. Climate change represents the greatest long-term threat to our planet and all of its people. Speed matters because climate change is what scientists describe as nonlinear, the devastation caused by climate change increases at an increasing rate. The US government reports that "Earth's temperature has risen by 0.14° F (0.08° C) per decade since 1880, and the rate of warming over the past 40 years is more than twice that: 0.32° F (0.18° C) per decade since 1981."[19] If you graph the average temperature for each decade, you won't find a straight line, you'll see a curve bending sharply upward as it moves rightward.

This means, in stark terms, that countering the challenge of climate change requires new technical knowledge and that we need that new knowledge to be developed and deployed faster than ever before. Acquisitions facilitate that speed, whether on the supply side of expanding technical capabilities or the demand side of moving those products to more markets more quickly.

Acquisition activity, particularly the integration of those acquisitions, has a lot to do with the relational perspective needed to build a truly sustainable world for all of us. Again, two elements from Ecolab's history stand out: the foundational role of respect and the power of humility to turbocharge the value creation process. "Being bought" carries with it any number of negative connotations, and many Nalco employees describe living through the dark days of life as a part of Suez. They described the Ecolab acquisition as not joining a new family, but a sense of coming home to one they already knew. A sustainable world for people must include workplaces based on respect and dignity. Respect fosters commitment to the cause, and a sustainable world requires our best commitment.

Humility allows that commitment to flourish. The conqueror's mentality destroys morale, but more insidiously it deters people from sharing the vital knowledge that builds great products and services that benefit people and the planet. If sustainability is the biggest challenge and puzzle of our time, then *anyone* withholding any necessary piece slows and stymies the progress of the entire effort. Humility encourages – literally instills the courage – that ensures those pieces come together. Humility also helps us keep in mind the breadth and depth of the sustainability challenge; humility encourages us to celebrate battles won while a larger war rages on.

LESSONS FOR LEADERS

I advocate the Ecolab acquisition model because it works. First, find a part of the solution that works for a particular market or sustainability challenge – think pest control or EL pre-Klenzade. Then look for targets that will broaden your market reach and buy them. This constitutes a "major acquisition" that substantially raises your market share, reach, and reputation. Then supplement that with a series of sustaining acquisitions that fill out the product portfolio or open new markets around the nation or the globe.

Ecolab has done hundreds of acquisitions over the past century, and it has learned to do it well. What should you take away? I'll offer several suggestions for your consideration. Buying and selling businesses helps with each of the 3Ps (profit, people, and planet) of sustainability. Successful acquirers have answers to the following questions:

1. *How will acquisitions play into our strategy?* As Table 7.1 notes, Ecolab began building its capabilities around acquisition in 1935, during the depths of the Great Depression. Calgon had developed a better solution for water softening and cleaning, and MJ felt that his customers deserved access to the best products on the market so he acquired a license to sell a competing product. Going outside the boundaries of his firm to get the best products and technology still motivates acquisitions at Ecolab, as evidenced by the number of sustaining acquisitions it makes.

   I've discussed the upsides of acquisition earlier in this chapter. Before you commit to acquisition as a strategy, you should know of at least two challenges of this strategic alternative. First, it takes time to master the internal processes and skills to become a serial acquirer. Doing a couple of deals does not make you an expert – that comes after a dozen or more deals over several years. You need capabilities in identifying targets and integrating them, but as I noted at the beginning of this chapter, the key skill lies in the acid test questions – how and why will both companies be more valuable because of the acquisition?

   My second warning is that M&A is a heady game. You'll have investment bankers telling you how prescient and talented you are, and you might begin to think that you've got the Midas touch when some early acquisitions succeed. The ancient Greeks had a word for this: *hubris,* or arrogance. The arrogant acquirer sees synergies where none exist and succumbs to the conqueror's mindset. You'll read in the next chapter about a couple of acquisitions Ecolab made that have a hint of hubris, but over the long haul, the core perspective and priority of humility have helped company leaders steer clear of the siren song of hubris.[20]

2. *Why is acquisition the best way to get what we need?* Ecolab paid a 32% premium for Nalco and acquirers pay, on average, a 35% premium over current market value to acquire a target. That is expensive! Before contemplating an acquisition, make sure that it beats the alternatives of expanding capabilities through greater investments in R&D or bringing sustainable products to market through organic growth. Acquisitions make sense when there's a quantum leap in capabilities or market entry (the fuel for transforming acquisitions), or dramatic reductions in time to market, the rationale for sustaining acquisitions. Sustainable profits require that you consider the opportunity costs of making acquisitions.

    This question naturally begets another: What's the source of new value from the acquisition? There are, in reality, only two options at the end of the day, whether an acquisition intends to expand internal capabilities or exploit new markets: The combined business either generates cost or revenue synergies. The whole must be cheaper to operate than the sum of the parts, or the acquisition must create new revenue, and in the case of sustainability, that means clean revenue, in ways that either company on its own could not generate.

3. *What's the cultural fit between our company and the target?* Remember Angela Bush's comment that Ecolab looks for cultural fit from the very beginning. It's the first, not the last, question to ask. Poor cultural fit results either in the loss of key stakeholders (customers leave, employees quit, or suppliers reduce their commitment to the firm) or in their passive acquiescence, rather than active embrace, of the acquisition. Creating synergies depends on active embrace; cultural misalignment slows the integration process and sabotages the value creation process of the new enterprise.

4. *How will we integrate the target into our operations?* Things like an investment thesis or the potential for synergies generates lots of buzz in the business press or among investors; however, for those who know, the ability to successfully integrate operations separates the

contenders from the pretenders. Successful integration begins with a vision of which B – bolt-on, bury, build, or blend – should define the combined entity. That decision creates a roadmap for integration. That map usually turns out to include lots of basic execution skills like hitting deadlines and learning a new corporate language, and it involves hard work and barrier-busting thinking. Blending a batch process-based technology like CIP with the continuous one that 3D TRASAR™ used required really smart people, lots of hours, and a willingness to think outside the traditional logic of engineering development. Your ability to integrate who you buy matters as much if not more than your ability to spot the right company to buy.

CONCLUSION

MJ Osborn dabbled in acquisitions; his EL competed in a single basic industry, dishwashing. His son and all successive CEOs realized that meeting the overall growth goals of the company required movement into new markets. The formula, as we noted earlier, turns out to be pretty simple: Prove the worth and viability of a new market through a small initial investment, then use acquisitions to garner a sizable share of that market. Continue to use acquisitions to fill out the product and geographic portfolio. Nail it, scale it, then refine it.

Ecolab is good at what it does, and acquisitions are no exception. That success derives from more than good luck, or the ability to hire acquisition-driven CEOs. It comes because the company's acquisition capabilities stem from, build on, and explicitly integrate the company's core RIGHT worldview and the priorities that flow from it. Acquisition capability is yarn-dyed into the fabric of Ecolab. The good news is that you can, over time and with significant effort, build a similar capability in your company.

EMILIO'S THOUGHTS

Harnessing the Combined Power of Two Global Leaders

In this chapter, Professor Godfrey writes about Ecolab's 2011 acquisition of Nalco and the synergies between the two companies. Having worked at Nalco since 1984 and at Ecolab since the acquisition, I had a front-row seat to all of this, and I can say that the seeds for this partnership began years earlier. In 2006, in my role as director of marketing for Nalco's global food, beverage, and pharmaceutical business group, I spent several weeks in California's Salinas Valley. Because of its ideal climate and fertile land, the area is often referred to as the fruit and vegetable basket of the country – so much of the nation's produce is grown there.

Back then, there were increasing concerns about water stress and how it was impacting Salinas Valley food and beverage processing plants. As the global leader in water management, Nalco was pursuing water re-use and recycling projects for large food processors, including bag lettuce facilities. From the fields to the plants, these processors work against the clock to get produce to market quickly and safely. Trucks filled with lettuce line up in front of plants ready to transfer their products into man-made flumes, filled with chilled freshwater, that transport lettuce through the plant.

In 2006, peracetic acid was increasingly being used in food and beverage plants as a sanitizer for food contact surfaces and as a disinfectant for fruits and vegetables. Peracetic acid (PAA) is a mixture of acetic acid (vinegar) and hydrogen peroxide (H_2O_2) in an aqueous solution. Ecolab had several patented peracetic acid solutions for a range of businesses, including food and beverage processing. One of these was Tsunami 100™. It helps prevent foodborne illnesses by eliminating pathogens in fruit and vegetable wash water, minimizes spoilage, and extends shelf life.

Siblings Reunited

Ecolab, the global leader in hygiene and cleaning products, held a market leadership position in the 1990s and 2000s in the food and beverage processing industry, while Nalco was the global leader in water management for this industry. With only 394 miles between headquarters, Ecolab and Nalco were long-lost siblings. They just didn't know it back then.

During the early 2000s, there was a rapid global expansion of consumer brands to meet the growing demand for products in new and emerging markets. Nestle, Unilever, Merck, Heineken, and others were looking for suppliers who could provide quality service, onsite expertise, and technology to support these expansions.

At the time, Nalco was experiencing double-digit growth in manufacturing markets, including food and beverage, pharmaceutical, biofuel, containerboard, semiconductor, and building materials industries. Investing in those markets made sense since they demanded more advanced water management expertise and automation driven by reliability, asset preservation, and awareness about conservation and corporate responsibility.

At about the same time, *Newsweek* and other media outlets began reporting on the greenest companies in America. Consumer brands were interested in aligning with service providers who supported their focus on natural resource conservation in their operations. This internal operational focus soon became a priority for the consumer-packaged goods industry, and companies like Ecolab and Nalco were developing site audits and other solutions focused on optimizing water and energy use. This presented an opportunity to develop new markets in cleaning and sanitation.

In 2005, Nalco launched 3D TRASAR™ Technology, a transformational innovation platform that revolutionized the water treatment market. In fact, it pioneered the concept of smart technology for water process and wastewater management. From 2007 to 2012, 3D TRASAR™ cooling and boiler automation technology grew rapidly among Nalco customers. Its value proposition focused on improving the total cost of operations and preserving critical systems and equipment. Water savings soon followed as a key benefit of delivering operational performance. (After the merger, the technology was expanded to include a cleaning and sanitation solution known as 3D TRASAR™ clean-in-place (CIP) technology.)

By 2008, Nalco's CEO, Erik Frywald, and its chief marketing officer, Mary Kay Kaufman, saw an opportunity to reposition Nalco from a chemical services provider focused on water and energy management to essential experts for water, energy and air, and as a partner in sustainability and corporate responsibility. One of the initial steps was to appoint the company's first director of sustainability. I was offered the role and jumped at the chance to help the company embed sustainability as a business growth accelerator. The repositioning was completed less than a year later in a shift that supported the growing demand for water and energy efficiency *and* sustainability.

Back then, many companies viewed the burgeoning sustainability movement as purely altruistic. Our commercial teams were challenged with communicating the holistic benefits of our approach to our customers. To substantiate the business, environmental, and resource efficiency benefits of technologies such as 3D TRASAR™, we developed eROI, which you already know about. At that time, it stood for *environmental* return on investment. But Ecolab soon realized that eROI supported the *total impact* of our solutions. Today, eROI refers to the *exponential* return on investment because it truly accelerates benefits for customers.

As Professor Godfrey so aptly states in this chapter, Ecolab acquires related businesses. And relatedness looks for similar "front ends" (customer groups, distribution channels, etc.) or "back ends" (suppliers, financing mechanisms, etc.). That leads to synergies for both companies by creating more value together than as separate entities. By leveraging similar business models and innovation, Ecolab and Nalco opened the door to new markets and increased our customer value and impact.

"We've long admired Nalco's capabilities, knowhow, and management team," said former Ecolab CEO Doug Baker in an interview before the merger, adding that he viewed Nalco as a strategic fit that would help the combined company address the global market for water treatment and management. Fast forward to the merger closing in December 2011 when Baker said, "We had been impressed with each other's strengths. The opportunity for both companies to serve industrial and institutional customers was clear. Our approach to food and beverage processing plants exemplified this. The merger brought Ecolab and Nalco together as one to create a company where $1 + 1$ is > 2." Doug Baker's and Christophe Beck's vision is now a reality.

Chapter 8

DIVESTITURE: SUSTAINABILITY THROUGH SUBTRACTION

Mistakes are how we learn.

— M'Shelle Lundquist Dixon[1]

On October 24, 1947, MJ submitted his annual letter to EL shareholders. He opened with a description of the difficulties the company faced as the US moved from a war to peacetime economy: four strikes, one lasting 50 days, drove up materials prices and made deliveries difficult. MJ compared the year's challenges to the dark years of 1931–1932, the early years of the Great Depression. Later, an upbeat MJ reported on changes in the postwar world. Procter & Gamble had convinced consumers to purchase dishwashing soaps and cleaners in grocery stores, rather than hardware stores. To capitalize on that trend, EL introduced a new product for home dishwashing machines: *Electrasol.*

EL had spent a decade's worth of research to develop Electrasol, a product designed to provide the same high-quality cleaning that *Soilax* provided commercial customers. In 1948, MJ reorganized his company into two divisions, Kitchen (institutional) and Package (consumer). EL entered a burgeoning consumer market fueled by the US Government's Servicemen's Readjustment Act of 1944, known popularly as the GI bill, which, along with other tax changes, lowered the cost of owning a home. The percentage of households owning a home grew from 44% in 1940 to 62% just 20 years later.[2] Those new homes usually featured the latest in labor-saving technologies, including a mechanical dishwasher.

EL dived into the growing market. Within a year, EB Osborn had negotiated deals with Hotpoint and General Electric, two major manufacturers, to provide a box of Electrasol, along with their recommendation for the product, with each new dishwashing machine sold. The Package division drove EL's growth over the next several years, and Electrasol grew its market share. EL had been selling a version of Soilax for home wall cleaning since the 1930s and had some familiarity with advertising in the consumer market; however, to sell Electrasol the company ramped up advertising expenditures, hired executives from major consumer goods companies to run the business, expanded the product line into laundry products with its Fun label, and learned to compete on price and promotion. In 1953, EL rolled out Finish, a companion to Electrasol that removed spots and left dishware clean and pristine.

EL bought and sold businesses and reconfigured its residential offerings over time. At one time, the company sold children's bath products, under the *Matey* brand name, and *Star* coffee filters. The company

157

would get out of most of these businesses; coffee filters, for example, had little connection to EL's core chemistry expertise. By the mid-1980s, the consumer division sales centered on a number of strong brands, Electrasol, Finish, and Jet Dry in dishwashing, Glass Free, Lime-Away, Mildew's Gone, and Scrub Free in household cleaning, Free and Soft fabric softener, and Clean & Smooth, a hand soap.

The consumer business had always been competitive, and over the years EL successfully went toe to toe with giants such as Colgate-Palmolive, Procter & Gamble, and Unilever. Its products held strong market positions – Electrasol and Finish held 20% of their combined market in 1983 – but as the recession and recovery of the early 1980s continued, company leaders wondered about the costs and benefits of market leadership.[3] As early as 1949, MJ noted that his Package division earned about a third of the company's kitchen products; however, consumer brands had always provided strong top-line growth and represented almost 28% of company sales in 1986.

Sandy Greve abruptly sold EL's consumer brands in 1987 for $250 million, 10% more than the division's 1986 sales and, by my estimates, a healthy multiple of 20–35X earnings.[4] Reckitt Benckiser bought Finish and Electrasol. Reckitt holds both brands today, and they continue to do well. In fact, the Godfrey family continues to use Finish in our home. Greve's sale represented a coming to grips with the reality that the residential market would become more, not less, competitive, and maintaining share would cost more each year. Ecolab, the new company name as of 1986, would be increasingly unable to match product development and advertising expenses with the giants.

The sale represented another turning point for the company, one that would drive growth for the next 35 years. After 40 years of success in the consumer market, Greve helped Ecolab see that good chemistry and great products represented only a portion of Ecolab's advantage; the other (larger?) portion came through personalized, expert service. The consumer market remained a "package" business, and Ecolab had no opportunity to earn its premium by providing homeowners with the customized, 24/7 service that its commercial customers valued. On that day in 1987, Ecolab stopped identifying itself as a dishwashing company; its new identity grew from its core competitive advantages of advanced chemistry and amazing personal service.

Twentieth-century crooner Neil Sedaka sang that "breaking up is hard to do." That proves true in both personal and business relationships.

The effort, energy, and substantial sums of money invested to buy a company create an organizational inertia that makes it hard to sell it, even when the reality of a failed acquisition stares leaders in the face. As EL's adventures in the consumer market illustrate, that inertia exerts a strong pull when those business units generate adequate and even excellent performance. Even knowing that consumer businesses would never be core to Ecolab, Greve and Al Schuman invested in two more consumer business, ChemLawn and a series of vehicle care businesses – car washes – that would generate another leading consumer product, Rain X.

Even if breaking up is hard to do, divestiture plays a key role in creating a truly sustainable enterprise, in terms of each of the 3Ps (profit, people, and planet). Selling businesses allows for redemption from mistakes, but also learning and growth from mismatched business models, poor market timing or competitive realities. Letting go stretches the core capabilities of managers and leaders and requires healthy doses of courage, foresight, and humility. As you'll see from the two major exits I'll focus on in this chapter, Ecolab's core perspectives and priorities encourage the type of rigorous self-analysis that leads to successful divestitures.

DIVESTITURE AND MARKET/CAPABILITY FIT

I'll do a deep dive into two major divestitures by Ecolab over the past 50 years. These two represent strategic mistakes, but they aren't the only businesses Ecolab has sold off. For example, Ecolab entered and built a strong presence in the commercial janitorial space, the vehicle care market (car washes), a business repairing commercial kitchen equipment, and the upstream oil and gas business it acquired as a part of the Nalco deal. It later divested each of these businesses. I focus on the two, high-profile mistakes of Apollo Technologies and ChemLawn because they illustrate the challenges inherent in the acquisitions game and how hard it is to let go of what seemed like a great deal.

Apollo Technologies: A Mistimed Market and Capability Stretch

EL had always dabbled outside of its dishwashing, cleaning, and sanitizing businesses. In 1961, the company began selling chemical solutions to the paper industry. That effort expanded into metal washing, automotive transportation, and military and commercial aviation. These early successes culminated in 1964 with the purchase of Magnus. EB explained the rationale of this purchase:

> Since its founding in 1921, Magnus has been a leader in the development of metal cleaning and processing methods that are "tailored for the industry." Its diversified line of industrial washing machines; acid, alkaline and solvent chemical cleaning compounds; metal stamping, drawing and cutting lubricant specialties; water treating chemicals and special finishes and coatings, are widely used by airlines, railroads, metal-working plants, steamship lines, paper mills, printers, refineries, truck and bus fleets and related industries. Its customer list reads like "Who's Who" in American Industry, and its direct sales effort is backed by 160 trained [representatives].[5]

In 1980, two years after EB's untimely death, Fred Lanners engineered the purchase of Apollo Technologies, "a leading developer and marketer of chemical systems to improve combustion efficiency and reduce pollution in oil and coal-fired electric utilities."[6] Apollo appeared to fit the Magnus mold. EL paid $72 million for a company that grew on the back of a single product, Pentron DC-8, a coal-scrubbing, coal-dust-reducing product for power plants that controlled pollution. Lanners relied on recent studies that coal production in the ensuing 20 years might triple. Apollo seemed to fit within the general rubric of the industrial division, selling specialty chemicals to heavy industry, and Apollo had some presence in core Magnus markets: metalworking, transportation, pulp and paper, electric utilities, mining, and metallurgical industries.

Sales grew from $45.2 million in 1979 to $83.2 million in 1981. They fell to $79 million by 1982. On the market side, a deep recession and initial concerns about coal's role as a pollutant belied studies predicting high growth. Coal production peaked in 1980 at 829 million short tons and fell the next two years. Sandy Greve took the reins at EL on January 1, 1983, and within his first week decided to sell Apollo. The move proved prescient. Coal production began to grow again in 1984, but prices remained flat, peaking in 1983 and falling for the rest of the decade. Production grew only 0.4% on an annual basis between 1984 and 1993.[7] An expansive market for Apollo's core product never materialized.

Greve recognized three failures in the Apollo deal. First, the market had shifted. The drop in coal production could be explained away as an impact of the deep recession of the early 1980s; however, Greve predicted that the coal-generated pollution would constrain the market over the long term, and the data proved him right. Coal's share of energy production fell from 45% in 1977 to 22% in 2021.[8] Coal power would never act as a growth engine.

Second, Greve realized that, while Apollo sold into some similar markets as Magnus, it provided few opportunities to create product solutions and synergies with Magnus. EL's strategy post-Apollo relied on its ability to "1) recognize [the] strengths of the company and to make sure those strengths are not dissipated, and 2) to find out how to play off those strengths and find new ones in promising markets for the future."[9] In terms of the RIGHT perspective, Apollo failed on both integration and growth.

Apollo failed on a third priority as well, humility. Greve noted that when he assumed command, others on the leadership team knew that Apollo represented a mistake. That mistake proved a hard pill to swallow for some, particularly given two events. First, the passing of EB Osborn left the company under new leadership and Apollo had been the first major strategic move for that new team. It may have been unreasonable to expect every acquisition to hit the jackpot, but having their first acquisition go south would be a tough pill to swallow. Other companies that I work with make this same mistake – they overgeneralize the degree to which management mistakes create the impression of misguided managers. Ironically, it's easier to be humble when we succeed than when we fail; it's the hubris thing I talked about in the previous chapter.

Second, what Greve found was an emperor with no clothes, and just like in the fable, none of the courtiers dared admit the failure of Apollo. Greve noted that he was not "the originator of the process . . . the process was clearly going on before I got here." I don't know, but I presume that process had morphed into an endless series of reviews of the business, ones where the potential for a turnaround still existed (those studies can't be all wrong!) or the synergies between Apollo and Magnus were about to be realized. Both of these represent manifestations of sunk cost thinking, and both become common ploys to delay decisions. The essence of humility is an honest admission of both strengths and weaknesses, and members of the C-suite had sidestepped that admission through an endless series of excuses.

Greve pulled the plug on the Apollo experience within days of becoming the CEO, noting, "I'm a decision maker."[10] I defined a leader as someone who acts, and Greve acted. EL would take a $42 million loss on the Apollo divestiture. He would go on to reduce overall debt at the company by almost one third and dramatically reduce nonoperating expenses at the company by almost two-thirds. He refined EL's strategy to focus on profitable, high-growth niches.

ChemLawn: More Market Mismatch and Company Misfit

Sandy Greve acted to abandon the failed Apollo acquisition in 1983. That makes it all the more surprising that he would (1) engage Ecolab in another misadventure in acquisition and (2) fail to recognize the mistake and move on in a timely manner.

In 1987, Ecolab paid $370 million for Columbus, Ohio-based ChemLawn. Founded in 1968 by the father-son combination, Paul and Richard Duke, the original ChemLawn offered liquid spray chemicals for residential lawn care. ChemLawn started in nearby Troy, Ohio, with one truck and 500 customers.[11] The company expanded nationally over the next two decades, limited only by the cash to buy more trucks and hire and train new service technicians. They grew on a mix of company owned and franchise operations.

Sales grew from $86 million in 1979 to $353 million in 1986, for a healthy 19% CAGR; however, net income fell from 5% to 6% to less than 3.5%, only $12.1 million in 1986.[12] With only 30 to 35% of a growing market, ChemLawn faced new, look-alike competitors and the costs of customer acquisition and retention soared. Its internal culture also decayed. The Dukes built a company grounded in dignity and respect for both customers and employees; however, by the time of the Ecolab purchase, a job at ChemLawn was "just a job" for most employees.[13] ChemLawn's stock traded around $17 per share in early 1987 when Waste Management Corporation made an unsolicited bid for ChemLawn.[14]

Ecolab accepted the role of white knight and eventually paid $370 million to rescue ChemLawn from Waste Management. The $37 per share price tag represented a 176% premium on a company whose margins had fallen more than 20% over the previous few years. Ecolab's debt load rose from 22% to 60%. Ecolab's shares dropped 10% at the announcement of the deal, a foreboding sign. ChemLawn would exert significant drag on Ecolab's stock until its divestiture four years later. Drought conditions in 1988 led to slower sales and higher costs – the company had to use more expensive dry chemicals during the drought, and that stretched out the time horizon to earn back that $200 million premium.

Ecolab struggled with the cyclical and regional nature of lawn care, and they never found the right customer service model. "'I used to think grass was grass,' [Michael] Shannon [ChemLawn president and Ecolab executive vice president] said, 'but the whole thing – from climate to the product itself, to the way it's delivered – is a complex business.'" By 1989, ChemLawn's profits turned negative and 80% of the core ChemLawn team had moved on to greener pastures. The continued downward pressure on Ecolab's stock forced Sandy Greve to find his own white knight in the form of a joint venture with Henkel KGA, a large European chemical company.

The companies combined their European operations, Ecolab supplemented its other international operations with Henkel units, and Henkel bought 30% of Ecolab's shares. It would take the company until 2008 to repurchase all those shares. Ecolab sold ChemLawn to ServiceMaster in 1991. The sale price of $107 million was less than ChemLawn's 1987 market value, and the $263 million loss Ecolab recorded meant that it realized none of the anticipated synergies with ChemLawn.

Why did Ecolab fail to create value at ChemLawn? Four reasons seem clear to me, and those four reasons all tie back to the RIGHT worldview and priorities that constitute the DNA of Ecolab: *Respect, Integration, Growth, Humility, and Technology*. The only part of the ChemLawn deal that made sense was growth, and I question even that. ChemLawn had great top-line growth; however, the math of growth – it becomes increasingly difficult to sustain high growth rates the larger you get – meant that capturing share beyond its one-third of the market would be a challenge. A closer look at the bottom line should have alerted Greve and his team to problems at ChemLawn; net income had fallen for multiple years.

The team chose to see those problems as solvable; however, as Ecolab VP and Treasurer Bruce Bentcover noted in 1989:

We recognized there were problems at ChemLawn when we bought it, . . The problems were a bit more widespread than we had anticipated, but there's nothing we've found that would lead us to question the wisdom of buying ChemLawn and using it as part of Ecolab's strategy of expanding the residential services business.[15]

Bentcover's comment hearkens back to Sandy Greve's confident proclamation I quoted in Chapter 3 that he saw nothing that made acquiring ChemLawn a foolhardy move.

That confidence, which seemed pervasive among senior leaders, revealed hubris, or the lack of humility, in action. Ecolab had strayed from its own recipe for success. When the drought of 1988 hit, the ChemLawn team laid off and then failed to hire back enough seasonal employees. This made short-term sense, but it left the company with too few trained employees when the weather improved and business ticked up. Mike Shannon tried to up the level of service at ChemLawn, but customers failed to appreciate, or pay more, for enhanced service. Finally, the fact that it took Ecolab's senior team four years, and finding its own white knight, to divest the business stands as evidence that, in this case at least, leaders failed to act with humility.

Ecolab lacked not only humility; they also seemed to abandon the core priority of respect. Letting 8 of 10 senior leaders at the acquired company – one with a complex business model that Ecolab did not grasp – leave does not indicate relationships of trust and respect between the two companies. A core tenet of respect for customers entails Ecolab associates knowing more about the business than their customers, but Ecolab never seemed to show a deep interest in figuring out the lawn care business. Perhaps the acquisition team paid too much heed to the Duke's platitudes about employee and customer dignity and failed to see the sea change toward a "just a job, just a customer" mentality that permeated ChemLawn.

Ecolab failed on humility and respect. Now let's add technology to the list. Ecolab's perspective views technology, high-technology and science-driven technology, as core to the company's identity. ChemLawn had chemical in the name, but lawn fertilizers and weed killers aren't specialty chemicals. They're bulk chemicals mixed into the right formulations. ChemLawn's advantage relied on using liquid versions of these mixtures – hardly grounded in research – and deploying those in bulk trucks. The nature of the task at hand, greening lawns, left little room for new, price premium-generating innovation to grow the business. In terms of the core Ecolab business model, ChemLawn would never be a good fit.

That lack of fit exposes the final failure of ChemLawn: it had no touchpoints to integrate with the rest of the business. Greve sold off the consumer products business because it didn't integrate well with the other parts of the business. He seems to have believed that that misfit arose from being in the consumer-*packaged-goods* business, and that a consumer-*service* business would integrate well with a commercial-service business.

This logic omits two key elements. First, integration requires overlap and lawn care and institutional service have no substantive overlap. The ability to translate learning or product solutions would never exist because the customers and the two product sets had no commonalities around which to build synergies.

Second, the type of service delivered differed. In lawn care, ChemLawn performed a convenience service; a homeowner could easily treat their lawn and keep it green; they just didn't want to. Economists characterize the demand for lawn care as highly elastic; if the price of the service went up, homeowners would just do it themselves. In contrast, managers running hotels and restaurants faced an inelastic demand curve and they willingly paid Ecolab a premium because they could not "just do it themselves." This meant that the core of Ecolab's service model – high touch and customized, would only lead to massive losses in lawn care. Consumer and commercial both start with C and the commonality ends there. Service means something different in a residence than a restaurant.

You might read about these two misadventures by Ecolab as my attempt to throw cold water on a remarkable company. I hope you'll see something very different, and that is that every company, even one with a clear recipe for strategic success in its core market, makes mistakes. I'd also argue that Ecolab's batting average in its divestiture activities is pretty good. It has divested more businesses at a healthy profit than at a loss. The major difference between successful and failed divestures? Consistency with the core perspective and priorities that do, and should, ground the company. In the next section, I'll put this discussion of divestiture in the context of sustainability. How can companies add to sustainability by subtraction?

DIVESTITURE AND SUSTAINABILITY

The benefits of acquisition that I described in the previous chapter include the ability to improve sustainability through reach and speed. Acquisitions allow companies to exploit new market opportunities at greater scale and/or enhance internal capabilities faster than through greenfield or organic entry. Divestiture, the necessary companion to any acquisition strategy, offers a different set of advantages. Divestiture improves sustainability performance in two ways: greater, smarter risk taking and a stronger sense of core identity.

Risk Aversion and Mistakes

The journey to create a sustainable company and world entails risk, as all journeys do. There will be the traditional risks that things won't work out as anticipated. Some technical solutions to biological and environmental challenges just won't work as intended, and potential fixes for human problems or health or income inequality often generate unintended consequences that limit their effectiveness. Those are very traditional risks of failure. Many challenges have no obvious solution, and it's uncertain whether a technology or organizational program will work. For people who hate to make mistakes, another way to cope with risk aversion, or risk as failure, is to constrain and delay action.

The ability to effectively divest mistaken acquisitions, or to shut down failing organic growth moves, mitigates that natural tendency to be risk averse because leaders know they can offload mistakes. Divestiture supports taking big bets and bold moves; if those moves don't work out, the company will take its lumps and move on. Risk aversion has both a cognitive (technical) and emotional (relational) component. Buying anything, from a car to a company, puts the quality of our judgment on display, and we all believe we possess good judgment. The ability to admit to and dispose of mistakes relieves the cognitive pressure that every judgment has to be perfect.

Acquisitions of any type also create an emotional commitment. We want our purchase to work out – which validates our sense of self as both shrewd and wise – and that desire engenders an often silent but very powerful emotional anchor to hold on to our new possession, even when it's the wrong thing to hold on to or the wrong time to hold it. We fear appearing incompetent. Admitting failure also becomes a source of social shame, not merely a case of an intellectual error in judgment, and shame is a powerful negative emotion. The knowledge that some acquisitions fail and the permission to sever our relationship with what we've bought help counter our natural tendency to remain committed to what in reality was a mistake.

Mistakes in the search for sustainable practices may appear as bets on external markets that don't behave as expected. We can, and should, cut Fred Lanners and his team some slack in the failure that was Apollo. Looking back, we see clearly both the decline of coal as a power source in the early 1980s and the economic and social causes for its decline.

Looking forward in 1980, a bet on coal carried risk but was not foolhardy. The United States had lived through two rounds of global gasoline price shocks, one in 1973 and one in 1979, and coal was a well-integrated domestic source of energy. Natural gas was just beginning to gain cost and distribution advantages, and the reality that it would displace coal was not a sure bet.

Other markets and technologies for sustainable production have and will face the same uncertainty. Solar and wind power have taken multiple decades and are only now beginning to operate at scale, and those markets have seen booms and busts. Ditto for hydroelectric and geothermal energy. Much of the western United States relies on hydroelectric power, and a decades-long drought, both a symptom and driver of a changing climate, have dried up revenue streams that once looked perpetual. Leaders shouldn't divest at the slightest sign of turbulence, but the emotional, intellectual, and organizational freedom to exit in the face of secular decline facilitates taking the initial risk to enter. Knowing it is OK to get out makes it easier to get in.

Corporate Identity and Vision

To many people, corporate identity means a logo, color scheme, and style guide. For me, corporate identity answers the most fundamental of all business questions: Who are we as a firm? What's core and enduring about us?[16] Firms, like people, have to figure out who they are, and what they really stand for; action, trial, and error mark the path to figuring out what's really core; and the decisions leaders make determine what endures over time. Whether in our private or professional life, identity does not appear fully formed. We only learn who we are as we see what we do and assess how we feel about what we've done. Identity creates a boundary between who we are and who we aren't; unfortunately, we usually recognize that boundary when we cross it.

Hindsight is always 20/20. When I look back at the ChemLawn acquisition from the Ecolab of the 2020s, it makes no sense, so far across the line that I want to ask, "What were you thinking?" I don't know for sure, but I can reconstruct a plausible story for making the acquisition. First, and probably foremost, on paper the companies looked like they shared the primary perspective of respect. The Dukes founded their company on the fundamental dignity of both employees and customers: If you do right by those two stakeholder groups, then profits will flow. What we see now might have been missed in the pell-mell crush and heady days of playing the white knight: Many franchisees, as well as company managers, viewed dignity as a great thought but neither central nor core in making money.

Second, Ecolab likely possessed the "ghost" of a consumer mindset. The company had just left a 40-year product-based relationship with the home consumer. The problem may have been in the product element of that relationship and the huge consumer market would still be viable if Ecolab moved to a service-based relationship. It took only one four-year experience to realize the mismatch lay in the "consumer" element and that consumers did not value the services Ecolab brought to the table. I see a strong analogy to the broad sector of sustainability where most problems have a hyphenated nature. Think poverty- or biology-based issues. The challenge for companies dyeing sustainability into the yarn of their identity comes from figuring out on which side of the hyphen the company creates value.

Identity underpins strategy, just as perspective underpins priorities. If you don't know who you really are, you have no deep sense of how you win with your customers. Identity helps clarify strategy, and strategy clarifies actions around organic growth, acquisition, and divestiture. Strategy guru Michael Porter noted 25 years ago that a company knew when it had a real strategy when it knew when to say no to an opportunity.[17] That kind of strategic clarity usually comes after leaders say yes to an opportunity and then realize that it's not where or who they want to be. Unfortunately, we usually have to cross that line before we realize we've gone too far, and acquisitions are one way companies cross those lines. A healthy divestiture process allows executive teams to step back across that line, with a better sense of why that line is where it is.

LESSONS FOR LEADERS

You should know by now what's coming under this header: so, what does this all mean for you? There are two major lessons, and I'll start with the most important one: Ecolab failed on some big-time acquisitions. But they're still celebrating a vibrant century. Most moves the company made over its first century worked out and helped create an exemplary organization. Some did not. That matters because you'll fail. You'll make missteps and have misadventures as you journey toward sustainability. Remember Apollo and ChemLawn. Put them up on your own wall of shame. Also, remember that Ecolab – albeit slowly – moved on from those failures.

That slowness to move on holds my second lesson: Humans are loss averse. We don't like losing, and we'll go to great lengths to not lose. That competitive spirit contributes to many of our successes. Like most good things, however, when taken to an extreme, our distaste for failure keeps us from further success. An extreme distaste for failure manifests itself as the failure to admit failure. Our natural tendencies allow us to hesitate in owning up to our mistakes, and most organizational systems reinforce that natural tendency. Pseudo-leaders routinely shoot the bearer of bad news. Few raises, bonuses, and promotions come to those who lead failed product lines or make losing bets in the acquisition game. When you want to divest something, or exit a line of business, you swim against a pretty strong current. I offer the following life vests to help you take the plunge:

- *Acknowledge emotions and hubris* in the acquisition process. Emotions are a dirty word in far too many corporate environments; all decisions have to be, or at least have to appear to be, rational. Leaders aren't arrogant conquerors, just shrewd gamblers. Fred Lanners presided over a company that had made few mistakes in acquisitions and, in some accounts, operated as a complacent family company. Observers described Sandy Greve as a demanding and driven manager, one reticent to hear about an emperor with no clothes. The mistake for both leaders was not the acquisitions, but rather the time it took to recognize and rectify when they failed.
- *Understand the risks* in growth through acquisition. For public companies, equity markets often focus on the downsides of an acquisition, from strategic misfit to challenges of implementation and they respond by driving down the share price. This creates a perverse situation where the pieces of the company hold more value individually than the combined whole. You become, like Ecolab in 1989, a takeover target, which jeopardizes your ability to fulfill your purpose and mission, and control your destiny. You find yourself, like Sandy Greve, looking for your own white knight.

  For private companies, venture capitalists and private equity investors dance a similar jig as stock markets. Your stock in trade is reputation, and your poor acquisition choice makes them more wary of future investment and more likely to engage in the kind of micro-management that can straitjacket operations and growth. The longer it takes you to divest, the more your reputation suffers.

  For both private and public companies, understand the risks that come with an acquisition premium. All acquisitions come at a premium or else no one would sell. Monstrous premiums, like the 176% one paid in the ChemLawn deal, create two risks. First, they raise the overall performance bar needed to earn back the premium, and sometimes there just aren't enough synergies to earn it back. Second, and more pernicious, the higher the premium, the shorter the time horizon. The drought of 1988 killed the ChemLawn acquisition because it stretched out an already tight time horizon for the deal to pay off.

- *Beware the sunk cost fallacy.* We've all sat through a movie that we loathed, and often knew minutes in that it deserved rotten tomatoes. What kept us in our seats? The fact that we laid out good money for the ticket, parking, popcorn, and soda. We often desperately hope for the plot to improve and justify our expenditures. We all engage in sunk cost thinking, and it pervades the world of acquisitions. Acquirers know the deal is heading south, but they hold out hope that with a little more investment and time things will turn around. They throw good money after bad. Sunk cost thinking operates with a perverse logic: The more we spend, the more time we are willing to give an investment before writing it off. Many acquirers are the opposite of smart gamblers who realize they've spent money and won't get it back. Be quick about cutting your losses.

- *Set up a system* to provide reliable information about when an acquisition fails. Conglomerates – those who buy companies with no intention of running them – have great systems and clear metrics for judging the value of acquisitions. I don't advocate becoming a conglomerate, but I do recommend their policy of having clear, primarily financial, metrics that provide hard evidence of the failure, or success, of an acquisition. When target companies don't hit their numbers, the natural tendency is to create a plausible excuse. I've already outlined the reason for that natural tendency. Even if you solve those issues, you'll still need a strong set of reporting systems to help you assess the overall fit of any acquisition into your strategic portfolio. And you need a system to help you divest things that don't fit as soon as possible.

CONCLUSION

I return to where I began to end the chapter on a positive note. Sandy Greve sold a 40-year-old consumer business because he realized that whatever the emotional attachment, historical nostalgia, and revenue growth that business provided, it was not – and would never be – central to the core identity of Ecolab. That divestiture, as I noted earlier, changed the company's identity in a fundamental way: Ecolab was no longer a dishwashing company. That became obvious in the consumer market, and over the ensuing decades the warewashing business would remain highly profitable and core to Ecolab's institutional business; however, its identity would become central to a cleanliness, hygiene, and, increasingly, water and energy saving company.

With its focus solidly in industrial and institutional markets, Ecolab could, and would, continue to create more value in each of its markets. As the company became more explicit about sustainability as a purpose and priority, it successfully engaged in Phase II sustainability, helping customers improve their performance in each of the 3Ps. The knowledge gained through its tight focus on institutional and industrial markets would, as the twenty-first century rolled on, allow the company to move to Phase III sustainability and work to make whole societies more sustainable. The next chapter focuses on a key element of that Phase III work: creating and leveraging multi-stakeholder collaborations.

EMILIO'S THOUGHTS

> *Skate to where the puck is going to be, not where it has been.*
> —Wayne Gretzky (hockey legend)

This quote has often been used by organizations to support their planning, innovation, and merger and acquisitions strategies. But it also applies to divestures – most notably, when to let go of businesses that negatively impact growth and profitability due to market and technology forces in the global economy.

Wayne Gretzky had a rare ability to sense where the puck was about to go. But many companies hang on to businesses too long and find themselves with below-par financial performance that negatively impacts their results. Former Ecolab Chairman and CEO Doug Baker often said: "Be mindful of the market currents versus the waves." His philosophy was that there are short-term situations (waves) that can cause business ups and downs (political instability, economic downturns, etc.), and that you should not overreact to those. But you should pay attention to the currents (resource scarcity, changing demographics, energy transitions, etc.), which will have a long-term impact on business risks and opportunities. Doug would remind us to stay focused on the currents as we developed and executed the business strategy.

A recent example of focusing on the currents versus the waves is Ecolab's 2020 divestiture of Champion Technologies, a global specialty chemical company that serviced the upstream oil and gas markets. In

October 2012, Ecolab agreed to buy Champion Technologies and move our cleaning-products company deeper into the energy industry chemical market. The purchase followed Ecolab's acquisition of Nalco in late 2011. The addition of Nalco marked Ecolab's expansion beyond its traditional business of manufacturing disinfectants and detergents for restaurants, hospitals, and other institutions. At the time, Nalco was a market leader in water-treatment chemicals used by oil and natural gas producers as well as the paper industry and other companies that consume or extract water.

From 2012 to 2019, Ecolab's upstream business, which was renamed Nalco Champion, experienced strong competitive and market currents, which moved it further away from Ecolab's core business strategy. The upstream business was competing against a different array of competitors than even four to six years earlier. It became more specialty chemical-like, requiring different value disciplines and customer preferences than other Ecolab businesses. Nalco Champion was also highly sensitive to business cycles. It was a challenge to manage fluctuating product costs, capital expenses, innovation, and formulation changes based on customer needs. In other words, it was very different from the rest of Ecolab's business.

One big market current over the last 10 years is the transition away from fossil fuels, as nations and companies advance efforts to move toward alternative energy sources. Renewable energy is the fastest-growing energy source globally. In the United States alone, it increased 42% from 2010 to 2020. By the end of 2020, renewables made up 29% of global electricity generation, according to the Center for Climate and Energy Solutions. During the previous decade, Doug Baker and his executive leadership team were closely monitoring the market currents related to the upstream business and the long-term impact on the rest of the enterprise. Many of the signs to divest the business were already there.

Fast forward to February 2019, when Ecolab announced that it would spin off Nalco Champion as a stand-alone publicly traded company. In June 2020, Ecolab finalized the separation of its upstream energy business when the previously announced spinoff company, ChampionX, merged with Apergy Corporation.

Earlier in this chapter, Professor Godfrey stated that identity underpins strategy. He said, if you don't know who you really are, you have no deep sense of why you win with your customers. Identity helps clarify strategy, and strategy clarifies actions around organic growth, acquisitions and divestitures. As he put it, divesture is the necessary companion to any acquisition strategy, and it offers a different set of advantages, including creating a stronger sense of core identity.

Letting go of a business that does not support a company's core identity is a necessity, even if it causes pain in the short term. I've seen that at Ecolab. However, because divesting a business that is not aligned with a company's core purpose is essential for future growth and for delivering customer and enterprise value, you just have to endure that pain. Corporate identities shift over time, and knowing when to let go is as important as knowing when to say yes to an opportunity. We expect our identity to continue to evolve and know that we'll eventually divest some of who we are today.

Chapter 9

CATALYZING SUSTAINABILITY THROUGH MULTI-STAKEHOLDER PARTNERSHIPS

Talent wins games, but teamwork and intelligence win championships.

—Michael Jordan[1]

As a member of the New York Stock Exchange, Ecolab enjoys certain privileges. One of those is access to the posh reception and meeting rooms at the exchange. On March 22, 2017 (World Water Day), Christophe Beck and Emilio hosted 65 of their largest customers, including BASF, Coca-Cola, Marriott, and Microsoft, to a half-day forum to announce and describe version 3.0 of Ecolab's Water Risk Monetizer (WRM), a tool that allowed customers to quantify the bottom-line implications of water quality and scarcity for their operations. In his opening remarks, Beck noted that this event represented a critical moment in water stewardship because it was now clear to the business community that water was not a free or taken-for-granted resource. It was a vital business issue; indeed, the top 150 global companies and their supply chains impacted one-third of global freshwater supplies.[2] Sustainable water management had moved from the backwater to the mainstream.

The ability to participate in, and lead, multi-stakeholder engagements – on display that day in 2017 – is the last of the five critical business processes through which Ecolab implements and achieves a sustainability advantage. (The other four processes include leadership throughout the organization, research and development and product solutions, mergers and acquisitions, and divestitures, which we've explored in the previous four chapters.) While the specifics of water stewardship were new to Ecolab in the 2010s, the principle of deep and meaningful engagement with nonbusiness stakeholders traces back to the earliest days of EL's history. The ability to design, nurture, and lead these partnerships represents Phase III sustainability, collaborative actions that move the dial at the societal level. They are the future for Ecolab and for our collective efforts to create a better world. As Doug Baker noted in introducing the Water Resilience Coalition, water stewardship will "be important to all of us individually, but you can't do it unless you act collectively."[3]

PARTNERING TO PROMOTE WATER STEWARDSHIP

That journey, at least for Ecolab, began about a decade before in a conference room in the Nalco Executive building. Nalco's customers had

177

been prodding the company to become more than just a chemical company, they wanted help managing water, energy, and meeting their own sustainably challenges. Nalco had already made great progress, but in late 2008 Emilio sat down with CEO Erik Frywald and Chief Marketing Officer Mary Kay Kaufman to think through how to strategically reposition the company around water and energy leadership. Frywald suggested that Emilio learn more about water stewardship outside industrial settings. Emilio called a friend at Coca-Cola – for whom water is a vital input – who pointed him toward their water partner, the World Wildlife Fund (WWF).

WWF, and its partners the Nature Conservancy and the Environmental Defense Fund, focused on watershed management because watershed vigor directly impacts wildlife vitality. Nalco engaged with the WWF in 2010, and began to learn what WWF knew and to share its own knowledge. The two partners found their knowledge and skills complementary and each provided part of a solution that had previously eluded the other. Over the next four years and an ever-expanding network of corporate and NGO partners, the Alliance for Water Stewardship (AWS) emerged; in 2014 the AWS published its first Water Stewardship Standard. Emilio described the experience of the group as "building the plane as we flew it." Ecolab's manufacturing facility in Taicang, China, became the first site in the world independently certified as meeting the AWS Standard.[4] As of 2022, over 160 businesses, NGOs, and government units belong to AWS, and its standard moves its members along the path to sensible and sustainable water management strategies.

Nalco's sustainability strategy took a giant leap forward in 2010 when Doug Baker and Eric Frywald connected at the World Economic Forum in Davos. Ecolab had a very small water unit and had known for years how critical water was to its portfolio of businesses, and Baker's conversation with Frywald allowed both to see how similar the companies were around sustainability as a core business strategy. Those conversations began the process that would see the companies merge less than two years later. In 2013, after a year of integration work, Baker and Ecolab Executive Vice-President Christophe Beck decided that the combined company's future strategy would focus on water. If a company can only be master of one thing, then that thing would be water; everything would build off that platform.

A part of focusing on water meant working beyond the confines of Ecolab's industrial and institutional businesses. They found another entry point in the UN Global Compact's CEO Mandate. Introduced in 2007, the Mandate, a public/private initiative, attempted to get CEOs to commit to water leadership in six areas: direct operations, supply chain and watershed management, collective action, public policy, community engagement, and transparency in reporting. Forward progress stagnated and the Mandate had very few signatories.

In 2018, Baker, Beck, and Emilio reached out to Jason Morrison, head of the UN Mandate and president of the Pacific Institute to see how they could help. Ecolab leaned in to rejuvenating the Mandate and began to engage with six partners, AB InBev, Diageo, Dow Chemical, Gap, Inc., Microsoft, and PVH Corp. Each used lots of water. The first two make beverages, Dow and Ecolab treat water, Microsoft uses water to cool its data centers – but what about the Gap and PVH, leading brands in the apparel world? As an industry, clothing uses about 20 *trillion* gallons of water each year.

In 2020, the seven companies founded the Water Resilience Coalition. To become a member of the Water Resilience Coalition, CEOs must pledge their company to a set of long-term (by 2050) and short-term (by 2030) goals.[5] These are (taken directly from the organization's website):

By 2050:

- *Net positive water impact*. Achieve a measurable and net positive impact in water-stressed basins on availability, quality, and accessibility through industry-leading water operations and basin initiatives.
- *Water-resilient value chain*. Develop, implement, and enable strategies to support leading impact-based water resilience practices across the global value chain.
- *Global leadership*. Raise the global ambition of water resilience through public and corporate outreach.

By 2030:

- Have positive water impact in over 100 water-stressed basins that support over 3 billion people.
- Equitable and resilient access and sanitation for at least 300 million people.
- Engage 150 companies with the potential to influence one-third of global water use.

Signatories, of which there are now well over 200, agree to become active stewards of water. That includes investing in facilities and tools to improve water management, raising awareness of the issue along their value chains, and building the coalition; in other words, members agree to do what Emilio and his colleagues did over a decade ago: continue to build and upgrade the plane as it remains in flight. The members of the WRC have learned to work together and operate at the appropriate scale for a global issue like water management.

THE EIGHT I'S THAT CREATE SUCCESSFUL WE'S

Working with others is a learned skill and we know a lot about how to help executives and organizations participate in and lead alliances with multiple and diverse stakeholders. I like a simple model developed by Rosabeth Moss Kanter, the Ernest L. Arbuckle Professor of Business Administration at the Harvard Business School. She's spent a career studying and consulting with companies about the challenges of innovation and leading change. Very early in that career, nearly 30 years ago, she looked at the traits of the most successful business alliances. She identified eight factors that permeated successful collaborations and named these the "eight I's that create successful We's." The eight are Individual Excellence, Importance, Interdependence, Investment, Information, Integration, Institutionalization, and Integrity.[6] Table 9.1 describes them.

Lest you think that these principles are just a cute alliteration or an artifact of the twentieth century, Kanter's latest work, written in 2022 after the global pandemic altered the societal landscape, highlights the traits successful leaders use to create powerful industry- and sector-spanning coalitions. She's dropped the alliteration, but the core concepts of the eight I's still provide the foundational recipe for success. The rest of this chapter illustrates how Ecolab employs each I to participate in, and more often lead, multi-stakeholder partnerships.

Individual Excellence

Each of the four core processes first described in Figure 3.1 (and the focus of the book to this point) should be considered a source of excellence. In its engagement with water stewardship, the company employed product solutions and research and development. This process builds on the core perspective and priority of technology as an element of

Table 9.1   Eight I's That Create Successful We's

* **Individual Excellence**
  * Both partners are strong and have something of value to contribute to the relationship.
  * Both parties enter the partnership for positive reasons.
* **Importance**
  * The relationship fits major objectives of both parties, so they want to make it work.
* **Interdependence**
  * The partners need each other. Neither can accomplish alone what both can together.
* **Investment**
  * The partners invest in each other to demonstrate their respective stakes in the relationship.
* **Information**
  * Communication is open. Partners share information required to make the relationship work.
* **Integration**
  * The partners develop shared ways of operating so they can work together smoothly.
* **Institutionalization**
  * The relationship is given formal status, with clear responsibilities and decision processes.
* **Integrity**
  * The partners behave toward each other in honorable ways that justify and enhance mutual trust.

Source: Adapted from Kanter, R. M. 1994.

positive change and progress. Ecolab's early partners, the WWF, Nature Conservancy, and Environmental Defense Fund, had deep knowledge about and advocacy for watershed management, a critical ecological habitat for wildlife. The people at Ecolab knew next to nothing about the intricacies of natural habitats, but they had forgotten more than their partners would ever know about industrial water and its management.

Everyone soon realized that each's area of expertise would play a vital role in a comprehensive water solution, one that entailed more than just regulation of natural habitats and needed to focus on downstream (no pun intended) uses of fresh water. The parties would later recruit organizations like Water.org to provide another critical piece of the water puzzle: safe, clean, and affordable access to water by individuals and families. The power of the partnership magnified as groups with distinct, critical knowledge and expertise leveraged each other's knowhow.

Ecolab brought two supporting elements of expertise to the emerging alliance: the willingness and ability to share knowledge in ways that others could understand and a focus on measurable results. They'd been doing this for over nine decades, and their thirst for knowledge facilitated knowledge sharing throughout the alliance. It's not enough for parties to bring individual excellence; they must share it throughout the network. Otherwise, knowledge and expertise remain siloed, and synergies across the alliance fail to form. Similarly, without the drive and pressure to measure results, alliances often bog down in words and abstract communiques that never lead to concrete action. Without knowledge sharing and measurement, an alliance becomes merely the sum of the parts, and the collaboration fails to realize its full value.

Sustainability represents a complex and multifaceted challenge that will require multiple sets of expertise and technical excellence to solve. Water stewardship illustrates the point that an end-to-end solution requires deep expertise to manage natural, economic, and human resources and make progress in specific areas. Other challenges are just as complex, from abandoning fossil fuels to ameliorating systemic racism in both word and deed. It will take our individual and collective best to get it done. The metaphor may seem trite, but a chain really is only as strong as the weakest link. The rate of progress on any of the 3Ps depends on skill and expertise, and alliances collapse when expertise does not exist or is not roughly equal across the collaboration. In the first case, the effort fails because it can't solve real problems; in the second, the alliance becomes driven by the partner who knows the most. Other partners contribute little, while the expert contributes everything and gains nothing.

Importance

Without water, Ecolab has a very small business. The way the company reports revenue doesn't reflect the true centrality of water to its business, but it provides a reasonable proxy. The company reports results for four distinct segments: global industrial, global institutional, global healthcare and life science, and other (primarily pest elimination). Water management products and services drive revenue in the industrial segment, which produced 49.5% ($6.3 billion) of 2021 revenue and 65% ($1.03 billion) of operating income.[7] Remember, these figures understate the impact because water matters for every business unit. At over half of total revenue and two-thirds of profit, water matters, and strategic stewardship represents a great source of new growth.

Nalco began working with the WWF in earnest in 2010 and over the next four years Emilio attended scores of meetings with an ever-broadening network of stakeholders. The group had a running joke, "Where's government?" Private-sector organizations joined and contributed but governmental agencies, particularly those with national reach, failed to show up. After some discussion, a reason seemed obvious. For the most part, domestic water use is subsidized by governments around the world, accounting only for the basic distribution and administrative costs of delivering water to users. Over time, poor water governance has compounded the challenges of aging infrastructure and in-efficient water management across public and private sectors. Put simply, water has low economic value. Inadequate management of water resources by governments, communities, and water users has led to the depletion and pollution of freshwater resources. Past and current approaches to water governance have created many of the shared water challenges we face making the global water crisis mainly a crisis of governance.

The data on governmental involvement in this multisector coalition reveals two lessons for the overall effort to build a sustainable world. The first seems trivial but matters nonetheless: Until a stakeholder sees sustainability as important *to them*, they won't get involved. I'm not talking here about just convincing the skeptics or browbeating those who deny climate change or the presence of systemic racism. That has been and will be tough sledding. Progress around each of the 3Ps (profit, people, and planet) accelerates when individuals and organizations begin to see the current and direct effects of these issues on the things they really care about most. Only then will these groups become involved.

The second lesson is that importance is a powerful sorting mechanism that defines natural boundaries for collaborative efforts. Groups that share perspectives and perceptions about the importance – economic, moral, and social – of different sustainability challenges have a common platform from which to work. Passion creates momentum that allows these groups to overcome a natural wariness or shared mistrust and begin to move forward. Importance correlates with contribution, and it influences some of the other I's in the model. It meters, for example, levels of energy and investment that stakeholders put in to collaborations. Progress toward a more sustainable world happens best when individuals, groups, or companies focus their efforts and energies on issues of critical importance to them. No one should work on everything, but everyone must work on something.

Interdependence

Interdependence means that each member of a coalition needs the others in order to succeed; the lack of interdependence leads to failure. Most businesses prize independence. Leaders like to do more than just call the shots in meetings; they want to be the masters of their own destiny. Relying on others signals weakness (never mind that any business depends on customers for revenue and employees for products, etc.). NGOs, on the other hand, often overemphasize their dependence on those who provide the resources that enable them to do their work. Collaborations usually begin with these two complementary mindsets of independence and dependence.

A toxic set of outcomes arise if businesses and their NGO partners carry these mindsets into partnerships. True collaboration never gets off the ground and a dominant-submissive relationship takes hold. Humility, a core tenet of Ecolab's worldview, provides the antidote to these dangerous defaults. Emilio reached out to the WWF and its partners because Nalco knew they didn't know everything and that they had a lot to learn. It must have been quite the culture shock to realize that, as good as they were at industrial water, Nalco didn't know much about watershed management. Both parties would have experienced another shock when groups like water.org joined the alliance. Without the knowledge of providing access to water, the alliance would not be able to work on social sustainability. Rather than a holistic solution targeting the roots of water stewardship, each would have continued to hack at branches.

All sustainability challenges share the characteristics of large scale, interrelatedness, and complexity. Whether we focus on increasing opportunities for women around the globe or reducing carbon emission, these problems are simply too big for any one group to solve. Systemic complexity defies simplistic understanding and single solutions; it requires the collective effort of many individuals and groups. That's just at the beginning. As the Alliance for Water Stewardship evolved, the group realized that the expertise they had in the room at any given time would not be enough to make a real dent in the problem. They needed more knowledge and more expertise to get to the point of issues a standard. The further they go down the road, the more they see another puzzle piece that's needed.

Before moving on to the next I, I'll highlight something about the eight I's that I hope you've noticed for yourself: The elements of the model build on and reinforce each other. Interdependence builds on the core RIGHT elements of *respect* and *humility*, and it requires trust, or the confidence that others will do their jobs.[8] When partners bring their best stuff, individual excellence, then competence-based trust can develop, and shared importance of the problem enhances commonality-based trust. Interdependence, a vital element for success, grows out of and reinforces not only individual excellence and importance, but every other I. The eight I's act as a reinforcing system to strengthen collaborative relationships.

Investment

Investment means skin in the game. Real skin and enough of it that it signals commitment to other members of the joint effort. Investments take many forms, including the lowest hanging fruit of financial resources or lending a logo and brand equity to the effort. Other types of investment are more subtle. Companies can invest intellectual property, they can designate human capital to a joint venture or collaboration, or they can invest social capital beyond just a logo or brand image. That's how Ecolab has invested in water stewardship. Doug Baker and Christophe Beck tapped Ecolab's stakeholders and put their own reputation on the line in inviting them to join the collaborative work.

Doug and Christophe drove the creation of the Water Resilience Coalition in the late 2010s in this way. About 2018, they witnessed the rise of another environment-based multi-stakeholder coalition, the Alliance to End Plastic Waste. Doug Baker, in particular, given his strategic vision of Ecolab as a water leader and his naturally competitive nature, watched the plastics alliance gain traction and realized he needed to do the same around water. Emilio reached out to Jason Morrison, the director of the UN CEO Water Mandate project and president of the prestigious Pacific Institute, and told him that Ecolab and other endorsing members were ready to help double the number of signatories to the Mandate.

Doug then reached out to Ecolab's key customers and began to persuade them to accelerate progress against the global water crisis. A question quickly arose about where to house the effort and how to measure progress. Working together with a half-dozen of its corporate partners, Ecolab became a founding member of the Water Resilience Coalition, an independent organization that now has over 30 members. Ecolab now invests in other efforts as a convenor; it brings leaders together to create change.

Being a convenor is one form of thought leadership. Leaders can stake out one of three (rough) positions of leadership. They can choose to be the "innovator" or "disruptor." Think Tesla or Google here; they exhibited clear leadership by driving commercialization of autonomous vehicles. The second option is "follow and adopt." Ford and General Motors occupy this position in autonomous vehicles. They hope to lead by scaling what others discover. Finally, a company can be a "platformer" or "convenor." In autonomous vehicles this is the US Defense Projects Research Administration (DARPA), an arm of the Department of Defense that sponsored the original contests that challenged others to design and push the envelope of autonomous vehicles. Ecolab sees its role going forward as creating cross-sector platforms for others to build on.

A sustainable future will require massive monetary investment. We see national governments around the world debate how much public money to invest in these efforts, where to invest, and over what time horizon. They're also trying to figure out what guardrails to put around those investments. Private industry will prove much better at making financial investments for at least two reasons. First, as I noted above, for businesses, water – and by extension every other sustainability issue – has a cost and price attached to it, and the platform for any wise investment will always be costs. Second, unlike government, businesses and their investors demand and expect positive quantifiable returns on those investments. Business is a better investor because it has more discipline than government and can better target funds to areas with high payoffs.

Businesses have another advantage in making these investments. They have more investment opportunities and ways to invest. Governments don't typically have intellectual property to invest. They can develop knowledge but have a hard time deploying it and other human capital. Given the demands for fairness and commitments to political agendas, government leaders lack access to the same types of social capital and reputational investments that private organizations have. Business leaders can call for and convene action without the baggage government leaders naturally carry.

Information and Integration

I put these two together because in the twenty-first century, the primary way we integrate partnerships is through information sharing and communication. In a manufacturing or service setting, integration would focus on things like rationalizing machinery, production schedules, software platforms, or sales processes. In the knowledge economy, information is the coin of the realm. Integration is a core element of Ecolab's worldview – you've read about how well the company performs on this dimension, from Klenzade in the 1960s to Nalco in the 2010s. In the new world of cross-sector sustainability partnerships, the most important component of integration lies in sharing information, creating common communication platforms, and clarifying how values and missions fit together across the membership.

In the water stewardship case, the first form of integration involved creating a common language. WWF and its partners used "conservation" as their simple term in use. Emilio and the Nalco team helped reframe that single concept into the 3Rs of reducing initial water use, reusing the same water as long as possible, and recycling water for eventual discharge. The change of language led to an evolution of mindset, from water management as one thing to many things, each with its own nuance, sophistication, and impact. That change in mindset changed the trajectory of any standard that would arise, and it also suggested other logical partners that needed to be involved in the ongoing effort.

The rubber hits the road at the integration stage of collaborations and, other than coming to grips with interdependence, represents the point of highest risk of failure. This is true for any endeavor, including efforts around sustainability. We could graph any organization in terms of Figure 3.1, perspective, purpose, priorities, processes, products, and performance. Products may be the most flexible, but from processes on down, inertia increases. Processes run well because they replicate the same sequences over time.[9] Each level of the pyramid represents a source of inertia; as you move toward the base of the pyramid, the level of inertia increase. Trying to change the core purpose and perspective of the organization creates financial, intellectual, moral challenges for any organization. Companies only change the core when the payoff exceeds all those costs.

The payoff to membership of a multi-stakeholder partnership increases, and the cost of involvement decreases as everyone artfully integrates processes rather than develops entirely new ones or simply adopts one partner's process lock, stock, and barrel. Artful integration has a distinctly minimalist quality – create as few new terms and new routines as possible, as well as an evolutionary one that allows members to continually adjust routines as greater levels of integration yield obvious results. Paradoxically, maximizing the sustainability value of a collaboration depends on minimizing the level of new processes each partner needs to adopt.

Institutionalization

To institutionalize something is to do two things. First, institutionalization formalizes relationships. Think about marriage as an institution. When two people marry, they don't formalize their love but they do formalize their relationship. Each person accepts a set of legal and cultural obligations, and each receives a set of legal and cultural benefits. This deepens the commitment partners bring to the collaboration in two ways. First, institutionalization publicly commits you to certain actions and obligations. Second, institutionalization makes exiting the relationship costly and difficult. Partners find themselves more willing to adjust their behavior in relationships because it proves cheaper to change than to exit.

Ecolab's involvement in multi-stakeholder relationships usually entails a formal commitment. They signed the CEO Water Mandate and publicly pledged to abide by its principles and work toward its objectives. Ditto for the Water Stewardship Standard. They've also been willing to certify facilities as compliant with various standards and their annual sustainability reports record and publicize progress. In their role as platform builder, they encourage others to make similar commitments.

Institutionalization has another meaning. Twentieth-century sociologist Philip Selznick argued that when something becomes an institution, it becomes value laden and taken for granted.[10] People no longer question its right to exist, and it will be seen, by many, as a worthwhile part of our society. Formalization creates obligations, but it also bestows legitimacy and a taken-for-grantedness on that formal organization. Ecolab's work on the Water Resilience Coalition represents an effort to make two things seen as both legitimate and just a normal part of life for a

CEO. The first is the actual commitment to water stewardship for their organization. As the 3Rs for water become taken for granted, mindsets and action sets both change in the right direction. The second, and more powerful, impact is that water stewardship, and by extension concern for the natural environment, becomes a legitimate concern of those who sit at the top of the organization. That also extends to the social element of the 3Ps. Sustainability belongs at the top. It is not merely a staff or engineering function; it constitutes a strategic issue for the long-term health of the enterprise. When sustainability in any area becomes institutionalized, progress accelerates.

Integrity

The eighth and final I is integrity. It may sound trite, but last is not least. Integrity means that partners behave toward each other in honorable ways and that their actions build trust and confidence, not destroy it. Ecolab's involvement in water collaborations presents a textbook case for how to act honorably with partners. Ecolab did not seek to highlight its foundational role in the development of the Alliance for Water Stewardship or the Water Resilience Coalition. While Ecolab's long-term business viability may depend on their ability to help customers achieve sustainable water stewardship, its involvement in founding these organizations was not some veiled sales pitch. Its goal has been to encourage other organizations, companies, NGOs, and governments to make a real commitment to water stewardship. There's a genuine dedication to Ecolab's purpose of protecting people and the resources vital to life. If this grows the long-term market for their products and services, it's a benefit, but not the reason behind these actions.

Second, Ecolab took the plunge and had its Taicang, China, manufacturing plant become the first facility on the planet to certify compliance with the Water Stewardship Standard. They walked their talk, and people of integrity do what they say they'll do. More importantly, however, people and organizations of integrity do what they tell others to do. Actions speak louder than words, and Ecolab exhibits commitment to the cause, not to finding its own angle or a set of quick sales.

Integrity also means alignment between espoused values and lived reality. One measure of integrity is the extent to which behaviors, policies, and procedures reflect the espoused values of the organization. Behaviors always reveal who a person or an organization really is; the relevant question becomes, "Are they who they say they are?" When we are who we say we are, or when we have integrity, we build trust. That's true for individuals, groups, or large organizations. When our actions belie our beliefs, we destroy trust, and we all know that rebuilding trust proves far more costly, and takes much longer, than we either expect or desire.

Trust operates at three different levels, and what level we operate at determines the speed and effectiveness of sustainability efforts. At the first level, we have confidence that our partner has our best interests at heart and they won't take advantage of us. This encourages us to enter into collaborations. The second level of trust entails confidence around reliability, that you'll do what you say you'll do when you say you'll do it. Level 2 trust speeds progress because no one has to monitor the other to ensure performance. The third level of trust manifests as a deep confidence that encourages risk taking and innovation. When we get to this level, we not only operate faster, we operate better and we jointly find new solutions to vexing business, environmental, and social problems.

Ecolab acts with integrity. They signal through their participation that they have the best interests of the planet and its people at heart. They deliver on commitments, whether its products or bringing people together to create a new set of water standards, Ecolab creates momentum and speeds progress; the Water Resilience Coalition has in fact more than doubled the number of signatories to the UN CEO Water Mandate between 2020 and 2022. Finally, the fundamental RIGHT perspective encourages others to join with Ecolab in finding new and innovative solutions to the problems facing people and the planet.

LESSONS FOR LEADERS

This chapter's Lessons for Leaders begin from a different starting point; Ecolab has not been engaged in multi-stakeholder partnerships for the entirety of its first century. As you've read above, its ability to succeed in this endeavor builds, like everything else, on the solid foundation of the RIGHT perspective and Ecolab's rich history of integration and growth across industries and markets. Some of the lessons I'll suggest draw on that foundation, while others draw on Ecolab's more recent experiences and learning.

1. *Foster humility*. Humility stands out as the most important perspective and skill for a successful collaboration. Humility allows an

organization to see clearly both the extent and limits of the individual excellence it brings to the party. The foundations of interdependence and integration won't happen unless an organization and its leaders have an accurate sense of who they are. Humility also begets respect; very few of us have long-term voluntary relationships with people or organizations we don't respect. Humility matters, a lot.

How can your organization develop and foster humility? The best way I know is through an honest self-audit and assessment that focuses on two questions. First, how do we really compare to competitors and companies we respect and aspire to be like? Go and collect data. It might help to hire third-party research firms to provide you with an objective assessment of where you are at. If you do the exercise internally, listen hard and call out any excuse making by your staff. One common excuse I often hear is that the best-in-class competitor competes unethically (somehow), and "We could be as good as them, but we have principles." That justification usually won't hold up to deep scrutiny. You need strong data to tell you where you really are.

Second, compare your performance today with a year ago, or five years ago. Avoid the simple question, "Are we better today than X years ago?" because it forces you into an artificial binary yes/no answer. Ask, "Where are we better and where are we worse than X years ago?" And, "Why are we better (worse) off than in the past?" Honest answers to these questions produce an accurate assessment of who you are, what you are good at, and where you need to work. That's humility, an honest and accurate assessment of your strengths and weaknesses.

2. *Prepare to work hard.* Businesspeople sometimes confuse multi-stakeholder collaborations with something akin to a cause-related marketing campaign. The company will lend its logo, attend a few meetings, and probably make some financial commitment to the organization. In return, the company should gain access to a customer or product segment, and if they affiliate with the right partners, they'll burnish their "authenticity" with the right audiences. What's not to love?

Collaborations and cause-related marketing both begin with C, but the commonality ends there. The eight I's require commitment on the part of a member to be authentic, not just to look authentic.

Each of the I's, when done well, involves developing and nurturing long-term relationships with others. They involve learning, much of it through mistakes, and they require patience through that ongoing process. Finally, membership in a collaboration requires faith – the faith that the endeavor will create real value for the people or part of the planet focused on. And faith that somehow, the business will learn things through its participation that will allow it to grow revenue and/or cut costs somewhere in the business. Faith is more than belief; it's work and action. Cause-related marketing requires none of these deep commitments or relational skills, so expect and prepare to work hard.

3. *Exercise judgment*. Collaborations take work and they carry risks, so be careful about which ones you enter into. Like many things in business, they're easier to get into than they are to get out of. Let importance and passion be your guide here. That may sound like an invitation to skip the due diligence and "go with your gut." Nothing could be further from the truth. Put simply, don't engage in these efforts unless the area of focus is strategically important to your business and you have some real and unique skill to offer. Ecolab's strategy centers on water, and it brings a century of expertise to the engagement. If a collaboration doesn't rise to this level of importance for you, then you'll always be on the periphery of the group. You'll spend much and gain little.

Cost/benefit mismatches represent one risk, but look hard for others as well. One comes immediately to mind: brand risk. Brand risk rises when your team fails to vet each member of a coalition. Only deal with solid partners, ones (largely) free from brand or reputational baggage, and take the time to investigate who you choose to deal with. Work to control membership decisions and onboarding processes to ensure that new partners meet your standards. As with any party, it's not your friends that cause the problems, it's when *their* friends and acquaintances show up – the ones you don't know and who don't know you.

You've invested a lot to build your brand. Don't let someone else squander it.

CONCLUSION

The ability to participate in and lead multi-stakeholder collaborations is the fifth and final Ecolab business process that I've discussed. Like the other four (leadership everywhere, research and development of product solutions, mergers and acquisitions, and divestitures), this one sinks its roots into and draws its strength from the company's RIGHT perspective. The company's ability to succeed in this new and important cross-sector activity both enhances and exploits skills the company has mastered around customer intimacy, knowledge mastery, science-driven products, and growth through acquisitions and divestitures. You should see the deeply dyed yarn that connects these four historical processes with an emerging mastery of societal-level, cross-sector work.

These collaborations focus Ecolab squarely on the future. The company's past strengths help it to engage in this arena, and the past decade has shown that Ecolab leads – it doesn't just participate. I've focused on water in this chapter, but that's only part of Ecolab's business. I'd bet that Christophe Beck, Emilio, or any other company leaders will engage in multi-stakeholder collaborations to solve sustainability issues across the business portfolio. The company's ability to develop and exploit physical chemistry drove its past success; future success likely depends on its ability to create and nurture social chemistry across a diverse group of global stakeholders.

EMILIO'S THOUGHTS

Rising to the Challenge: Business as Usual Is Not a Sustainable Option, and Collective Action Is Hard

Public-private partnerships are a way for like-minded individuals and organizations to collaborate on challenges and achieve greater impact jointly than they could individually. These partnerships, by definition, require collaboration, and it's no secret that they're hard. Working together to achieve a common objective can be difficult, especially when organizations have conflicting interests.

On World Water Day 2017, Christophe Beck, then executive vice president and president of Nalco, urged 60+ water influencers from the public and private sector at a New York Stock Exchange Water Forum to move from awareness to action on water scarcity and to make water risk management an integral part of their business strategies. "It's good for your business and good for the world," he said.

Those words still resonate today as we confront an escalating global water and climate crisis. For example, Europe is dealing with record-breaking droughts and increasing water scarcity. In the United States, in Nevada and Arizona, Lake Mead's water level dropped more than 1,000 feet as of the end of July 2022, continuing a 22-year downward trend. That same month, Utah's Lake Powell was at its lowest level ever. The Yangtze River, the most important river in China, is drying up, and the Horn of Africa is facing an unprecedented drought. The 2017 Water Forum in New York was one of a growing number of water scarcity events catalyzed by what was happening at the time, namely the threat of places like California, Cape Town, and India running out of freshwater. The social and governance issues linked to water, such as human rights and environmental justice, are also precipitating factors. Gender equality also comes into play; for example, in many countries, women are responsible for the time-consuming process of gathering water resources.

Earlier in this chapter, Professor Godfrey chronicled our water stewardship journey and my quest to develop a multi-stakeholder engagement strategy on water for Nalco and Ecolab. Our early engagement started with collaborations – with organizations as varied as the World Wildlife Fund, the Nature Conservancy, the UN CEO Water Mandate, the Coca-Cola Company, Nestlé, and other companies. It was focused on developing a universal standard for water stewardship, which later became the Alliance for Water Stewardship (AWS) Standard.

Before we consider this topic in more detail it's important to define water stewardship. According to the AWS, it is the use of water that is socially and culturally equitable, environmentally sustainable, and economically beneficial, and achieved through a stakeholder-inclusive process that includes both site- and catchment-based actions. It acknowledges water as a local resource shared by multiple stakeholders in a watershed. Water stewardship also refers to caring for something we do not own through collaboration with other stakeholders in the basin.

For Ecolab, it means improving water stewardship within our own operations and within the watersheds in which we operate. It's a commitment that extends beyond our operations and our customers' operations to partnerships with thought leaders and prominent organizations that support responsible use of the world's limited freshwater resources to the benefit of nature, communities, and business. Becoming a water steward enables companies to understand all their water-related risks – physical, reputational, financial, and regulatory – and implement strategies to minimize those risks and promote a sustainable business strategy.

In response to emerging water challenges, more and more companies are engaging in corporate water stewardship and working with others to achieve more sustainable water management. That brings me to the convening role that Ecolab has had for more than a decade to raise awareness and action to address the water crisis. There were three pathways to Ecolab's water stewardship strategy involving public-private partnerships:

- *Promote water stewardship in our internal operations and through our customers to meet the goals of the United Nations Sustainable Development Goals (UNSDG), in particular UNSDG 6, on clean water and sanitation.* These efforts were set in motion through Ecolab's role as a founding member of the Alliance for Water Stewardship Standard and Certification, launched in Lima Peru in 2014. One year later, our plant in Taicang, China, received the world's first AWS certification for adopting the International Water Stewardship Standard, which promotes sustainable freshwater use. The fact that the plant operates in the water-sensitive region of the Taihu basin of the Yangtze River made this certification even more significant. With our 2030 impact goals, we are now on a path for AWS certification in our top 15 water-stressed locations globally.
- *Work collectively.* We can't do this alone. Partnerships and coalitions are essential for tackling the global challenges that impact people, planet, and business health. A case in point: the UN Global Compact Water Resilience Coalition. As a founding member, Ecolab is urging other industry leaders to join the Coalition by signing a Net Positive Water Pledge and working toward four overarching 2050 commitments and actions:

- *Leading the way with corporate water leadership.* We have pledged to deliver measurable net-positive impact in water-stressed basins where we operate, with a focus on the availability, quality, and accessibility of freshwater resources. By holding ourselves accountable and always striving to do better, we are setting bolder environmental performance goals that align with our business growth strategy as we continue to work to decouple resource use from growth.
- *Creating water-resilient value chains.* We are developing, implementing, and facilitating strategies to support leading impact-based water resilience practices across the global value chain. Through a UN CEO Water Mandate and McKinsey assessment in 2020, we found that 150 of the largest water users and their supply chains can impact one-third of the freshwater use.
- *Enabling sustainable water, sanitation, and hygiene (WASH) access for the most vulnerable communities.* We are driving collective action to pursue interventions that will impact 300 million people.
- *Advocating for change.* We are raising the ambition of water resilience through public and corporate outreach as well as by inspiring other industry leaders to join the coalition and sign the pledge.
- *Help companies determine the true value of water.* A big challenge for water stewardship is that water is undervalued and underpriced in much of the world and is often cheapest where it is most scarce. This makes it difficult to make the business case for investing in water-saving technologies or to make informed decisions about where to locate or expand operations. In 2014, as droughts and water stress were capturing headlines in the media, Ecolab jumped in to help industry tackle this challenge. With the help of S&P Global Sustainable 1 and partners such as Microsoft, Dow, Ford, the UN CEO Water Mandate, the World Resources Institute, and other stakeholders, Ecolab created the Smart Water Navigator (SWN) portal. It is the publicly available web-based tool to monetize water stress, risks, and externalities at the local level for business. This free, easy-to-use tool guides companies in their journey

toward "smart water management." It helps businesses adopt practices that can reduce risk by tackling underlying local, shared water challenges through:

- Meaningful water reduction target setting
- Strong accountability
- Industry best practices
- Preparing facilities for engaging with other basin stakeholders

Ecolab's Smart Water Navigator™ (SWN) portal addresses two main underlying challenges:

- Enhance a company's understanding of water risk, using the Water Risk Monetizer (WRM) tool, and guide a response that is proportional to the problem.
- Help industry build trust and credibility with stakeholders to drive more effective governance and collective action on shared water resources.

Ultimately, the SWN portal helps companies on their smart water management journey by providing industry specific examples of how the tool can be applied to reduce risk, increase resilience, and contribute to solving local shared water challenges. Our goal: to help companies understand water's full value and deliver insights to drive holistic water management that enables growth.

Water became our rallying cry in 2013, and we centered on the principle of water stewardship. With the help of the business, corporate marketing, brand, communications, and insights teams, Ecolab Sustainability established a glide path to drive Ecolab's water thought leadership through partners such as the Alliance for Water Stewardship, UN CEO Water Mandate, World Resources Institute, the Nature Conservancy, Bluerisk, World Environment Center, GreenBiz, and a host of other leaders and influencers.

Beth Simermeyer, Gail Peterson, Nigel Glennie, Kari Bjorhus, Shannon Pettitte, Steve Lauring, Meredith Englund, and the sustainability team were invaluable resources in helping us pursue our ambitious goal of becoming the world's foremost water and trusted sustainability company. They are the collective team that helped sustainability develop the insights, tools, and thought leadership engagement to bolster Ecolab's brand and reputation as a leading global water company.

Our confidence in our ability to save water has led us to establish an equally ambitious customer impact goal: conserving 300 billion gallons of water annually by 2030. That's equivalent to the annual drinking water needs of more than 1 billion people. It's ambitious, yet achievable. Like everything else it takes hard work. As Doug Baker always said, we should set ambitious goals, but in the end, what Mother Nature really cares about is what we do and the impact we can have together. But through these efforts and through partnerships with our customers, we know we can get there. As a convenor behind many different public-private partnerships, it's what we do. And we'll continue to work collectively to achieve even greater impact in the years to come.

Chapter 10

LOOKING FORWARD TO ECOLAB'S SECOND CENTURY

Every time that wheel turn around, bound to cover just a little more ground.

—Jerry Garcia

By the mid-2010s, Ecolab's value proposition and strategy centered on helping customers achieve all of their 3P goals: a positive impact on people, planet, and profit. As Christophe Beck explained it to me, "The essence of sustainability is the fundamental proposition that you improve business performance and lower cost as you reduce the use of natural resources. It's a win-win-win proposition."[1] The customer, Ecolab, and the environment would all win through sustainable solutions. The synergies that accompanied the Nalco acquisition earlier that decade led Emilio and the executive team to recast Ecolab's strategy in terms of "four pillars," an integrated approach that highlighted key challenges that lay at the intersection of its business and sustainability goals. Those four pillars were Clean Water, Safe Food, Abundant Energy, and Healthy Environments. They became, in 2015, the basis for Ecolab's 2020 Sustainability goals and vision:

- Customer impact:
  - Help customers save 300 billion gallons of water annually by 2030.
  - Help customer prevent more than 1 million foodborne illnesses each year.
- Operational goals:
  - Reduce water withdrawals by 25%.
  - Reduce greenhouse gas emissions by 10%.

The four pillars anchored Ecolab's strategy and they supported the United Nations Sustainable Development Goals (SDGs) around Gender Equality (SDG 5), Clean Water (SDG 6), Affordable and Clean Energy (SDG 7), Good Health and Well-Being (SDG 3), Responsible Consumption and Production (SDG 12), and Climate Action (SDG 13), Decent Work and Economic Growth (SDG 8), and Industry, Innovation, and Infrastructure (SDG 9).

In late 2018, Emilio and his eight-person corporate sustainability team began the process of setting new impact targets for the next decade. The 2030 goal-setting process provided the team with the opportunity to rethink how sustainability contributed to Ecolab's overall strategy and could spark sustained revenue growth. The first innovation, which

I described in Chapter 3, came as they began to think of the three phases of sustainability: the four walls, the value chain, and societal benefit. Foremost for Tenuta, however, was the reality that *sustainability* was such a broad notion that a company could become stretched too thin by trying to be all things to all people. To avoid this loss of focus, Emilio used four questions as guardrails to tighten the scope of the new goals:

1. *What's relevant and good for Ecolab's success?* In 2019, Ecolab's sales were around $13 billion, and the company had ambitious growth goals. Sustainability needed to become a driver of strategic evolution and revenue growth, building on the company's core assets and capabilities.

2. *How do we work with our customers to improve their business performance?* Customers bought from Ecolab, and paid more for its products, because the company's solutions improved their business results, either by reducing costs or increasing revenues. Customers increasingly set their own ambitious sustainability goals and relied on Ecolab to help them achieve those goals. The new 2030 goals, as with everything else at Ecolab, had to center on customer needs and value.

3. *How does our work impact the planet?* Thinking about global impact on the planet would be the essence of a bold and ambitious goal and the water business would be central to that effort. If, for example, Ecolab could find new ways to scale its water business, the impact on arid countries and regions of the world could be dramatic, in the provision of clean drinking water and sufficient water for economic growth.[2]

4. *What are the implications of our work for people and society?* Some 2020 goals had a human focus, such as preventing foodborne illnesses, but ambitious and bold meant helping more people and being more explicit about the ways in which people's lives would improve through Ecolab actions. Every aspect of Ecolab's business touched consumers in some way and the 2030 goals needed to stretch the company's impact in enhancing the lives of all.

While Emilio and his team refined the 2030 goals, the company spun out its upstream oil and gas business, Nalco Champion. The spinout effectively removed the "abundant energy" pillar as a core area of work, and the team replaced abundant energy with climate as a bolder and more expansive "fourth pillar" for the company. The new 2030 sustainability goals built on each pillar:

- Conserve 300 billion gallons of water annually, a 28% increase from the company's 2021 performance of 215 billion gallons conserved. The 2030 goal would be the equivalent of the annual drinking water needs of 1 billion people.
- Help provide safe food, free from bacteria or other microbial pests, for 2 billion people, which translates into 11 million fewer food-borne illnesses each year, a 30% increase from Ecolab's 2021 performance.
- Ecolab's hand hygiene solutions aim to clean 90 billion hands by 2030. The goal would be to increase that by 33% over the coming years, preventing 2.2 million healthcare-related infections. The work of Ecolab's healthcare business units would result in helping 70 million people receiving safer medical care.
- For climate, as the plan took shape, Ecolab products and services have helped customers reduce greenhouse gas emissions by 3.6 million metric tons each year. The 2030 goal would be a 40% increase to 6 million metric tons avoided, preventing over 10 million pollution-related illnesses.

The 2030 impact goals connect Ecolab's past with its emerging future. The goals play the role of Janus, the Roman god of beginnings and endings. Janus had two heads, one facing backward (endings) and one facing forward (beginnings). Our modern month of January takes its name from him, and the month provides us with the opportunity to pass from, and reflect on, the year just past and plan for, and anticipate, the year ahead. Our goal in this chapter is to play Janus. I'll look back and provide a summary of core lessons you should carry forward in your own work and Emilio will close the chapter with a look at the road just ahead for Ecolab.

PAUL'S KEY LESSONS FROM ECOLAB'S FIRST CENTURY

I've studied Ecolab for over five years. I've spent time in the corporate offices meeting with executives, reviewed archives studying history and lab meetings with researchers, and followed up in the field with the boots on the ground that make Ecolab what it is today. Each interaction I've had with Ecolab people leaves me with three strong impressions about what every company can learn: the power of a relationship-based view of business, the solid foundation of the RIGHT perspective, and the critical role that leaders at all levels play in creating value for customers.

Relationships First

I noted in Chapter 2 that all management challenges have a relational and technical aspect. You can't truly deal with challenges unless you deal with both elements, and the sequence you employ impacts how effective you'll be. I made the case throughout the book that when leaders adopt a "relationships first" mentality, they'll see technical solutions, but they'll see them in a different light. A "technical first" mentality, however, doesn't naturally invite working on the larger context of relationships. I'll highlight five different types of relationships that your company should focus on.

Relationships between *individuals* come first. If individuals can't build working relationships based on common interests, respect, and trust, nothing else happens – in business or sustainability. Both MJ Osborn at EL and Herb Kern at Nalco recognized the fundamental role that seeing other people as people with real needs and interests played in a winning company. You saw in Chapter 5 how that plays out in training and development; Ecolab associates get exposure to others from across the company and world in virtual trainings sessions. They then enter into real, one-on-one mentoring relationships with their own managers. Chapter 6 focused on how the company creates similarly deep and meaningful business relationships with customers.

Relationships between *organizational units* constitute the second area of focus. In Chapter 6 you saw how Ecolab takes great care to integrate RD&E teams and those selling in the field. They've solved a common problem that plagues product development in businesses across industries. The common organizational form is the silo, where groups work independently and with high doses of suspicion toward those in other silos. At Ecolab, field associates report back to researchers and researchers get out into the field. As you saw in Chapter 7, each acquisition is integrated into the "family" in the way that makes the most sense for that business.

Relationships with *stakeholders outside* those in the traditional value chain stand next in line. As you read in Chapter 9, these relationships build on respect, but they require heavy doses of humility and time to make them work. Partners need time to learn how to work together, and each must be willing to invest in building the relationship.

A fourth type of relationship exists between people and *data* and results. At too many organizations I've been a part of, real, broad data is frowned upon and measurement focuses on selected areas where the results will always turn out well. Ecolab, in contrast, relentlessly measures everything. A core part of its value proposition, embodied in eROI, entails sharing that data with customers.

The final relationship type juxtaposes people, the organization, and *technology*. Ecolab, as Economics Laboratory before it, is a research- and science-driven company. Technology fuels value creation; however, customer and human needs guide that process. The company doesn't roll out marginal "new and improved" products just to drive revenue; the improvement must be substantive and focused on real customer needs. Technology must also integrate with human, organizational, and social elements to craft an integrated product solution, as you saw with healthcare acquired infections (HAIs) in Chapter 6. Technology serves people, not the other way around.

I'd invite you to ask yourself how your company rates on each of these types of relationships and begin to develop plans for change and improvement. Relationships are, and will continue to be, core to creating a sustainable world in each of the 3Ps.

The RIGHT Perspective and Its Children

The 1982 business class *In Search of Excellence* represented a sea change in business thinking on many levels.[3] Authors Tom Peters and Robert Waterman made a strong case that "values" mattered, and that companies that are managed by and for values tended to be excellent financial performers as well. They proved agnostic about values, however. Whether it was innovation or quality or solving hard problems, as long as a company had some deep values, it should be on the road to success. I don't think that holds for sustainability. Having a specific set of values matters.

In what you've read to this point, Emilio and I have made the case that the RIGHT perspective, and the values it naturally begets, provide the best foundation on which to build a sustainable enterprise. It all begins with respect, for people as subjects in themselves, with real needs and worthy goals. *Respect* extends to all living things, and a deep level of respect also sees the nonliving natural environment as worthy of respect for the role it plays in supporting all forms of life. The opposite view portrays everything but the viewer as an object, just a thing to be manipulated and used for self-benefit. Treating the natural environment as an object of our use and abuse has led us to our current state. Wildfires destroy homes and communities, as do hurricanes and tornadoes. Nature itself revolts against its manipulation and issues a call for us to treat her as a subject worthy of respect. Respect comes first in RIGHT for a reason; it provides the viewpoint that clarifies everything else.

Integration holds that everything connects to and interacts with everything else. This perspective rejects the strict categories that have served as the foundation for much of Western thought (think the mind-body separation introduced by Descartes centuries ago), and market-driven economic behavior (think of the distinct roles of producers and consumers). Integration invites people to move beyond an "either/or" mentality and embrace a "both/and" worldview. MJ's core strategy built on the notion that his customers would pay higher prices *and* generate higher returns. His successors at Ecolab see a trade-off between positive people and planet outcomes and profit as deceptive reasoning; they've spent decades proving that doing good for nature and others leads to doing well financially. The world really is interconnected, we now operate at a scale where this reality reveals itself to even the most casual observer.

Growth views progress as not just a part of human existence, such as maturation from childhood to adulthood, but as a morally praiseworthy outcome. Growth can be negative (think a cancer cell) or positive (think of a child learning to read). Businesses grow or die because others in the market either see the value in their operation and participate, or they don't and the company starves for resources. There is no cruise control in business or markets – they are always evolving and changing, growing in either scale, scope, or sophistication. At Ecolab, a focus on growth leads to finding the next customer need to satisfy and developing integrated product solutions that fill that need. Yesterday that need was for clean dishes. Today it's for clean hands. Today and tomorrow it's for clean energy and water.

Humility grows out of our interconnectedness, complements respect, and softens the hard edges of growth and technology. Humility celebrates strengths and invites us to work on weaknesses. As you saw in Chapter 8, divesting acquisitions or exiting markets requires humility in the admission that we didn't judge right or we couldn't build what we thought we could. Chapter 9 explained how humility drives the types of societal collaborations that we need to solve the challenge of our time – creating a truly sustainable society. What lies ahead requires multiple skill-sets, knowledge bases, and strategic visions, more than any individual or organization can pull off on their own. Working together works best when everyone brings a healthy dose of humility to the endeavor.

Technology completes the RIGHT perspective. MJ came of age when the full impacts of the Industrial Revolution changed the world. He worked in the pharmaceutical industry as it transitioned to a scientific basis. He sold cars during the decade when the automobile moved from margin to Main Street. EL operated on the cutting edge of hygiene and sanitation during a time when mechanical appliances like dishwashers and laundries first exhibited their potential. His perspective saw technology as just a part of life. Osborn saw its positive potential and worked to leverage that as he built his business. As I've argued throughout the book, a sustainable world will incorporate technology; we can't turn the clock back to the eighteenth century, nor would we want to. When bounded by *respect and humility, technology* can benefit people, planet, and profits (the 3Ps).

The Power of Leadership

Leadership matters. Chapters 2 through 9 each included lessons for leaders that summarized ways your organization could apply the principles that helped Ecolab become what it is today. Table 10.1 provides a review of 28 things. That's a lot. When I read a book, I'm impressed if I can find one to three things I want to work on. If you choose three things to work on first, the others will fall into place at the right time. Several of those 28 suggestions revolve around leadership. I'll highlight two things you should understand about leadership.

First, understand the critical role that senior leaders play. The advantage that senior leaders have is that they see things those lower in the organization don't, and sometimes can't, see. They manage the needs of several different stakeholder groups, they should define the overall strategy of the organization, and keep everyone focused on implementing it.

Table 10.1 Lessons for Leaders: A Summary

Chapter	Lesson	Key Implication
2	Be realistic.	Focus first on what you can achieve; build momentum.
	Begin at the beginning.	Respect is the foundation for everything that follows.
	Top-down matters.	Top management must set the tone.
	Overcommunicate.	Share the message multiple times in multiple ways.
	Embed.	Make RIGHT real through policy and procedure.
3	Priorities then processes.	Processes grow out of priorities; sequence matters.
	Processes commit you.	Real commitments carry real consequences; think hard.
4	Leadership is the strategic factor.	Leadership provides the direction and fuel for action.
	Leadership can be learned.	Develop leaders thoughtfully and systematically.
	Leadership can be a team sport.	Leverage different skills through the team.
	Ideal leader changes over time.	Match leader skills with what your company needs.
5	Hire smart.	The alternative, managing tough, always cost more.
	Link development to perspective.	Training reinforces culture; align it with your core.
	Integrate training throughout.	Find the right balance between center and periphery.
6	Use the job-to-be-done model.	Focus products on customer needs.
	Fit technology to the company.	Technology serves the organization, not vice versa.
	Create a vitality index.	Measuring R&D makes it more productive.

Chapter	Lesson	Key Implication
7	Align M&A with strategy.	This prevents drift and wasted energy.
	Why is acquisition best?	Account for premiums and consider alternatives.
	Cultural fit matters.	Cultural misalignment prevents value creation.
	Be clear about integration.	Integration drives synergies and value.
8	Acknowledge emotion and hubris.	Either the head or heart can lead to poor choices.
	Understand the risks.	Plan for the downside and be ready for it.
	Beware the sunk cost fallacy.	Cut bait early; don't wait.
	Set up a system.	Be metric guided in your evaluations and choices.
9	Foster humility.	It's the most important skill for partnering.
	Prepare to work hard.	Collaborations take work to succeed – so do it.
	Exercise judgment.	It's easier to get in than out; be thoughtful.

They should also look 7–10 years into the future and work to prepare the organization for several potential futures. Given all of this, and given the importance of moving our economy and society onto a sustainable path, senior leaders must recognize the need to incorporate, if not embed, sustainability in and through the organization.

Interestingly enough, they best move toward a sustainable future by not saying no to sustainability initiatives. Leaders don't have to get the future exactly right, nor must they allow 1,000 flowers to bloom for the organization to move ahead. What they must do, however, is allow sustainable strategies to form and gain momentum and not shut them down prematurely. People deeper in the organization will prove incredibly adept at generating ideas and sorting out failures; executives allow that process to proceed by not picking winners and losers in advance. It's best to say nothing at all and let the process proceed.

Second, understand that the role of leaders at every level is to move that process forward. Those on the front lines, be it logistics, operations, sales, or research, enjoy access to cutting-edge problems and potential solutions and to critically examine what they see in the market and discover ideas and solutions with real merit; they can use their real-time access to stakeholders and markets to see what gets traction and what gets tossed aside. They must also answer the "so what?" question for the enterprise. This involves thinking through the implications of what's new for the business. If top managers need to avoid saying no, leaders throughout move the dial when they say yes to the reality of potential opportunities and threats. They also say yes to dedicating their best efforts to the innovation and risk taking that will bring out the substantive change. They must say yes and become the drivers and champions of change.

BEYOND 100: EMILIO'S PREDICTIONS FOR ECOLAB'S SECOND CENTURY

Doing well by doing good stands the test of time.
                                              —Christophe Beck

As we prepared for our June 2021 investor webinar, Christophe Beck, CEO and chairman, Mike Monahan and Andrew Hedberg, SVP and VP of Investor Relations, and Laurie Marsh, chief HR officer, and I were planning our program and remarks. This perennial webinar is designed to introduce and highlight the release of our annual corporate sustainability and social responsibility report. During the preparations, Christophe began to share his key thoughts on Ecolab's environmental, social, and governance (ESG) leadership and what makes Ecolab stand out to investors. For several years, Ecolab has been recognized by many of the more prominent raters and rankers as an ESG leader. It's a testament to the fact that for Ecolab, profit and purpose can be harmonious. They don't have to compete. "If you align your organization to that premise, it will enable us to sustain both business growth and corporate social responsibility," Christophe said. He went on to say that "ESG is core to our growth," and we are a company that can demonstrate to the world that "Doing well by doing good" is a reality.

Those statements are even more relevant today than they were then. Right now, it sometimes seems as if the world has been turned upside down. As this book goes to press, we're facing so many global challenges at once – geopolitical, supply chain, and inflationary – that it's hard to stay focused on the most pressing challenge of our time: climate change.

But it's essential that we keep our eyes on the ball and maintain our focus because the news around climate is not getting better. It's getting worse. And as we learned coming out of COP26, there is a growing chorus of consumer and stakeholder outcry about corporations making pledges without a defined path to achieve them and, as a result, falling short of their goals.

That's no surprise, given the urgent need to address this issue and the dire consequences of inaction. In 2021, global energy-related carbon dioxide emissions rose by 6% to 36.3 billion tons, their highest level ever and the largest increase in global CO_2 emissions in absolute terms, according to the International Energy Agency (IEA). And the planet continues to get hotter, with this year so far ranked as the fifth warmest ever, according to the National Oceanic and Atmospheric Administration (NOAA).

Let's not forget water. Climate change, population growth, and economic development have led to increased competition for water resources. As a result, water has become scarcer and costlier – with a projected global freshwater deficit of 56% by 2030, according to the World Resources Institute (WRI). In many ways, water is the number one physical risk that companies will face in a changing climate.

Climate, water, and energy are tightly connected; address one and you address the others. While water scarcity would exist even without climate change, climate change exacerbates it significantly. The effects of climate change are mostly expressed in water: droughts, excessive precipitation, sea-level rise, salt-water intrusion, glacier melt-off, and so on. As a result, if you use less water, you are less vulnerable to climate change. But at the same time, if you use less water, you will also use less energy, because water use requires energy (i.e., pumping, heating, cooling, treating). And because most energy generated in the world still comes from fossil fuels, if you use less water, you will lower your carbon emissions and help mitigate climate change. In other words, if you help mitigate climate change, you will minimize water stress and increase operational resilience.

Based on the findings from approximately 500 Ecolab Total Plant Assessment (TPA) water and energy audits, mostly in the food and beverage and light manufacturing sectors, we estimate that:

- A typical facility's potential water usage reduction is 30–40%, on average.

- The resulting potential energy savings is, on average, 15–20% in thermal energy (mostly natural gas) and 1–4% in electricity.
- Results vary from facility to facility (depending on the fossil fuels used and how a facility's utilities generate electricity), but industrial facilities can reduce their carbon emissions by up to 15% just by lowering their water consumption.

Here's the best part: Facilities experience cost savings from reduced energy and water use as well as productivity and quality improvements. The "green premium," or the notion that sustainable solutions cost more, is a myth. We can deliver business, sustainability, and climate results at the same time while maximizing the exponential return on investment (eROI). For many companies, there is a disconnect between commitments and actions, something that's been referred to as the "say/do gap." This inability to move the needle on sustainability actions is an obstacle toward progress and the source of so much consumer and stakeholder frustration.

Among the questions these stakeholder groups want businesses to answer are:

- What is your current baseline?
- What is your ambition?
- What is your roadmap for getting there?
- How do you measure your progress?

It's imperative for businesses to have clearly defined action plans with achievable goals and support from the highest levels of their organizations to ensure that they can achieve their objectives. At Ecolab, we're working to advance a sustainable future together with our customers. In 2021, despite the many challenges facing us, we made tremendous progress toward our ambitious customer outcome goals. We've also made great progress in our efforts to achieve a net positive water impact and tackle carbon emissions. As a result, we're on a glide path toward accomplishing our 2030 impact goals, which include achieving 100% renewable electricity and a positive water impact. We continue to exponentially grow our positive impact through initiatives such as the following:

- Ecolab is a founding member of the Water Resilience Coalition, a CEO-led movement that collectively addresses global water challenges.

- Alliance for Water Stewardship (AWS) certification was awarded for two additional manufacturing sites in Mexico, and we received our first-ever platinum certification for our facility in Taicang, China.
- We signed a virtual power purchase agreement (VPPA) in Finland to enable us to achieve 100% renewable energy by 2030, instead of by 2050.
- An employee-led Global Sustainability Network was launched to accelerate Ecolab's growth and impact.

As we look outward, Ecolab has a vital role to play in helping our customers and industry close the say/do gap. There are proven, tangible solutions available to operate more efficiently, reduce water and energy use, and accelerate growth and advance a more sustainable future. That's why our next big initiative is Ecolab Water for Climate™.

Ecolab Water for Climate™ is an impactful new program designed to help companies lower their environmental footprint to meet their climate goals and advance sustainable business growth. It helps drive long-term success in a resource-constrained world by providing outcome-based water solutions to help manage the use of water, energy, and other natural resources. Its solutions include the Ecolab Global Intelligence Center, which helps customers make sense of their data so they can take concrete steps to accelerate their sustainability journeys while meeting their productivity and profitability objectives. Like a NASA control center, the Global Intelligence Center offers 24/7 monitoring – providing an extra set of eyes on a customer's facility and operations.

Through the program, we helped a consumer package goods facility in an extremely water-stressed region in India address its climate, water, and business challenges, including production expansion that would increase water use by 50% in the next few years. At the same time, the company pledged to achieve net zero carbon by 2050 and get halfway there by 2030.

Ecolab was called in to create a roadmap to address the facility's resource challenges and growth targets. As part of the plan, Ecolab recommended digitally enabled solutions to continuously monitor the plant's water and energy flow. Real-time monitoring solutions such as Ecolab Water Flow Intelligence and 3D TRASAR™ smart technology played a major role in boosting water and energy efficiency in critical utility and automated equipment cleaning operations, which improved cleaning turnaround times and increased production. Our solutions also included interventions to reuse and recycle water at the site level. The company is now able to increase production in a highly water-stressed area by conserving and reusing water. We also managed to deliver reduced carbon emissions at a return of greater than 50% eROI. (See Figure 10.1.)

I'll be the first to say that it isn't easy for a company to achieve sustainability goals while simultaneously growing its business and creating value for stakeholders. But it can be done. First, companies need to develop a culture that enables them to achieve and operationalize ambitious sustainability goals. It also takes:

- An unwavering commitment from senior leadership
- Alignment with business strategy
- Readiness of an organization to act

At Ecolab, we've learned that having our CEO and executive leadership committed to supporting us on our sustainability journey is critical. And what helps get senior management on board is understanding the implications to our business strategy in terms of risks and opportunities. If we don't address the challenges posed by water scarcity and climate change, we can't continue to succeed and grow. Ecolab is a growth company, and as we move Beyond 100 into our second century,

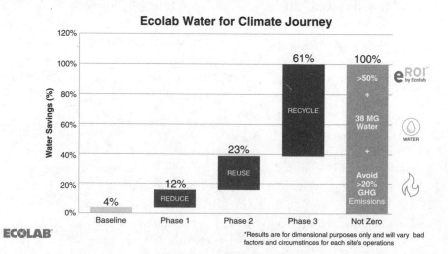

Figure 10.1 Ecolab's Water for Climate Journey

we will continue to increase our positive impact in our own operations and through our customers.

We end where we started. Doing well by doing good. Christophe has set an ambition for the company to be the world's trusted sustainability company. Last year, we worked with our customers to help conserve 215 billion gallons of water – enough drinking water for 734 million people – and avoid 3.6 million metric tons of greenhouse gas emissions – preventing 5.7 million pollution related illnesses. These results were achieved while avoiding the so-called "green premium." Through broader industry collaboration, information sharing, and new mechanisms for accountability, we can help advance a more sustainable future.

The journey isn't an easy one and the challenges are many, but when the course is set by leaders like Christophe, we can achieve seemingly unsurmountable tasks. We have a lot of work to do to overcome the gap between where we are today and where we need to be in the not-so-distant future. But with a leadership commitment, a timeline, and clearly articulated goals, it can be done. And when that happens, everyone will benefit – businesses, people, and the planet. I'll leave the last word to Christophe, who sums it up best in this statement:

At Ecolab, we see an unparalleled opportunity to grow both our business and positive impact in the world, and to help our customers do the same. We are proud of our progress and what is still to come. Together, with our customers, we plan to continue to grow and deliver on our purpose to protect people and the resources vital to life.

NOTES

CHAPTER 1

1. Air quality improvements from COVID lockdowns confirmed, United Nations UN News, 03 September 2021. Available at https://news .un.org/en/story/2021/09/1099092#:~:text=4.5%20million%20pollution%20victims&text=Analysis%20showed%20decreases%20 of%20up,same%20periods%20in%202015%E2%80%932019

2. Data on the data centers from Ecolab internal data, estimates of electricity usage from Home-X (https://homex.com/ask/how-many-households-can-1-mw-power) and water usage from California state University Santa Barbara (https://watertalks.csusb.edu/how-much-water-do-people-use#:~:text=How%20Much%20Water%20 Does%20One,and%20182.5%20gallons%20per%20year.)

3. Data on the Digital Realty Project from Ecolab and Digital Realty internal documents.

4. WCED (World Commission on Environment and Development), *Our Common Future* (Oxford: Oxford University Press, 1987), p. 47.

5. This data, as well as our discussion of the history of sustainability, comes from Jacobus A. Du Pisani, "Sustainable Development – Historical Roots of the Concept," *Environmental Sciences* 3 (2) (2006): 83–96.

6. The quote is misattributed to management guru Peter Drucker. For the correct version of Drucker's quote, see https://www.drucker .institute/did-peter-drucker-say-that/

7. I am indebted to my BYU colleague Kim Clark, who taught me about the power of thinking about leadership this way.

8. Ecolab, "Celebrating 75 Years of History," internal company document (1998): 5–6.

9. See "Ecolab Timeline," https://www.ecolab.com/about/our-history/ecolab-timeline

10. Data for Ecolab comes from its annual reports over those years. Data on the comparison metrics can be found as follows: Industry data for ROS/ ROA from Mergent Key Business Ratios, $n = 600+$ companies in SIC 28; Industry data for ROE (81 companies/ speciality chemicals) from NYU Stern School of Business, January 2022, available at https://pages.stern.nyu.edu/~adamodar/New_Home_Page/datafile/roe.html; Industry data for CapEX/ Sales and CapEx/ EBIT (81 companies) from NYU Stern School of Business, January 2022, available at https://pages.stern.nyu.edu/~adamodar/New_Home_Page/datafile/capex.html

11. Stock price data for EL gathered by relevant date searches of the *Minneapolis Star-Tribune* and/ or *Wall Street Journal*.

12. Data on Ecolab's environmental performance taken from its 2020 Sustainability Report, available at https://www.ecolab.com/corporate-responsibility/sustainability-reporting-resources. Comparison data taken from various Google searches for the relevant topics, such as the average size of households in the United States, US city population sizes, number of vehicle registrations, etc.

13. Economics Laboratory Annual Report, 1970.

CHAPTER 2

1. Data on the Osborn family genealogy and family history taken from familysearch.org, with a search leading back from Merritt J Osborn. Information on dates, times, and locations also cross-checked with US Census and Birth, Marriage, and Death records on Ancestry.com

2. This, other quotations, and the data found in the remainder of this opening came from a personal letter from MJ Osborn to Bill Henry, dated June 22, 1959. Letter located in the Archives of the Minnesota State Historical Society. Dates also supplemented by MJ's Obituary, *Minneapolis Star Tribune*, January 24, 1960.

3. Osborn recounts his early life during EL's 25th anniversary party, a transcript of which can be found in the Archives of the Minnesota State Historical Society.

4. See note 2.

5. The rest of the quotations in the introduction come from the letter cited in note 2.

6. German definitions taken from Langenscheidt's German-English Dictionary, available at https://en.langenscheidt.com/german-english/weltanschauung; see also https://www.encyclopedia.com/philosophy-and-religion/philosophy/philosophy-terms-and-concepts/worldview-philosophy

7. I take this from my friend and mentor Clayton Christensen. See C. Christensen and M. Raynor, "Why Hard-Nosed Executives Should Care About Management Theory," *Harvard Business Review* 81 (September 2003): 66–74.

8. See F. Herzberg, *Work and the Nature of Man* (Cleveland: World Publishing, 1966).

9. See W. G. Ouchi and R. L. Price, "Hierarchies, Clans, and Theory Z: A New Perspective on Organization Development," *Organizational Dynamics* 7 (2) (1978): 2544.

10. See R. A. Power and M. Pluess, "Heritability estimates of the Big Five Personality Traits Based on Common Genetic Variants," *Translational Psychiatry* 5 (7) (2015): e604.

11. Tribute to Merritt J. Osborn, January 1960. Folio available at the Archives of the Minnesota State Historical Society.

12. EL 1966 Annual Report.

13. See J. Collins and J. Porras, *Built to Last: Successful Habits of Visionary Companies* (New York, Harper Collins, 1994).

14. The Lanners account can be found in the EL News, an internal publication. Available at the Archives of the Minnesota State Historical Society. Baker's quotation comes from Burl Gilyard, "2017 Person of the Year: Doug Baker Jr." *Twin Cities Business* (December 2017): 33.

15. Data on automobile penetration from PJ Hugill, "Good reads and the automobile in the United States," *Geographical Review* 72 (3) (1982): 327–349.

16. Letter from MJ Osborn, January 26, 1953. Available in the Archives of the Minnesota State Historical Society.

17. T. Fred, "Products and Services for a Cleaner World": The Story of Economics Laboratory, Inc. (New York: Newcomen Society of America, 1981), (Accessed via the Internet Archive, https://archive.org/details/productsservices0000lann/page/21/mode/1up?view=theater).

18. See B. Friedman, *The Moral Consequences of Economic Growth* (New York: Vintage, 2005), 592 pages. For specifics on the link between poverty and both environment and health degradation, see PC Godfrey, "Community Enterprise Solutions: Replicating the Micro consignment Model," William Davidson Institute Case Study, April 1, 2013.

19. See J. P. Tangney, Humility. In S. J. Lopez & C. R. Snyder (Eds.), *Oxford Handbook of Positive Psychology* (Oxford University Press, 2009), pp. 483–490; and K. Konkola, "Meek Imperialists: Humility in 17th century England," *Trinity Journal* 28 (1) (Spring 2007): 3–35.

20. M. Myers, "Ecolab on New Turf with Chemlawn Purchase," *Minneapolis Star Tribune*, June 29, 1987, page 1M.

21. See Ecolab's 2020 Annual Report.

22. This is our own research based on Ecolab and P&G data over the previous decade.

23. Taken from the EL 1943 Annual Report to shareholders.

24. Ecolab Obtains First-to-Market EPA-Registered Laundry Disinfectant Claim against Clostridium difficile, Ecolab News Release, available at https://www.ecolab.com/news/2018/10/ecolab-obtains-firsttomarket-eparegistered-laundry-disinfectant-claim-against-clostridium-difficile

CHAPTER 3

1. Alexia Wulff, "A Brief History of Las Vegas as We Know It Today," *Culture Trip*, January 13, 2017. Available at https://theculturetrip.com/north-america/usa/nevada/articles/a-brief-history-of-las-vegas-as-we-know-it-today/, visitor statistics from the Las Vegas Convention and Visitors Bureau, Associated Press, 26 March 2022. Available at

https://www.usnews.com/news/best-states/nevada/articles/2022-03-26/tourism-board-charts-upswing-of-las-vegas-visitor-diversity

2. Paulie Doyle, "The 25 Most Visited Tourist Spots in America," *Newsweek*, October 8, 2021. Available at https://www.newsweek.com/most-visited-tourist-spots-america-disney-new-york-california-1616737 Data on hotel rooms from https://downtown.vegas/myth-buster/fifteen-of-the-worlds-25-largest-hotels-by-room-count-are-on-the-strip-true/#:~:text=In%20total%2C%20Las%20Vegas%20offers%20over%20150%2C000%20hotel%2Fmotel%20rooms. The number of restaurants comes from https://www.casino.org/vitalvegas/las-vegas-reportedly-has-most-restaurants-per-capita-sorta/. The number of slot machines from https://www.huntingtonandellis.com/companyblogpost/54/578/How-Many-Slot-Machines-Are-in-Las-Vegas?#:~:text=Did%20you%20know%20there%20are,casinos%20come%20from%20slot%20machines. The cost of alcohol at Mandalay Bay from https://www.lasvegasadvisor.com/faq-dining-beer/

3. For data as of late 2022, see https://earthobservatory.nasa.gov/images/150111/lake-mead-keeps-dropping#:~:text=Continuing%20a%2022022%2Dyear%20downward,just%2027%20percent%20of%20capacity.

4. Taken from Ecolab's Internal branding guidelines and documents. Ecolab was in the process of updating its website as we went to press.

5. E. Freeman, *Strategic Management: A Stakeholder Approach* (Boston: Pittman, 1984).

6. The business roundtable's statement of corporate purpose can be found at https://www.businessroundtable.org/business-roundtable-redefines-the-purpose-of-a-corporation-to-promote-an-economy-that-serves-all-americans

7. Fred Lanners, *Products and Services for a Cleaner World* (New York: The Newcomen Society North America, 1981), 28 pages.

8. EL report to shareholders, 1935.

CHAPTER 4

1. This opening story is based on private interviews with Doug Baker held during the summer of 2022.

2. Quoted in Burl Gilyard, "2017 Person of the Year: Doug Baker Jr.," *Twin Cities Business*, December 1, 2017, https://tcbmag.com/2017-person-of-the-year-doug-baker-jr/

3. All quotations in the next two paragraphs taken from Chester I. Barnard, *The Functions of the Executive* (London: Oxford University Press, 1938). The strategic factor is discussed on page 203 and the moral factor defined on p. 259.

4. From a bulletin to shareholders, dated December 19, 1925. The bulletin is in the Archives of the Minnesota State Historical Society.

5. EL 1984 Annual Report.

6. For a discussion and definition of dynamic capabilities, see D. J. Teece, G. Pisano, and A. Shuen, "Dynamic Capabilities and Strategic Management," *Strategic Management Journal* 18 (7) (August 1, 1997): 509–533, doi:10.2307/3088148.

CHAPTER 5

1. Donald H. McGannon was a contemporary of EB Osborn. He worked as an executive in the broadcasting industry as television emerged as the dominant medium of its era. This quotation is taken from https://kengreencpa.medium.com/yes-everyone-is-a-leader-here-are-20-leadership-quotes-to-encourage-you-as-a-leader-e35802e7c179

2. This quote, as with the other information in this section, came from an interview with Paul Langlois in late August 2022.

3. Definition from the Oxford English Dictionary. Available at https://www-oed-com.byu.idm.oclc.org/view/Entry/13500?redirectedFrom=autonomy#eid

4. You can find many definitions of this online. I took mine from https://www.merriam-webster.com/dictionary/strategus

5. This is one of my all-time favorite quotes. It comes from Pierre Mornell, *45 Effective Ways for Hiring Smart!: How to Predict Winners and Losers in the Incredibly Expensive People-Reading Game* (Berkeley, CA: Ten Speed Press, 1998).

6. Interview with Laurie Marsh, August 2022.

7. Information on Herzberg taken form a variety of sources, including the British Library (https://www.bl.uk/people/frederick-herzberg), and various business sites (https://www.businessballs.com/improving-workplace-performance/frederick-herzberg-background/, https://www.business.com/articles/management-theory-of-frederick-herzberg/).

8. You can read the core book or, for those with shorter attention spans, Herzberg wrote a classic *Harvard Business Review* article on this model. The book is Frederick Herzberg, Bernard Mausner, and Barbara Bloch Snyderman, *The Motivation to Work* (New York: John Wiley & Sons, 1959), reprinted by Routledge in 2017. The HBR article is reprinted as Frederick Herzberg, "One More Time, How Do You Motivate Employees," *Harvard Business Review* 81 (1) (2003): 87–96.

9. For more on adult learning, see Tonette Rocco, M. Cecil Smith, Robert Mizzi, Lisa Merriweather, and Joshua Hawley, editors, *The Handbook of Adult and Continuing Education* (Sterling, VA: Stylus, a publication of the American Association of Adult and Continuing Education, 2020).

10. Information on the impact of automation to workforce NCCI Insights, "The Impact of Automation on Employment – Part I," October 10, 2017, https://www.ncci.com/Articles/Pages/II_Insights_QEB_Impact-Automation-Employment-Q2-2017-Part1.aspx

CHAPTER 6

1. Data in this paragraph taken from internal Ecolab product development and marketing documents.

2. Mortality Analysis, "Coronavirus Resource Center," Johns Hopkins University, https://coronavirus.jhu.edu/data/mortality (accessed October 18, 2022).

3. S. Zhang, S. Palazuelos-Munoz, E. M. Balsells, H. Nair, A. Chit, M. H. Kyaw, "Cost of Hospital Management of *Clostridium difficile* infection in United States – A Meta-Analysis and Modelling Study," *BMC Infect Dis.* 16 (1) August 25, 2016: 447. doi: 10.1186/s12879-016-1786-6. PMID: 27562241; PMCID: PMC5000548. For HAI's in general, the figures come from Health Topics – Healthcare-

Associated Infections (HAI), N.D., Office of the Associate Director for Policy and Strategy, Center for Disease Control, available at https://www.cdc.gov/policy/polaris/healthtopics/hai/index.html

4. Clayton M. Christensen, Scott Cook, and Taddy Hall, "What Customers Want from Your Products," *Harvard Business School Working Knowledge*, January 16, 2006, https://hbswk.hbs.edu/item/what-customers-want-from-your-products (accessed March 18, 2019).

5. MJ Osborn, letter to EL employees, January 26, 1953. Minnesota State Historical Society Archives.

6. To be fair, most people got five of six. Different people omitted different elements, but I was impressed at how quickly each person rattled off five or six standards.

7. This quote and others in this section come from answers to questions by Larry Berger to Paul Godfrey, August 2022.

8. Jeff Dyer, Hal Gregersen, and Clayton Christensen, *The Innovators DNA* (Boston: Harvard Business School Press, 2011). See also David C. Robertson and Bill Breen, *Brick by Brick: How LEGO Rewrote the Rules of Innovation and Conquered the Global Toy Industry* (New York: Crown Business, 2013), 268–269.

9. MJ Osborn, EL 1927 Annual Report, available at the Minnesota State Historical Society Archives.

CHAPTER 7

1. Graham Kenny, "Don't Make This Common M&A Mistake," *Harvard Business Review* 16 (March 2020). Available at https://hbr.org/2020/03/dont-make-this-common-ma-mistake#:~:text=According%20to%20most%20studies%2C%20between,integrating%20the%20two%20parties%20involved

2. Data on company sizes found at https://americanbusinesshistory.org/largest-companies-1917-and-1929/

3. Nalco Chemical Corporation History, Funding Universe, available at http://www.fundinguniverse.com/company-histories/nalco-chemical-corporation-history/, accessed 07 July 2018.

4. "Suez Buys Nalco for $4.1 Billion," *CNN Money*, June 28, 1999. Available at http://money.cnn.com/1999/06/28/worldbiz/suez/, accessed 07 July, 2018.

5. "Suez Sells Nalco for $4.35 Billion," *Water World*, September 4, 2003. Available at https://www.waterworld.com/articles/2003/09/suez-sells-nalco-for-435-billion.html, accessed 07 July 2018.

6. Internal Nalco materials available at file:///C:/Users/pcg/Downloads/B-1435_Galaxy_3D_TRASAR_Automation_Cooling_Water_pdf%20(1).pdf, accessed 07 July 2018.

7. The above paragraphs use data from an interview with Emilio Tenuta, October 11, 2017.

8. See Kenny, "Don't Make This Common M&A Mistake."

9. C. K. Prahalad, and R. A. Bettis, "The Dominant Logic: A New Linkage Between Diversity and Performance," *Strategic Management Journal* 7 (6) (1986): 485–501.

10. The notion of adopting into the family came from Paul Godfrey interview with Angela Bush in 2022, the original quote about Nalco's similarity came from his interview with Bush in October of 2017.

11. Private interview with Doug Baker, October 2017.

12. My BYU colleague Nathan Furr published a book by this title in 2011. https://www.nailthenscale.com/

13. Quotation taken from Ecolab website, https://investor.ecolab.com/investor-story/business-model, accessed 06 July 2018.

14. Estimates found in the Ecolab merger with Nalco.

15. Private interview with Emilio Tenuta, October 2017.

16. Information on microbial fouling can be found at https://www.luminultra.com/industry/upstream-oil-gas/, accessed 10 July 2018.

17. Christophe Beck, interview, August 2, 2018.

18. See Ecolab's 2017 Annual Report for the quotations noted here.

19. Rebecca Lindsey and Luann Dahlman, "Climate Change: Global Temperatures," NOAA Climate.gov, June 28, 2022, https://www

.climate.gov/news-features/understanding-climate/climate-change-global-temperature

20. For the impact of hubris on M&A performance, see M. L. A. Hayward and D. C. Hambrick, "Explaining the Premiums Paid for Large Acquisitions: Evidence of CEO Hubris," *Administrative Science Quarterly* (1997): 103–127; R. Roll, "The Hubris Hypothesis of Corporate Takeovers," *Journal of Business* (1986): 197–216; P. R. Rau and T. Vermaelen, "Glamour, Value and the Post-Acquisition Performance of Acquiring Firms," *Journal of Financial Economics* 49 (2) (1998): 223–253.

CHAPTER 8

1. M'Shelle Lundquist Dixon was my neighbor several years ago. She's still a great friend. She told our children this and I've never forgotten its power.

2. M. Chambers, C. Garriga, and D. E. Schlagenhauf, The New Deal, the GI Bill, and the Post-War Housing, Economic Dynamics (2012). Available at https://economicdynamics.org/meetpapers/2012/paper_1050.pdf

3. "Economics Laboratory tries a comeback without 'crapshoot acquisitions,'" *Business Week* 3 (September 1984): 95–96.

4. A Barron's article, "Shaping up: Economics Laboratory is putting its house in order," November, 11, 1985, noted that the margins in the consumer business were about 3%.

5. EB Osborn, writing in the EL 1965 Annual Report.

6. Fred Lanners, EL 1980 Annual Report.

7. See the Annual Energy Review, 2011, for historical coal production, available at https://www.eia.gov/totalenergy/data/annual/pdf/aer.pdf, page 199. Data on decadal growth from the Coal Industry Annual, 1994. Available at https://www.eia.gov/coal/annual/archive/05841993.pdf

8. Data for 1977 found at Energy in Transition, 1985–2010: Final report of the committee on nuclear and alternative energy systems,

National Academies Press, Chapter 4, p. 147. Available at https://nap.nationalacademies.org/read/11771/chapter/5#147. Data for 2021 comes from US Energy Information Administration, available at https://www.eia.gov/tools/faqs/faq.php?id=427&t=3

9. "Outsider Puts Energy to Work at Economics Laboratory," *St. Paul Pioneer Press Dispatch*, January 24, 1983.

10. See note 7.

11. The company resettled to Columbus as it grew, but started as a side business in Troy. See "Interview with Paul G. Duke," Troy (Ohio) Historical Society, December 1, 1983. Available at https://thetroyhistoricalsociety.org/oral%20histories/interview_with_paul_duke.html

12. The $86 million figure can be found in the source noted in note 11. For 1983 sales, see Susan Fryder, "Ecolab OKs 'White Knight' role," *Minneapolis Star and Tribune*, March 21, 1987, p. 7, 11B; Profit numbers from Mike Myers, "Ecolab on New Turn with ChemLawn Purchase," *Minneapolis Star and Tribune*, June 29, 1987.

13. "The personality that ignited the industry," Landscape Management, October 1992. Available at https://archive.lib.msu.edu/tic/wetrt/page/1992oct51-60.pdf; see also "ChemLawn, under Ecolab, found out it 'couldn't go home again'" Landscape Management, December 1992. Available at https://archive.lib.msu.edu/tic/wetrt/article/1992dec27.pdf

14. "COMPANY NEWS; ChemLawn Bid of $33 a Share," *New York Times*, March 20, 1987.

15. Susan Feyder, "Ecolab Still Trying to Revive ChemLawn," *Minneapolis Star and Tribune*, May 22, 1989, 4D.

16. My colleagues Dave Whetten and Stuart Albert noted that a company's identity isn't what it claims, but what it does over time – the core, central, and enduring actions it takes result in identity. See S. Albert and D. A. Whetten, "Organizational Identity," *Research in Organizational Behavior* 7 (1985): 263–295.

17. M. Porter, "What Is Strategy?" *Harvard Business Review* 6 (Nov/Dec 1996): 61–78.

CHAPTER 9

1. Quotation available at https://blog.hubspot.com/marketing/team work-quotes

2. Data from presentation announcing the Water Resilience Coalition, available at https://www.youtube.com/watch?v=zC2pNYXWCt4.

3. Doug Baker, see note 1.

4. See Ecolab's 2017 Sustainability Report, p. 25. Available through https://www.ecolab.com/corporate-responsibility/sustainability-reporting-resources

5. The CEO Water Mandate Pledge: https://ceowatermandate.org/resilience/sign-the-pledge/

6. Rosasbeth Moss Kanter, "Collaborative Advantage: The Art of Alliances," *Harvard Business Review*, July-August 1994: 96–108.

7. Data from Ecolab's 2021 Annual Report and 10-K filing. Available at https://s24.q4cdn.com/931105847/files/doc_financials/2021/ar/Annual-Report-2021.pdf

8. For the importance of trust, see Stephen M. R. Covey, *The Speed of Trust* (New York: Free Press, 2008). Covey, son of guru Stephen R. Covey of the 7-habits fame, argues that any collaboration will work more smoothly, more quickly, and more effectively when the partners have confidence in each other.

9. Richard Nelson and Sid Winter made this observation over 40 years ago. It has now become a foundational part of thinking about wise strategic management. See Richard Nelson and Sid Winter, *An Evolutionary Theory of Economic Change* (Cambridge, MA: Harvard University Press, 1982).

10. See Philip Selznick, *Leadership in Administration* (Berkley, CA: University of California Press, 1957).

CHAPTER 10

1. Interview with Christophe Beck, October 12, 2017.

2. See the World Wildlife Fund data on water scarcity at https://www .worldwildlife.org/threats/water-scarcity#:~:text=Only%203%25%20 of%20the%20world's,one%20month%20of%20the%20year

3. Tom Peters and Robert Waterman, *In Search of Excellence* (New York: Harper Business, 1982).

ABOUT THE AUTHORS

Paul C. Godfrey, PhD (Salt Lake City, UT; https://marriott.byu.edu/directory/details?id=5330) currently serves as the William and Roceil Low Professor of Business Strategy in the Marriott School of Management at Brigham Young University. He is the author of two trade books, *More Than Money* (Stanford University Press, 2014) and *Strategic Risk Management* (Berrett-Koehler Press, 2020). *More than Money* garnered a Silver Medal in 2016 by Axiom Business Book Awards. Dr. Godfrey is a co-author of *Strategic Management* (John Wiley and Sons, 2015, 2018) and *Ethics in Business* (John Wiley and Sons, 2022).

Emilio Tenuta (St. Paul, MN; ecolab.com) is the chief sustainability officer at Ecolab, a provider of food and water safety, hygiene, and sustainability products and services for over 3 million customer organizations around the world. Ecolab employs approximately 50,000 people and operates in more than 170 countries. Tenuta's tenure at Ecolab is 35 years, and he now leads Ecolab's strategic sustainability journey focused on corporate responsibility, internal environmental stewardship, and helping customers operate more sustainably.

He sits on the board of directors for the World Environment Center and the leadership council of the Corporate Eco Forum. Tenuta has strong partnerships with the United Nations Global Compact (UNGC), and a number of NGOs to support management of water and energy risks in the industrial sector, including the World Wildlife Fund (WWF), Alliance for Water Stewardship (AWS), UN CEO Water Mandate, the Nature Conservancy, and World Economic Forum (WEF). Tenuta is a graduate of the Northwestern University Kellogg School of Management.

INDEX